Transatlantic Tensions

Transatlantic Tensions

The United States, Europe, and Problem Countries

Richard N. Haass

Editor

BROOKINGS INSTITUTION PRESS
Washington, D.C.

Copyright © 1999
THE BROOKINGS INSTITUTION
1775 Massachusetts Avenue, N.W., Washington, D.C. 20036
www.brookings.edu

Library of Congress Cataloging-in-Publication data
Transatlantic tensions : the United States, Europe, and problem
countries / edited by Richard N. Haass.

   p.   cm.
   Includes bibliographical references (p.) and index.
   ISBN 0-8157-3352-6 (alk. paper)
   ISBN 0-8157-3351-8 (pbk. : alk. paper)
   1. Europe, Western—Foreign relations—United States. 2. United
States—Foreign relations—Europe, Western. 3.
Terrorism—History—20th century. 4. Human rights—History—20th
century. 5. Europe, Western—Foreign relations—20th century. 6.
United States—Foreign relations—20th century. I. Haass, Richard.
   D1058 .T724 1999
   327.1´09182´109045—dc21

            99-6239
            CIP

9 8 7 6 5 4 3 2 1

Typeset in Adobe Garamond

Composition by Cynthia Stock, Silver Spring, Maryland

Printed by R.R. Donnelly & Sons, Harrisonburg, Virginia

THE BROOKINGS INSTITUTION

The Brookings Institution is an independent organization devoted to nonpartisan research, education, and publication in economics, government, foreign policy, and the social sciences generally. Its principal purposes are to aid in the development of sound public policies and to promote public understanding of issues of national importance.

The Institution was founded on December 8, 1927, to merge the activities of the Institute for Government Research, founded in 1916, the Institute of Economics, founded in 1922, and the Robert Brookings Graduate School of Economics and Government, founded in 1924.

The Board of Trustees is responsible for the general administration of the Institution, while the immediate direction of the policies, program, and staff is vested in the President, assisted by an advisory committee of the officers and staff. The by-laws of the Institution state: It is the function of the Trustees to make possible the conduct of scientific research, and publication, under the most favorable conditions, and to safeguard the independence of the research staff in pursuit of their studies and in the publication of the result of such studies. It is not a part of their function to determine, control, or influence the conduct of particular investigations or the conclusions reached.

The President bears final responsibility for the decision to publish a manuscript as a Brookings book. In reaching his judgment on competence, accuracy, and objectivity of each study, the President is advised by the director of the appropriate research program and weighs the views of a panel of expert outside readers who report to him in confidence on the quality of the work. Publication of a work signifies that it is deemed a competent treatment worthy of public consideration but does not imply endorsement of conclusions or recommendations.

The Institution maintains its position of neutrality on issues of public policy in order to safeguard the intellectual freedom of the staff. Hence interpretations or conclusions in Brookings publications should be understood to be solely those of the authors and should not be attributed to the Institution, to its trustees, officers, or other staff members, or to the organizations that support its research.

Foreword

I am not usually drawn to edited volumes, preferring instead to read the sustained thinking of one person. In some instances, though, edited volumes are not only unavoidable but desirable. This is one of them. Few if any individuals could capture American and European thinking on so wide a range of topics and countries as this volume requires.

By 1997, it became obvious that, with the notable exception of developments in the Balkans, it was often issues outside Europe that were having the greatest impact on—and often causing the most friction for—relations across the Atlantic. Five case studies—Cuba, Iran, Iraq, Libya, and Nigeria—were selected for study, and in each case an American and a European author (or, in one case, a pair of authors) were sent a common set of questions by Richard N. Haass, editor of this volume and director of the Brookings Foreign Policy Studies program. A conference was then convened at the Brookings Institution on March 9–10, 1998. A good many country and transatlantic specialists joined the case authors at that time. In the aftermath of the discussions at the conference, all of the authors were asked to revise their draft chapters. These revised case studies—as well as a draft introduction and conclusion containing insights and prescriptions gleaned from the cases and the conference—were then reviewed by experts in the field and again revised. This book is the result.

The editor's thanks begin with the eleven authors, who were asked to produce multiple drafts on what were in most instances moving targets. Indeed, all of the cases examined underwent significant evolution during the project, as the situation on the ground, transatlantic politics, or both, changed in important ways.

Second, appreciation is owed to those who attended and contributed to the initial March 1998 conference: Ronald Asmus, Harald Braun, Richard Burt, Patrick Clawson, Anthony Corso, Ivo Daalder, Jonathan Davidson, Nicholas Davidson, Karen Donfried, Kimberly Ann Elliott, Heike Fuller, Michael Gadbaw, Hubert Knirsch, Sebastian Mallaby, Charlotte Quinn, Wolfgang Reinicke, Nicolas de Riviere, Robert Satloff, Richard Sawaya, Helmut Sonnenfeldt, Stefano Stefanini, Alfonso Tena, Jennifer Tufts, and Randall Weidman. Herve Magro of the embassy of France in Washington deserves special credit for presenting his country's position when Dominique Moïsi could not attend.

Thanks also go to those who read and commented on one or another of the drafts: Zalmay Khalilzad, Rocky Suddarth, Lisa Anderson, Mark Falcoff, Peter Lewis, Ivo Daalder, and Philip Gordon.

Special recognition is given to Karla Nieting, research assistant in the Brookings Foreign Policy Studies program, who took responsibility for most of the logistics and administration while at the same time managing to comment on all the drafts. This book would not have seen the light of day without her. Candice Geouge assisted with administration, editing, and verification. Susan Jackson, Bridget Butkevich, Mica Kreutz, Sara Sezun, and Catherine Thie verified the manuscript. Theresa Walker ably edited the prose of twelve different voices, Carlotta Ribar proofread the book, and Susan Fels prepared the index. Susan Woollen coordinated the cover design.

Just as critical was a different kind of support. I want to thank the German Marshall Fund of the United States, the GE Fund, and the Arca Foundation, whose interest and financial assistance made this undertaking possible.

The views expressed in this volume are those of the authors and editor and should not be ascribed to the organizations whose assistance is acknowledged above or to the trustees, officers, or other staff members of the Brookings Institution.

Michael H. Armacost
President

April 1999
Washington, D.C.

Contents

Transatlantic Tensions

RICHARD N. HAASS

1 | *Introduction*

A t first glance, little is new in the notion that
developments beyond the continent of Europe
often constitute a source of tension between the United States and the
countries of western Europe. Throughout the four decades of the cold
war, NATO and transatlantic relationships were more often rocked by
developments far afield—the Korean War, Indochina, the Suez crisis,
Lebanon, the Cuban missile crisis, Vietnam, the 1973 Middle East war
and oil crisis, Lebanon, and then Libya in the 1980s—than they were
by what took place inside Europe or, more narrowly, within the treaty
area of the North Atlantic Treaty Organization.[1]

This pattern can be readily explained. The Soviet challenge was more
immediate in Europe and provided needed glue to the alliance. But it
did not guarantee harmony in Europe, much less beyond. Little sympa-
thy arose in the United States, especially in the initial years following
World War II, for what turned out to be the final vestiges of European
colonialism—and Europe had little interest in what was seen as American moralizing and meddling in Europe's affairs. As the years passed,
U.S. prosecution of cold war competition around the world often met
with European apathy or opposition—reactions that were the source of
more than a little American frustration, anger, or both. The net result

1

was mostly the same: the United States and its European allies often worked at cross purposes. This tendency to disagree on what to do in other parts of the globe inevitably affected allied ability to cooperate inside of Europe, in spite of the mostly common front against the Soviet Union.[2]

The first major challenge of the post–cold war era came from outside of Europe—the August 1990 Iraqi invasion of Kuwait—and, for the most part, the transatlantic relationship displayed a high degree of unity and utility. Two European states, Great Britain and France, proved to be among the most valuable political and military allies of the United States during the 1990–91 Persian Gulf conflict. Despite differences—Prime Minister Margaret Thatcher was impatient holding off military action while new UN Security Council resolutions were sought; French President François Mitterrand was more anxious than President George Bush to avoid a land war and more willing to distance himself from Kuwait's ruling family if that was the price of persuading Saddam Hussein to accept UN demands—the overall pattern was one of collaboration among the three Western members of the UN Security Council.

The breakup of Yugoslavia presented a different kind of challenge—more a source (and a reflection) of transatlantic friction than a successful experience. In Europe but "out-of-area" from NATO's perspective, Bosnia was a venue where for years the United States and Europe were unable to concert either their diplomacy or the use of military force. (The American inclination to avoid entanglement and hand responsibility for Bosnia to a Europe that proved unable and unwilling to take it on only made matters worse.) Not until the situation grew dire—for both the local inhabitants and the Western alliance—did matters begin to improve, as NATO air attacks, led by the United States, on Bosnian Serb positions helped to bring about new realities that made the Dayton Accords possible.[3] In 1998, a similar pattern unfolded in Kosovo. In this case, both Americans and Europeans were slow to react to the large-scale repression and aggression, directed primarily against the mostly Albanian inhabitants of Kosovo. Here, again, the United States and Europe often found themselves at odds over the proper ends and means of policy, most notably the use of military force.[4]

The 1990–91 Gulf War collaboration and the eventual cooperation in Bosnia should not obscure a larger reality. Increased friction (and decreased cooperation) characterizes relations across the Atlantic on policies toward problem countries. This trend has, if anything, accelerated with the passage of time, and with it the gradual passing from the scene of a generation informed by the habit of transatlantic cooperation. This development worked to reinforce trends already accelerated by the demise of the cold war, the disappearance of the Soviet threat, and the reduction of tension in Europe, all of which reduced the obvious necessity and momentum for transatlantic cooperation, especially in the security sphere.[5]

Yet the reduced threat to European security does not mean the absence of stakes. To the contrary, how the United States and the countries of Europe work with one another beyond Europe matters in at least three important ways. First, a good deal hangs in the balance. Four of the five countries examined in this volume are major energy exporters. Three pose major challenges to global efforts aiming to stem the proliferation of weapons of mass destruction. All five offer substantial markets for European and U.S. exports. Second, the United States and Europe are potential partners in shaping the post–cold war world. Their ability to cooperate will have a major impact on whether the emerging era of international relations turns out to be one that is more or less violent, prosperous, and democratic. Economic and political sanctions (as well as various supplier or export control arrangements designed to thwart proliferation of weapons of mass destruction) will inevitably have less impact in the absence of transatlantic cooperation; so, too, will diplomacy premised on the notion of providing rewards or incentives only if certain behavioral standards are reached. Military action becomes far more expensive (in human and financial terms) and more difficult to sustain domestically if burdens are not shared. Third, disagreements on particular out-of-area issues will inevitably affect the ability of Americans and Europeans to cooperate on other issues, regardless of their venue. Thus, differences over the best approach to one conflict can frustrate cooperation in another if patterns of unilateralism prevail. This concern is anything but hypothetical. At one point, the United States considered abandoning the Bosnian arms embargo. Whatever the merits of a policy change for Bosnia, such a decision could well have led France and others to reconsider their support of Iraqi sanctions. Similarly, secondary sanctions—the introduction of sanctions against third parties who do not participate in primary sanctions against a designated target—by nature expand the area of disagreement. Indeed, several of the cases in this volume look at secondary sanctions and their impact on such common interests as strengthening the capacity of the World Trade Organization to regulate international trade.

This book examines five prominent non-European challenges to U.S.-European relations after the cold war: Cuba, Iran, Iraq, Libya, and Nigeria. These countries do not constitute the complete universe of such problems, but they are some of the most important and representative.[6] How the two poles of the transatlantic relationship manage these issues will directly influence the evolution of these five important countries as well as the ability of the United States and Europe to act together in the post–cold war world.

Cuba is the problem country of longest standing. It has been a subject of transatlantic policy debates for nearly four decades. A basic discrepancy exists on the seriousness of the situation. For most European governments, Cuba constitutes a normal country, whereas for the United States, it is anything but normal given its location, history, and role in domestic American politics. Not surprisingly, this perceptual gap has led to fundamental policy differences—differences that would have remained readily manageable except for the American decision to introduce secondary sanctions, as part of the Cuban Liberty and Democratic (LIBERTAD) Act of 1996, or Helms-Burton Act, against those European individuals and firms doing business with expropriated property.[7]

Iran has been a problem for U.S.-European relations for only about half the time that Cuba has. Like Cuba, differences exist over how much of a threat it poses and, even more pointedly, over how best to deal with Iran. Europeans have favored engagement. Until recently, the U.S. bias was for sanctions. (The gap between these two orientations was reflected in how the policies were labeled: "critical dialogue" as opposed to "dual containment.") Also, like Cuba, transatlantic policy differences have been exacerbated by the American threat to impose secondary sanctions (using the Iran and Libya Sanctions Act of 1996, or ILSA) against those non-American firms investing in Iran's energy sector.

Iraq constitutes a fundamentally different problem from both of the above two countries in important ways. As alluded to earlier, the United States and the governments of Europe have not disagreed fundamentally over how to deal with Iraq ever since Saddam Hussein attacked Kuwait more than eight years ago. Time, however, has taken its toll, and the strain between the United States and France in particular is increasing, in large part over the desirability and necessity of maintaining comprehensive sanctions and over how best to bring about Iraqi compliance with its international obligations.

Libya in some ways resembles both the Iraq and Iran cases. Libyan terrorism provided inspiration for considerable common policy; explicit UN Security Council backing further facilitated transatlantic cooperation. But as is true with Iraq, transatlantic cooperation has weakened somewhat with the passage of time. As is also true with Iran, some European governments argue that the current policy—political and economic isolation of Libya—risks bringing about worse political leadership in that country. Also, like Iran, Europeans strongly reject secondary American sanctions instituted to discourage investment in Libya's energy sector.

Nigeria is a special case. It has been less an actual source of disagreement between Americans and Europeans than a potential one. Still, the deaths of General Sani Abacha and his democratic opponent Moshood Abiola have not eliminated the policy questions or differences, and Americans and Europeans need to determine how best to promote a democratic transition in one of Africa's most important countries. As a result, Nigeria brings to the surface basic questions common to all five of these cases and to those that might emerge in the future. Should Western policy emphasize commerce or the internal politics of a country? How, if at all, should economic sanctions be employed?

The book's conclusion sets forth ideas for bridging Atlantic differences in each of these settings, both to increase the possible impact of American and European diplomacy and to limit the potential of these issues to poison the overall transatlantic relationship. The conclusion also suggests some more general steps for Americans and Europeans to consider, again with the goal of making the post–cold war world a more stable and prosperous place. With great power relations within Europe mostly stable, these issues are likely to have the greatest import for—and impact on—transatlantic relations in the years to come.

Notes

1. For background on the traditional out-of-area issue, see Peter N. Schmitz, *Defending the NATO Alliance: Global Implications* (Washington, D.C.: National

Defense University Press, 1987); Elizabeth D. Sherwood, *Allies in Crisis: Meeting Global Challenges to Western Security* (Yale University Press, 1990); and Douglas Stuart and William Tow, *The Limits of Alliance: NATO Out-of-Area Problems Since 1949* (Johns Hopkins University Press, 1990).

2. Suez and Hungary are two examples; another is the pervasive impact of differences over the October 1973 war in the Middle East. For analyses of difficulties in the alliance, see, for example, Robert Endicott Osgood, *NATO: The Entangling Alliance* (University of Chicago Press, 1962); Henry A. Kissinger, *The Troubled Partnership: A Re-Appraisal of the Atlantic Alliance* (McGraw-Hill, 1965); Anton W. DePorte, *Europe between the Superpowers: The Enduring Balance* (Yale University Press, 1986); and Josef Joffe, *The Limited Partnership: Europe, the United States, and the Burdens of Alliance* (Ballinger, 1987).

3. For analyses of U.S., European, and NATO involvement in Bosnia, see the chapter entitled "America, Europe, and Bosnia" in Richard Holbrooke, *To End a War* (Random House, 1998); Ivo H. Daalder, *Getting to Dayton: The Making of America's Bosnia Policy* (Brookings, 1999); and Carl Bildt, "Europe and Bosnia: Lessons of the Past and Paths for the Future," address to the Netherlands Association of International Affairs, The Hague, May 27, 1997.

4. See, for example, William Drozdiak, "U.S. European Allies Divided over NATO's Authority to Act," *Washington Post*, November 8, 1998, p. A33; and Roger Cohen, "Kosovo Crisis Strains Relations between the U.S. and Europe," *New York Times*, November 10, 1998, p. A13.

5. See Stephen M. Walt, "The Ties That Fray: Why Europe and America Are Drifting Apart," *National Interest*, no. 54 (Winter 1998–99), pp. 3–11.

6. The former Yugoslavia was not included given its location in Europe; for this same reason, Cyprus is omitted. Both are technically but not politically "out-of-area." India and Pakistan (in the wake of their nuclear tests) would have made good cases but were left out because the project was too far along to accord them equal treatment. North Korea was excluded as it has largely been a subject of concern mostly for the United States, the Republic of Korea, and Japan. Russia and China were excluded for a different reason, namely, that their importance already accords them a special place in transatlantic relations.

7. To date, the United States has not actually applied these secondary sanctions, having agreed to waive portions of Helms-Burton in an agreement signed May 18, 1998. See "Understanding with Respect to Disciplines for the Strengthening of Investment Protection," London, May 18, 1998, as found on the Internet (http://www.eurunion.org/news/invest.htm.). Also, see James Bennet, "To Clear Air with Europe, U.S. Waives Some Sanctions," *New York Times*, May 19, 1998, p. A6.

RICHARD A. NUCCIO

2 | *Cuba:*
A U.S. Perspective

One of the most strongly held opinions about U.S.
Cuba policy is that it is based on outmoded
conceptions of Cuba as a cold war threat. Once Cuba's ties to the Soviet
Union were severed by the collapse of the "evil empire," the argument
goes, Cuba no longer represented a strategic asset to Soviet power. Cuba's
retrenchment from global engagement in wars of national liberation,
guerrilla training, and military and intelligence support for revolutionary governments is usually cited as evidence that Cuba is no longer a
threat to U.S. interests and merits a changed relationship with the United
States. Sometimes conditions laid down by U.S. policymakers twenty
years ago for normalization of relations are cited as now having been
met by Cuba, justifying an automatic U.S. response. A typical statement is that by Wayne Smith:

> The Cold War is over. The Soviet Union has disintegrated. Its former
> ally, Cuba, no longer represents even a potential threat to the security
> of the United States or to that of any other country. In fact, all U.S.
> foreign policy concerns with respect to Cuba have been overcome,
> our objectives met: Cuban troops are out of Africa; Cuba is no longer
> assisting revolutionary movements in Central America or anywhere

else in the world; Cuba's military ties with the former Soviet Union have been reduced to near zero.

Given all this, one would have expected U.S.-Cuban relations to take a turn for the better.[1]

This view ignores the fact that the end of the cold war also affected the U.S. national interest and definition of its national security. This is true for the Latin American and Caribbean region as a whole as well as for Cuba.

For example, the Presidential Review Directive process (PRD–21) for the Latin American and Caribbean region, conducted in the first year of the Clinton administration, identified five national interests of the United States, including the following:

—The promotion of democracy, accountability, and transparency, and the protection of human rights;

—The expansion of free markets and free trade;

—Combating narco-trafficking;

—Controlling illegal immigration; and

—Protecting the natural environment.

Communism or, for that matter, any other kind of ideological definition of threat was absent from the PRD–21 document.

Given this definition of U.S. interests, an active Cuba policy to promote a peaceful, democratic transition should have been among the top priorities for U.S. policymakers responsible for the region. There were two principal reasons.

—One, Cuba was by 1993 the only state in the hemisphere that did not accept the ideal of electoral democracy and market forces as the defining characteristics of legitimate governments.

Some might argue that imposing a new priority of democracy and free markets on Cuba is just another example of the United States "moving the goalposts" for Cuba policy: when Cuba meets one set of conditions, a new set is imposed. However, these goalposts moved for the entire region in the 1990s as citizens held authoritarian governments from Mexico to Guatemala to Paraguay more accountable. And in 1993 the Santiago Declaration at a meeting of the Organization of American States committed the region to the promotion and defense of democracy.

It is true that for other "difficult states"—China, North Korea, and Vietnam being obvious examples—the Clinton administration relented on policies that conditioned improved relations on progress in human rights and democratization. Yet, for each of these states very important national interests were at play, interests far more important than any in the entire Latin American and Caribbean region. Managing China's emergence as a world power is one of the Clinton administration's highest priorities. Friendly relations with China are seen as important in themselves as well as for their ability to affect other regional issues, such as discouraging the development of nuclear weapons by North Korea.

The size of these Asian markets as well as the adoption by some of free market reforms encouraging foreign investment helped to build significant U.S. domestic lobbies supporting less conditioned engagement policies with each of these countries. In contrast, there was until 1998 no politically significant lobby for less conditioned engagement with Cuba. To the contrary, until the pope's visit to Cuba in January 1998 and the weakening of the Cuban American lobby after the death of Jorge Más Canosa, those attempting to promote normalization of relations with Cuba usually became political punching bags.

—Two, the fragile prevalence of democratic values in the Western Hemisphere could be reversed by a disastrous transition in Cuba. This is because Cuba has great symbolic importance for Latin American nationalists and the left. From the CIA-engineered coup in Guatemala in 1954 through the campaign to destabilize Salvador Allende's Chile, U.S. Latin American policy gave ample evidence that it would not tolerate victories by leftist candidates even through democratic processes. Viewed from this perspective, President Bill Clinton's statements about the candidacy of Luís Inácio da Silva ("Lula") in Brazil and that of Cuauhtémoc Cárdenas in Mexico—that the United States would find a way to work cooperatively with anyone elected through a free and fair process—are historic. They contributed to ending the association of U.S. Latin policy with support for right-wing dictators. But U.S. success in promoting a democratic, peaceful transition in socialist Cuba would have an even greater impact. Conversely, a violent transition in Cuba that drew in U.S. forces or residents and required a long U.S. tutelage or even occupation could reignite a cycle of anti-U.S. sentiment in the region. The return of anti-Americanism to the hemispheric agenda would threaten many U.S. objectives such as controlling illegal migration and fighting narcotics trafficking that require regional governments' cooperation to succeed.[2]

Nevertheless, Cuba did not come to occupy such a prominent place in the administration's priorities. Various factors contributed to this situation such as the fact that Latin American policy, like most foreign policy issues, was not a central focus of the Clinton administration's first term. The successful campaign to pass NAFTA and the invasion of Haiti—largely a response to domestic pressures—were the only regional preoccupations of the upper reaches of the administration. An issue as politically difficult as Cuba was even less likely to receive high-level attention.

But Cuba's hesitant experiment in economic reform did not mobilize any countervailing domestic interest among U.S. investors. Without any overriding economic interest, the unrelenting opposition of the Cuban government to two principal U.S. interests in the region, democracy and human rights, meant that there would be no "automatic" normalization of U.S.-Cuban relations.

The Emergence of a Post–Cold War Cuba Policy

The fundamental national security threat facing the United States from Cuba is of a societal collapse that leads to widespread violence. This scenario is the most likely to produce either significant outflows of refugees, or active involvement of U.S. forces and/or Cuban Americans in Cuba. U.S. policy should, therefore, attempt to promote a transition in Cuba, but in a way likely to maximize a peaceful outcome.[3]

These words are from a Cuba memo prepared for Assistant Secretary of State for Inter-American Affairs Alexander Watson. The memo was prompted by a request for testimony from the Western Hemisphere Subcommittee of the House Foreign Affairs Committee in August 1993. Cuba was the first subject on which the subcommittee sought testimony from the new administration's Inter-American Affairs Bureau.[4]

This statement of U.S. interests was nearly identical to that in another Cuba memo written for the Clinton transition team some months earlier. This October 1992 memo conveyed to the transition team the conviction of this author that the incoming Clinton administration would face an imminent challenge from Cuba:

A Clinton administration will very likely confront a crisis in Cuba during its first two years. That crisis could involve the following:

—Threats of massive illegal migration to Florida and other Southern states;

—Use of the island for drug trafficking with or without Cuban government collaboration;

—Civil unrest on the island that creates pressure for U.S. military action or encourages "freelance" military action against Cuba by exiles from U.S. shores; and/or

—Provocative actions against the United States by a failing regime driven to desperate measures.

—Timely initiatives by the administration may preempt the most drastic of these options, but will probably not be able to avoid completely the negative impact of these developments on the United States.

A 1993 memo to Watson laid out the strategy that could advance U.S. interests while mitigating the possible threats to the United States from Cuba.

The principal instrument to promote change in Cuba that is more likely to be peaceful is to strengthen the civil society that has been so devastated by 30 years of dictatorship. This was the fundamental lesson of *Ostpolitik*. The poets, playwrights, labor leaders, human rights activists, students, party professionals, military officers, and disillusioned middle class professionals who were reached by the programs of the West formed the democratic core of the post-communist transitions. Where they were weakest, anti-democratic forces were more likely to have the resources to maintain power in the new societies and to restrict the depth of democratic transformation or, in some cases, to reverse it.

It is doubtful that European Cuba analysts would disagree fundamentally with this description of U.S. interests. If imitation is truly the sincerest form of flattery, Europeans should also not object to the proposal to focus U.S. Cuba policy on the strengthening of civil society and promotion of the kinds of contact and exchange that characterized *Ostpolitik*.[5] Beginning with Watson's testimony in the fall of 1993, the language of promoting a peaceful transition through an emphasis on civil society worked its way into the testimony of other administration officials, including Secretary of State Warren Christopher.

Yet few Europeans know that this objective was the driving concept of U.S. policy. Instead, most European analysts consistently decry U.S. Cuba policy as mired in cold war thinking and reliant on a discredited embargo. How can this be?

There are several reasons why the gap between U.S. and European thinking on Cuba was perceived as being much greater than it really was during the period from 1993 until the signing by President Clinton of the Cuban Liberty and Democratic Solidarity (LIBERTAD) Act, or Helms-Burton law, in March 1996. Part of the explanation is the timidity of senior Clinton administration officials who perceived—correctly— that their own careers would be threatened by too public and too aggressive an attempt to reorient U.S. Cuba policy. There was a pervasive conviction within the career bureaucracy that one must "administer Cuba policy from the right." (The official who gave this advice must remain anonymous but had direct responsibility for Cuba policy.) Senior officials responsible for Cuba policy only moved policy forward when they believed they had the support or at least acquiescence of key Cuban American lobbies such as the Cuban American National Foundation. They consistently portrayed Clinton administration policy as "unchanged" from previous policy. The ritualistic citation of the 1992 Cuban Democracy Act (CDA, sometimes known as the Torricelli Act) as the basis for policy also reinforced the impression of continuity in U.S. policy. The Bureau of Inter-American Affairs referred to the CDA as the "scapular." With the exception of the *Foreign Affairs* article by David Rieff discussed below, most analysis of the CDA focused on its provisions tightening the U.S. embargo. This ignored the important changes in U.S. policy represented by its emphasis on peaceful change, authorization of long distance telephone service, and support for humanitarian assistance to Cuba. Thus, by describing all policy decisions as flowing from the CDA, the State Department would protect itself from political attack by the Cuban American community while taking advantage of the usefulness of the CDA in facilitating new initiatives in Cuba policy.

This cautiousness of senior officials was reinforced by President Clinton's reluctance to assume any personal responsibility for his administration's Cuba policies. With rare exceptions, decisions on Cuba policy were announced by spokespersons or lower-ranking officials, and the president never delivered a speech outlining his Cuba policies to a national audience.

A second reason why European perceptions of U.S. Cuba policy were at variance with actual policy was the success of the Cuban regime in winning the propaganda battle with the United States. Cuba continued to portray itself as a victim of U.S. aggression even as important changes in U.S. policy beneficial to Cuba's government took place. These changes eventually made the United States the largest humanitarian donor to Cuba, dramatically increased Cuban American and other licensed travel to the island, and authorized direct payments to the Cuban government worth hundreds of millions of dollars. (In 1998 annual revenues to Cuba from long distance telephone service are in the range of $70 million, and the trend is upward.)

Another element of the disparity in perceptions was a key difference between *Ostpolitik* and the U.S.'s *Surpolitik* for Cuba: official state-to-state relations. In the European context *Ostpolitik* was a kind of bargain in which the West gained access to the East's hearts and minds while the East's leaders gained the legitimacy of formally negotiating this access with Western governments. U.S. Cuba policy under Clinton sought at least rhetorically to divorce its opening to the Cuban "people" from its continuing isolation of the Cuban "government." Until the Cuban migration crisis of 1994, the Clinton administration avoided direct negotiations with the Cuban government and then insisted that these migration "talks" dealt exclusively with migration issues.

However, perhaps the most important reason why U.S. and European approaches to Cuba were perceived to be so different was that a major initiative in U.S.-European cooperation was launched in 1995 that had to maintain a low profile if it were to succeed. This initiative put to one side the key issue dividing Washington and most of its European allies, that is, the U.S. economic embargo of Cuba. It sought European cooperation in areas of U.S. policy where there was virtually complete agreement: recognition of the legitimacy of peaceful dissent, promotion of human rights, and encouragement of a peaceful transition through an emphasis on strengthening civil society. This initiative made important progress between January 1995 and February 1996. It collapsed after the European Commission, with U.S. knowledge and approval, attempted direct face-to-face negotiations with Castro to obtain his personal commitment to a program of political and economic reform and was rebuffed. The subsequent decision by Castro to launch a wave of repression against a group of dissidents to whom the European Union (EU) had extended protection and to shoot down two U.S.-licensed civilian aircraft, killing three U.S. citizens and a U.S. resident, brought to an end this European initiative. It also undermined U.S. domestic support for the Clinton administration's openings in Cuba policy and led directly to the passage of Helms-Burton.

Ironically, these actions by Castro and the U.S. response of Helms-Burton reversed the terms of the disparity between perception and reality in U.S.-European approaches to Cuba. Under the gun of Helms-Burton, Europeans are now at pains to portray their Cuba policy to a skeptical U.S. Congress as consistent with U.S. goals of democracy, human rights, and protection of U.S. private property. Yet the United States and Europe are further apart than ever on the goals of Cuba policy and the means to be used to achieve them. The current disconnect between Europe and the United States could still lead to a confrontation over Cuba policy that would inflict real damage on U.S.-European relations on substantive matters of much greater importance to both parties than Cuba. The inclusion of Europe in the domestic equation of U.S. Cuba policy also undermines any contribution the EU might make to encouraging peaceful change in Cuba and perpetuates U.S. isolation.

A European Initiative on Cuba and an Uncharacteristic U.S. Response

As Felipe Gonzalez's socialist government prepared to assume the EU's presidency in 1995, Spain decided to carry out a major opening to Cuba. When U.S. policymakers became aware of this push for a "cooperative agreement" to encourage trade between Cuba and the EU, they debated two possible responses. One, a long U.S. tradition, was to marshal support from those EU members sympathetic to U.S. concerns and block or delay the Spanish effort. The second option, the one chosen, was to work quietly with Spain and the EU to strengthen the conditions attached to any agreement, in particular to include a "democracy clause" that the EU had itself added to other trade accords.

Throughout 1995, senior U.S. officials traveled to Madrid, Brussels, Rome, and London to explain U.S. policy on Cuba. In conversations with their European counterparts they acknowledged disagreement over the utility of the U.S. economic embargo in achieving the shared objective of a peaceful and democratic outcome in Cuba. But they also stressed new aspects of U.S. policy where the United States and its European friends could agree:

—Selective openings in the embargo to encourage contact and communication with the Cuban people;

—Recognition that the development of Cuba's civil society—those institutions between the state and the family that are the wellspring of modern, democratic values—was the best way to encourage change.

—A commitment by the Clinton administration to making "carefully calibrated responses" to any movement in Cuba toward reform, as argued by the Cuban Democracy Act of 1992.

The Europeans were skeptical of U.S. sincerity and confident that they could achieve in Cuba what U.S. policy had not. But over time the logic of the U.S. position had its effect. The United States was only holding the Europeans to standards of democracy and human rights that they themselves practiced. Several governments were wary of Castro's real intentions and made it clear that they wanted meaningful conditionality on any agreement between the EU and Cuba.

This year-long effort culminated on February 7, 1996, in a meeting between this author; Stuart Eizenstat, then the U.S. ambassador to the EU; and Manuel Marín, the vice president of the European Commission, a leader in Spain's ruling Socialist Party and the force behind the EU initiative. Marín was leaving that day for Cuba to meet privately with Castro.[6] He had told his Cuban interlocutors that he also would meet with the newly formed human rights group, the *Concilio Cubano* [Cuban Council], and extend to it the protection of the EU.

In his meeting with Castro, Marín would stress the importance of Castro's personal commitment to specific economic and political reforms. These included the revision of Cuba's laws criminalizing speech and thought and the encouragement of microenterprise. Marín explained that he would bring to the Cuban leader not only the prospect of a cooperative trade agreement with the EU but also the offer of an observer seat in the Rio Group, an organization of the largest and most powerful Latin American countries.

The closing of the gap between the U.S. and EU positions startled

U.S. officials in the room. Without time to consult Washington, they nevertheless gave Marín a commitment that, if his mission were successful, they would work to obtain from President Clinton some important signal recognizing that real reform was under way in Cuba.

Marín's meeting with Castro did not go well. After eleven hours of contentious debate, Castro rejected every item on Marín's agenda. As Marín's plane cleared Havana air traffic control, Castro ordered the arrest of Cuban Council leaders, including those who had met with Marín. Sometime during those early days of February, Castro also gave Cuba's air force the authority to shoot down two U.S.-licensed civilian planes on February 24.

As provocative an assertion as it may seem, many in the U.S. and European governments believe that the Cuban government chose to shoot down the exile planes because it would end this U.S. initiative. The U.S. success in closing the gap with its European allies on Cuba and rallying meaningful domestic support for Castro's opponents on the island was perceived as too threatening by Havana.

David Rieff, one of very few who seems to have grasped the content of U.S. Cuba policy at the time, explains what may have been the Cubans' mindset:

> The Clinton administration's emphasis on a Track II approach alarmed the Castro regime more than the original passage of the Torricelli bill. If the U.S. government turned its attention from supporting the heroic but largely impotent dissident movement to overtly or covertly sponsoring or even just actively encouraging the activities of nongovernmental humanitarian organizations, the regime might find itself faced with powerful opposing forces. Something must be done, Cuban leaders decided, before the country was deluged by international aid and human rights organizations more likely even than the church to share Washington's desire for Castro's departure.[7]

By February 1996 U.S. Cuba policy was advancing along three fronts. It had successfully linked with developments within Cuba and the emergence of *Concilio Cubano* as a legitimate opposition voice. *Concilio's* call for a national day of dialogue on February 24 captured the imagination of many in the exile community. People as far apart politically as Ramon Cernuda, whose gallery had been bombed by right-wing exiles for displaying "communist" art and who was a Miami-based ally of socialist dissident Elizardo Sanchez, and U.S. Representative Lincoln Diaz-Balart (R.-Fla.), whose aunt was married to and abandoned by Castro, both endorsed *Concilio's* day of dialogue.

Within the United States moderate voices of the exile community were emerging. Outside the Cuban community a broad range of nongovernmental organizations responded to the administration's efforts to encourage the growth of Cuba's civil society. Marín's visit, his official recognition of *Concilio*, and insistence on an agenda of political and economic reform must have seemed to the Cubans to be the final blow to their careful strategy of isolating the United States.

Whatever the motivation for the Cuban government's actions, the shootdown overwhelmed administration support for its own policies.[8] Though some argued that signing Helms-Burton would destroy the possibility of a constructive Cuba policy, in the aftermath of the shootdown another logic prevailed: Clinton's political advisers determined that signing Helms-Burton would make the president appear "tough" and protect his reelection chances in 1996.[9]

U.S. Cuba Policy under Helms-Burton

Most of the European ire over Helms-Burton has focused on Titles III and IV. Title III permits U.S. citizens whose property was expropriated without compensation by the Cuban government, including those who were not citizens when the expropriation occurred, to sue in U.S. court those foreign corporations that "traffic" in these properties. (Trafficking includes a broad range of activities from outright ownership to indirect benefit.) Title IV permits denying entry to the United States to the corporate officers and their families of companies engaged in such trafficking. When the president decided to seek a face-saving compromise to permit him to sign Helms-Burton, his senior aides sought a "waiver" of two aspects of Title III. One was the initiation of a time period after which those covered by the trafficking provisions of Helms-Burton could be sued in U.S. courts; the other was the entry into force of U.S. citizens' "standing" in court. After signing the legislation on March 12, 1996, President Clinton exercised his option to waive the right of citizens to sue but did allow the clock to start. If the president at some future point does not waive—as he must every six months—the two-year clock will have run its course, and U.S. citizens will be able to begin the process of litigation.

In the negotiations over Helms-Burton, Congress sought to restrict the president's ability to exercise his waiver by insisting that it not merely meet the test of being "in the national interest" but also that it "expedite a transition to democracy in Cuba." As the drafters of the legislation made clear in their report on the bill, they intended this language to make the waiver an unusual and difficult decision.

> In the judgment of the committee of conference, under current circumstances the President could not in good faith determine that suspension of the right of action is either "necessary to the national interests of the United States" or "will expedite a transition to democracy in Cuba." In particular, the committee believes that it is demonstrably not the case that suspending the right of action will expedite a transition to democracy in Cuba, inasmuch as suspension would remove a significant deterrent to foreign investment in Cuba, thereby helping prolong Castro's grip on power.[10]

In practice this legislative intent has been ignored by the White House, which has waived it every six months since passage of the bill.

The loophole that permits the White House to continue the waiver is an extension of the effort described earlier to win European support for the U.S. strategy of promoting a peaceful, democratic transition. This was to seek public commitments by the Europeans to the positions represented by Marín's undisclosed Cuba initiative. If the administration could demonstrate to Congress that other governments were prepared to endorse the objectives of U.S. Cuba policy—and realistically only the Europeans were potential candidates—then suspending the sanctions against these governments would contribute automatically to advancing the cause of democracy in Cuba.

However, there were two problems with this approach. The first was that U.S. policy officially opposed foreign investment in Cuba. How could the United States adopt a code of conduct for investment it did not want to see? This inherent contradiction had prevented the administration from publicly endorsing the Arcos Principles earlier. (The Arcos Principles are a code of conduct for investors in Cuba that were developed by two Cuban American professionals with the Inter-American Development Bank. The prominent Cuban human rights activist

Gustavo Arcos reviewed and endorsed the principles.) The authors of Helms-Burton clearly opposed on principle any foreign investment in Cuba whether in expropriated property or not. However, criticism of the extraterritorial reach of the legislation forced the bill's supporters to narrow the legislation to investment in U.S. expropriated property. To use a code of conduct as the basis for a waiver, U.S. policy would have to overcome the awkwardness of condemning all investment, while conceding that if investment in nonexpropriated property was to occur its adherence to the Arcos Principles did make a contribution to democracy. Eizenstat adopted this argument, compiled a list of "best business practices" loosely based on the Arcos Principles, and thus provided the basis for Clinton's first and subsequent waivers.[11]

There were, however, two intrinsic problems with this conceptual basis for the waiver that have been ignored by the administration. First, it did not provide a long-term solution to the inherent conflict between the desire of Congress to eliminate all foreign investment in Castro's Cuba and the European belief that foreign investment in Cuba is a mechanism to promote peaceful change. European governments, irked by the requirement to pay public obeisance to U.S. Cuba policy, maintained that their goal was to obtain a *permanent* waiver of Title III and add a waiver to Title IV. Only Congress can change the existing legislative requirements, and it has demonstrated great skepticism about the Europeans' efforts so far.

In a press statement issued at the time of President Clinton's fourth consecutive waiver of Title III in January 1998, Senate Foreign Relations Committee Chairman Jesse Helms (R.-N.C.) described Clinton as "abetting profiteers who are propping up Castro at the expense of the Cuban people." Helms also said that his committee would "schedule a hearing early this year [1998] to examine the administration's failure to enforce this law, and to press for action to hasten the end to Castro's brutality."[12] More recently a report on a trip to Cuba by Senator Helms's principal Latin American adviser Roger Noriega and two other Senate and House staffers denounced the EU efforts on Cuba. "The EU's performance has been little talk and even less action," said the report. It added, "The president's repeated suspensions of Title III make a mockery of U.S. law, and could invite a legal challenge from Americans whose right to sue is being arbitrarily denied." The editor of the newsletter reporting these remarks commented, "The tone of the report contrasts sharply with remarks in January by Undersecretary of State Stuart

Eizenstat, who hailed the 'unprecedented multilateral effort' to push for democracy in Cuba."[13]

A second problem is more fundamental and reveals the true dilemma of U.S. Cuba policy under Helms-Burton. Public commitments by other governments to the United States that they will undertake efforts to support human rights and advance democratic practices in Cuba may help justify a Helms-Burton waiver, but it undercuts these same governments' ability to actually carry out such commitments *within* Cuba. The strategy behind the approach to the Europeans in 1995 was to coordinate the Europeans' policy of engagement with the Cuban government with the U.S. policy of isolation of that government. The Europeans would be the "good cop" since the U.S. policy environment condemned it to being solely the "bad cop." U.S. policy, for the reasons described earlier, was constrained politically from conducting face-to-face negotiations with the Cuban government over the U.S. interest in having access to the Cuban people. Europe had no such constraints. Whatever the merits of the engagement versus isolation debate, the Europeans and United States were more likely to produce results in concert. But, as in real efforts to outmaneuver a police suspect, it was important that Cuba be convinced that in responding to the "good" cop—Europe—it was not succumbing to the threats and intimidation of the "bad" United States. Institutionalizing European efforts on human rights or economic and political reform within the context of Helms-Burton gives the Cubans a perfect excuse for resisting what they otherwise might have felt some pressure to accept because it came from their European "friends" and not their gringo enemy.

By forcing the administration to "recruit" Europe into its waiver decisions, Helms-Burton has transformed European Cuba policy into the same ineffective sop for domestic public opinion that U.S. Cuba policy long was. Neither U.S. nor European officials are concerned with whether public postures taken to satisfy Helms-Burton's requirements actually translate into productive efforts inside Cuba.

Is a Peaceful, Democratic Transition Still the Objective of U.S. Cuba Policy?

These are the obstacles, both political and conceptual, that Titles III and IV present to any policy to promote a peaceful, democratic transition in Cuba. However, these two titles are not the most damaging aspect of Helms-Burton to the goal of a peaceful transition, nor what separate U.S. and European approaches to Cuba. That dubious distinction belongs to a relatively neglected aspect of Title II that mandates among other things that a transition government in Cuba cannot include Fidel Castro or his brother Raul.

Some clarification is needed. The Castro brothers probably are not interested in carrying out a democratic transition. But U.S. policy should not discard the opportunity for Cuba's leaders to choose a path that would advance the interest of the vast majority of Cubans and of the United States in a peaceful transition. The behavior of Cuba's leaders, not their genetic makeup, should determine U.S. policy. Stated another way, though it may not matter to Senator Helms whether Fidel leaves "horizontally or vertically," it surely does to the interests of the United States.[14] The objective of U.S. policy should be to encourage a peaceful transition, to remove all unnecessary obstacles to Cuba's leaders choosing to lead such a transition, and to demonstrate to the world and to key sectors in Cuba that Castro, not U.S. policy, is the obstacle to a brighter future for the Cuban people. From 1996 until 1998 restrained U.S. enforcement of Titles III and IV and a desire by both parties to avoid provoking a crisis in the World Trade Organization postponed the emergence of tensions resulting from the latent contradictions in U.S. and European approaches to Cuba. A new compromise, discussed below, announced by U.S. and EU officials at the special EU-U.S. summit in May 1998 that deals with conflicts over U.S. sanctions of Iran, Libya, and Cuba should push off the day of reckoning further.

But détente with Europe assumes a static situation in Cuba, something the United States should not assume. Cuba is in a transition process that is likely to produce new challenges to U.S. policy and perhaps new confrontations with an administration nearly out of diplomatic options to demonstrate "toughness" and subservient to a militantly anti-Castro Congress. It is far from clear that this latest compromise with the EU will survive a new crisis in U.S.-Cuban relations that prompts military strikes against Cuban targets or an oil blockade of Cuba—two options debated seriously at the time of the February 24 shootdown.

From Détente to Entente on Cuba

With leadership from Washington and Brussels it may be possible to move from the current precarious détente to meaningful cooperation on Cuba policy. The first requirement for a constructive Cuba policy based on national interests is for the president of the United States to reassert his responsibility for the conduct of U.S. foreign policy.[15] This is not gratuitous criticism. The president speaks about Cuba policy as if someone else were in charge of it. When questioned about U.S. Cuba policy during his Latin American trip in October 1997, Clinton described current policy as being the product of "the hardest-line people in Miami." He suggested during this trip, subsequently on a national news interview program, and to fund-raising audiences shortly before the visit of Pope John Paul II to Cuba that he had endorsed the Cuban Democracy Act in 1992 to encourage a process of change in Cuba. However, according to the president, the Castro regime's failure to respond positively to his initiatives led to a change in policy by Congress. Consistent with this view that others are responsible for his Cuba policy, President Clinton has even called on President Castro to help him change it.[16] All of these statements suggest that the administration is unwilling to do the hard work necessary to lead the country toward a more responsible Cuba policy. If Castro himself has to supply the political constituency for U.S. leadership, we will wait a long time for such a change.

A more constructive approach and one more likely to attract international support would follow the suggestion of Secretary of State Madeleine K. Albright when she said in March 1998, "The Cuban people are beginning to think beyond Castro. We need to do the same."[17] "Thinking beyond Castro" means recognizing that the Cuban government's reluctant experiment in enclave capitalism offers opportunities for U.S. objectives. Foreign investment in Cuba is not a panacea for dictatorship or repression. But if highly conditioned to encourage the spread of capitalism beyond the sectors and regions to which the Cuban regime would like to restrict it, foreign investment would be an ally of change and democratization in Cuba. A policy based on this concept would draw on America's strengths in the power of its ideas and the openness of our society. In its desire to topple the Castro regime, Helms-Burton mimics the mean-spiritedness and absolutism of the dictatorship itself. Yet three years after Helms-Burton was passed it should be clear that the legislation's goal of destabilizing the regime is neither within its reach nor desirable.

The May 1998 EU-U.S. accord appears to confirm the analysis made earlier. It avoids conflict over Helms-Burton but does nothing to advance the cause of a peaceful, democratic transition in Cuba. In return for commitments by the Europeans that will "chill" future investment there, the United States has agreed to seek changes from Congress that would give the president greater authority to waive certain sanctions against European countries doing business in Cuba.

The administration's promise to seek congressional authorization for changes in Cuba policy is the best news in the agreement. This chapter has argued against the negative impact of Helms-Burton on U.S. Cuba policy and congressional "hijacking" of executive branch authority. Now that the administration's prestige is on the line, it may make the political effort required to secure congressional support of its compromise with the Europeans. If successful on this first step, it may discover the courage to do more.

However, early congressional reactions are not encouraging. Senate Foreign Relations Committee chairman Jesse Helms, coauthor of Helms-Burton, said after the agreement was announced, "It will be a cold day in you-know-where before the EU convinces me to trade the binding restrictions in the Helms-Burton law for an agreement that legitimizes their theft of American property in Cuba."[18] Representative Lincoln Diaz-Balart said the administration "should not assume this has the support of Congress."[19] In a joint letter to Secretary Albright in June, Helms and House International Relations Committee chairman Benjamin A. Gilman (R.–N.Y.), listed seven concerns they had about the EU-U.S. deal and appeared to close the door on congressional approval of the EU-U.S. "understanding." "The Europeans should not expect us [to] cede protections for our citizens under Title III in exchange for their doing their utmost to help the Cuban people. We trust that you will convey that message to make clear that Title III is not on the table."[20]

More troubling is the fact that the enormous political capital expended by the administration to protect the American owners of expropriated property does nothing to promote the more vital U.S. interest in a peaceful, democratic transition. To do so the administration must challenge Helms-Burton's assumption that foreign investment cannot contribute to a solution to Cuba's transition crisis. This would require the administration to *endorse* foreign investment in Cuba *if* it is strongly conditioned. Such strengthened conditionality would follow the recommendations of the Arcos Principles and encourage investors to deal directly with their employees in the setting of working conditions, rather than through the Cuban government agency that now contracts with foreign companies to provide workers, collects their pay in dollars, and pays the workers a reduced compensation in Cuban pesos. It would recognize the right of employees to organize independently to represent themselves, make available the goods and services they provide in Cuba to all Cuban citizens, and enforce existing environmental legislation and press for additional environmental protections. In exchange for such an important change in U.S. Cuba policy, the Europeans should acknowledge that their détente with the United States to avoid conflict over Helms-Burton is not a contribution to real change in Cuba. They should pledge to undertake more serious and subtler cooperation with the shared objective of a peaceful, democratic transition.

This begs the question of what administration policy should be with regard to U.S. investment. The logic that expanding the impact of capitalism in Cuba would increase pressures for democratic change applies to U.S. policy as well as the EU's. However, there are two problems with dropping all restrictions on U.S. investment. The first is political. By signing Helms-Burton, President Clinton transferred the power to lift the U.S. embargo to Congress. Its judgment about whether developments in Cuba fulfill the strict conditionality of Helms-Burton, not that of a future president, will determine the pace and content of the executive branch's response. Yet even the most enthusiastic advocates of unbridled U.S. investment in Cuba acknowledge that the positive effects of such investment on political and economic reform will not be seen for many years. It seems unlikely that U.S. politicians will be willing to pay the short-term political price for making such a change when they may not be around to collect the political dividend. Second, massive flows of U.S. investment might well have the immediate effect of stabilizing Castro's government and perpetuating his rule. How ironic it would be if all the United States had to show for ending the trade embargo was a handful of lucrative business deals.

A more politically palatable and principled shift in U.S. policy that permits greater coordination with the Europeans would advocate selective lifting of the U.S. embargo such as has already occurred in certain areas. As mentioned earlier, long distance telephone service was expanded to Cuba through authorization of direct payments to the Cuban phone company. The original telecommunications regulations promulgated under the Cuban Democracy Act anticipated that a logical next step for

U.S policy was to authorize U.S. telecommunications companies to invest in Cuba's internal telecommunications infrastructure. Such investment by U.S. companies could expand opportunities for ordinary Cubans to communicate with the outside world through hard bargaining for universal access throughout the island and by insisting that there not be government restrictions on Internet access. Similarly, U.S. investment could be encouraged in the health industry and in food production in ways that might encourage the growth of microenterprise. U.S. business schools should be permitted to set up training programs in Cuban universities to teach business management skills and to expand dramatically exchange programs for students and faculty of business and technical schools. The full lifting of the embargo would have to wait until the conditions of Helms-Burton were met or, more likely, until progress in Cuba's evolution toward an open society supported efforts to repeal Helms-Burton's unrealistic and intrusive Title II provisions.

If Cuba were a static place of no consequence to the United States and located thousands of miles from American shores, it would not matter if both the United States and Europe were to pursue ineffective policies that at best do nothing to further a peaceful, democratic transition on the island and at worst increase the possibility of a violent and chaotic transition. It might be cruel to condemn 11 million Cubans to economic privation and political repression to placate domestic constituencies; it might even be stupid. But it would not necessarily be a criminal neglect of the national interest.

However, Cuba is not a distant country or one in stasis. It is ninety miles from U.S. shores and already a decade into a post-Soviet transition toward something other than what it has been for nearly forty years. Historically since the end of World War II, 10 percent of the population of the Caribbean Basin has migrated permanently to the United States. Roughly that percentage of Cubans has already fled Castro's Cuba. We do not know precisely how many more would join their fellow exiles if they could, but the number is surely in the millions. If Cubans cannot solve Cuba's future problems in Cuba, they will try to solve them by migrating to the United States. It is that simple. Therefore, it is at once important and urgent for both the United States and Europe to take responsibility for encouraging deep, structural change on the island.[21]

The United States and Europe have demonstrated that they can reach agreement to adopt Cuba policies that address their own domestic political constituencies rather than Cuban realities. This resolves the threat to important U.S.-European relations presented by the unwise decision to pass and sign Helms-Burton, but it does nothing to advance and may well retard the U.S. interest in promoting a peaceful, democratic transition in Cuba. It will be difficult to overcome years of bad U.S. policy and the straitjacket of current legislation to fashion policies in Washington and Brussels that reinforce each other and what should be the objective of Cuba policy. However, because what happens in Cuba matters to 11 million Cubans and to the democratic progress made in the Western Hemisphere in the last decade and a half, this is a task worth undertaking.

Notes

1. Wayne Smith, "Our Cuba Diplomacy: A Critical Reexamination," Washington, Center for International Policy, October 1994.

2. Some analysts might argue that the U.S. invasion of Haiti to restore President Aristide to power demonstrates that there is regional support for U.S. intervention when it is on the side of democracy. This is a significant misreading of Haiti's significance for Latin America. Because of its distinctive racial, cultural, and linguistic heritage, Haiti is not viewed by the rest of the Latin American and Caribbean region as relevant to their national situations.

3. I entered the State Department as a political appointee in July 1993. This language and the other quotations included below are from private papers I wrote as a staffer to then-Representative Robert G. Torricelli or from contributions to the Clinton-Gore campaign or transition team. This particular language on national security was repeated many times in internal government documents. It also appeared in official statements by Watson and other senior officials.

4. "Recent Developments in Cuba Policy: Telecommunications and Dollarization," Subcommittee on Western Hemisphere Affairs of the House Foreign Affairs Committee, August 4, 1994.

5. I used *Ostpolitik* in this memo as shorthand for diplomatic initiatives undertaken by European leaders to lessen the risk of war while increasing ties between the divided halves of Europe. *Ostpolitik* refers properly to a number of interrelated diplomatic moves undertaken by West German Chancellor Willy Brandt. These included the negotiation of a treaty with Poland to settle the question of the Polish border and the status of German minorities; signaling to Moscow that West Germany did not seek to undermine the Soviet position in Eastern Europe; reassurance of West German public opinion that the freedom of West Berlin would not suffer from a consolidation of the Federal Republic's relations with Eastern Europe; and direct negotiations with East Germany.

Another critical part of *Ostpolitik's* strategy of the engagement with the East was the Conference on Security and Cooperation in Europe and the complex array of Western and Eastern demands included in its agenda. In developing a section of the Cuban Democracy Act called "Support for the Cuban People." I drew on the third "basket" of the CSCE's agenda: broadening of contacts between people, freer flow of information, and the broadening of cultural and educational cooperation. During the period I was drafting the Cuban Democracy Act I drew ideas from a discussion of these negotiations by Alastair Buchan, *The End of the Postwar Era* (Saturday Review Press/E.P. Dutton and Co., 1974).

6. Eizenstat was at the time U.S. Ambassador to the European Union. In 1996 he was named an undersecretary of commerce and then undersecretary of state for economic, business, and agricultural affairs. He subsequently became the principal administration spokesperson for its Helms-Burton strategy.

7. David Rieff, "Cuba Refrozen," *Foreign Affairs*, vol. 75 (July-August 1996), p. 73. I do not know how Rieff came to view U.S. Cuba policy as it was seen by those carrying it out. I have never met Rieff nor spoken with him.

8. Another explanation for the shootdown, as articulated in the *New Yorker* magazine, is that the Cubans were forced to shoot down the two aircraft because their complaints about the overflights had gone unheeded by the United States and/or that a secret, back channel communication through a U.S. journalist had guaranteed the Cuban government that the overflights would be stopped. See Carl Nagin, "Annals of Diplomacy, Backfire," *New Yorker*, January 26, 1998, pp. 30–35. To my knowledge, no such back channel message was ever sent by the White House. If someone authorized it above me, which in the case of Cuba could only mean Tony Lake or Sandy Berger, it was done without understanding the limitations of U.S. law and without any implementation to deliver on the promise. Despite the declaration by the president of a national state of emergency after the shootdown, it is still impossible for U.S. authorities to *prevent* someone from flying from the United States because of a mere suspicion that he or she might violate the international airspace of another country.

9. At the cabinet level meeting immediately after the shootdown to review recommendations to the president on Helms-Burton most cabinet officers, including Attorney General Janet Reno, Defense Secretary William Perry, and Joint Chiefs Chairman John Shalikashvili, were shocked to learn that Helms-Burton codified the U.S. economic embargo. The attorney general's first reaction was to suggest a review of the bill's constitutionality. However, all objections to signing the bill were overruled first by George Stephanopoulos and Leon Panetta, then by National Security Adviser Tony Lake. At the time Helms-Burton was signed there was some debate within the administration about how restrictive the legislation was. Some held that the executive branch retained its ability to promulgate regulations and, hence, change Cuba policy without prior approval; others that Helms-Burton was an intolerable, even unconstitutional, intrusion on the president's ability to conduct foreign policy. Those who recommended signature to him did not understand the full implications of Helms-Burton.

10. "Joint Explanatory Statement of the Committee of the Conference," Conference report to accompany H.R. 927, "Cuban Liberty and Democratic Solidarity (Libertad) Act of 1996," 104 Cong. 2 sess., March 1, 1996, p. 26.

11. "Let me note that the U.S. discourages investment in Cuba. We don't believe that investment under the current circumstances would promote change; it would only strengthen the Castro regime. However, we recognize that some foreign companies are going to seek investment opportunities in Cuba." Stuart Eizenstat, "Speech to the North American Committee of the National Policy Association," Washington, January 7, 1998.

12. "Helms Blasts Clinton's Failure to Enforce Cuba Law," Senate Committee on Foreign Relations, press release, Washington, January 16, 1998, cited in George Gedda, "Study: EU Violates Cuba Pledges," *Associated Press*, March 4, 1998.

13. Ralph Galliano, *U.S-Cuba Policy Report,* vol. 5 (January 31, 1998), p. 9.

14. In the press conference, February 28, 1996, immediately after the successful negotiation of the administration compromise on Helms-Burton, Senator Helms summed up the bill by saying that it was "Farewell Fidel." He continues to reaffirm his position that the manner of Castro's departure is irrelevant to Cuba's democratic prospects. "I don't care how he leaves there. Horizontally or vertically," Helms said on CNN's *Evans & Novak.* "I want him out of there, and the Cuban people want him out, too." As quoted in Kalpana Srinivasan, "Helms: Cuba Embargo Will Stand," *Associated Press*, January 31, 1998.

15. See Richard A. Nuccio, "Mr. Clinton, Take the Lead in Shaping up U.S. Policy on Cuba," *Miami Herald*, February 1, 1998, p. 3L.

16. Sonya Ross, "Clinton Seeks Better Cuba Relations," November 10, 1997, the Associated Press, reported the president's statements on *Meet the Press*, November 9, 1997, this way: President Clinton says he would like the United States to develop ties with Cuba, provided Fidel Castro first takes steps toward democracy. In a television interview aired that Sunday, Clinton envisioned "an ongoing relationship" with Cuba much like the one the United States has built with China, also under communist rule. "But we have to have some basis for opening. It can't be a one-way street," he said on NBC-TV's *Meet the Press.* And "There has to be some sense that there's an evolution going on in Cuba, and it can turn into a modern state."

17. Press conference by Secretary of State Madeleine K. Albright, Washington, March 20, 1998.

18. Dan Balz, "U.S. Eases Stand on Cuba, Iran Sanctions, Helms Condemns, Europe Hails Move," *Washington Post*, May 19, 1998, p. A15.

19. Ibid.

20. Jesse Helms and Benjamin A. Gilman, *Letter to the Honorable Madeleine Albright*, June 17, 1998.

21. Europe, like the United States, believes that how a transition occurs in Cuba has profound implications for the rest of the region. This is still not the prevailing view in Latin America and the Caribbean itself, which has adopted the attitude that Cuba is a U.S. problem of only marginal concern to them.

JOAQUÍN ROY

3

Europe: Cuba, the U.S. Embargo, and the Helms-Burton Law

O n May 18, 1998, the European Union and the
United States announced at the end of the sum-
mit held in London by British Prime Minister Tony Blair (doubling as
president of the European Union) and U.S. President Bill Clinton that
they had agreed to a compromise that in essence would freeze the application of the controversial Cuban Liberty and Democratic Solidarity
(LIBERTAD) Act of 1996 (Helms-Burton Act) and the Iran and Libya

This paper should recognize the generous and unconditional encouragement received
from my colleague and friend Enrique Baloyra in what probably was his last editing activity
before his untimely death in July 1997. The result was an article, "The Helms-Burton Law:
Development, Consequences, and Legacy for Inter-American and U.S.-European Relations,"
Journal of Inter-American Studies and World Affairs, vol. 39 (Fall 1997), pp. 77–108, and a
shorter, essay version published in Spanish, "Auge y caída de la ley Helms-Burton," *Leviatán*
(Madrid), vol. 68 (Verano 1997), pp. 33–42; *Archivos del Presente*, Buenos Aires (Abril-
Junio 1997), pp. 117–30; and *Encuentro*, Madrid, vol. 4-4 (Primavera/Verano 1997), pp.
68–77. Among those who have contributed to this chapter according to their generosity
and special capacities are Ambler H. Moss, Angel Viñas, Robert Kirsner, Anna Krift, and
the staff of Richter Library and the Law School Library of the University of Miami, the Law
School Library of the University of Barcelona, the CIDOB Foundation of Barcelona, IRELA,
the DGI and DGVIII of the European Commission, and the Oficina de Información
Diplomática of Spain's Ministry of Foreign Affairs.

Sanctions Act of 1996 (ILSA or D'Amato Act) in reference to investment in Cuba, Libya, and Iran.[1] On Cuba, the understanding confirmed
the promise by the EU not to pursue retaliatory measures against the
United States in the World Trade Organization (WTO) and to discourage investment in certain questionable, that is, expropriated, properties. The White House, in exchange, promised to pressure the U.S.
Congress to further neutralize the application of the Helms-Burton legislation, which allows lawsuits against investors in previously U.S.-owned
properties in Cuba and denies visas to executives of foreign firms dealing
with such properties. The United States and the European Union agreed
to establish a Registry of Claims and to work jointly in the context of
the Multilateral Agreement on Investment (MAI). In sum, the agreement
confirmed the path taken in 1997 when both parties sought a compromise to avoid a serious commercial confrontation with unpredictable
political consequences. However, as far as the Cuban dimension is concerned, the agreement is not free of problems. It has been relunctantly
accepted by some of the EU member states, different commentators,
U.S. sources, and Cuba.[2] Moreover, the agreement still depends on congressional cooperation and is linked to the overall development of policies regarding sensitive European interests in Libya and Iran.[3]

Introduction

Any analysis of the European links with Cuba has to consider the
peculiar relationship between the United States and the Caribbean nation. When Cuba became a Marxist-Leninist state just ninety miles from
the U.S. shores, Washington took this as an offense that no U.S. president has managed to cope with successfully. In contrast, Europe has
pretended to deal with Cuba almost as a totally "normal" state. For
Germany, Cuba has simply meant one more Latin American opportunity for trade and investment. For France and Great Britain, Cuba has
historically signified an important territory of the Caribbean region
where they competed for hegemony with Spain and with each other.
Cuba has been for Spain something very special, "the ever faithful island." In executing a practical, explicit policy of commercial engagement, Europe has given the United States a clear message of its opposition
to the embargo.

In view of the matter-of-fact policy of European states toward Cuba during the cold war, the contrasts with U.S. policy became more evident with the dissolution of the Soviet Union, the protector of the Cuban Revolution. However, some new obstacles have become apparent for European interests.

A "Normal" Relationship Disturbed by a "Problem"

Since late in 1995, when the U.S. Senate and House of Representatives inserted a number of adjustments and touches into the basic text of the Helms-Burton bill, some major developments have to be taken into account. The first event is the criminal shooting down of two Cuban exiles' planes a few miles off Havana on February 24, 1996, an act that shattered all possibilities of rapprochement between the United States and Cuba. As a result, President Bill Clinton signed Helms-Burton on March 12, 1996. The Helms-Burton law aims to discourage foreign investment in Cuba through the threat of lawsuits (Title III) and the imposition of restrictions to travel to the United States on foreign executives whose companies "traffic" in "stolen" properties (Title IV). It seeks to generate a deeper economic deterioration in order to accelerate the fall of the current Cuban regime.

The European Union decided in the fall of 1996 to enact a Regulation (complemented by a Joint Action) as a blocking measure. Simultaneously, the EU announced its intent to insert this issue in the framework of the WTO. As a confirmation of its policy of conditioning economic aid, the EU also issued a Common Position detailing the requirements to be met by Cuba in order to become a beneficiary. As a sign of mutual concern for the looming confrontation between close economic and political partners, on April 11, 1997, the EU responded to the U.S. partial suspension of the law (Title III) by agreeing on a pact that would in essence freeze the move toward the WTO. A serious international confrontation was defused.

The history of how matters arrived at such a point is instructive and began more than a decade ago when Cuba decided to foster economic reforms and investment. In 1982 Havana approved a law to regulate the activities of business consortia.[4] In September 1995, Law no. 77 was issued to regulate foreign investment.[5] According to the Cuban government, at the end of 1995, 212 joint ventures were operating in Cuba, with European interests in the lead. At the end of 1997, the most optimistic figures of foreign investment in Cuba topped $5.5 billion in "announced" and $1.2 billion in "committed/delivered" operations.[6]

These investments could not skirt some relationship with expropriated properties, on which Washington and Havana never came to terms in negotiating a settlement. Investments became potential targets for future confiscation and retaliation emanating from a new twist in U.S. policy and its immediate translation, the Cuban Democracy Act (CDA) of 1992, the "Torricelli law."[7] Although it placed limitations on the ability of U.S. subsidiaries to deal with Cuba, it also left the door open for a rapprochement. Helms-Burton would redress this gap.

Cuba's Trade Dependency with Europe

In the 1960s and 1970s, European states were dealing with Cuba in clear violation of U.S. pressures and admonitions. The search for pragmatism and the consideration of Cuba as a "normal" state prevailed. In global terms the figures of Western Europe–Cuba trade were modest. Yet in strategic terms, they were crucial for Cuba.[8]

With the economic reforms that took place in Cuba after the end of the cold war, the Cuban economy began to shift to a sort of normalization of relations with Western European states. In the absence of a decisive road to democracy and a market economy, a sort of stable Cuba became the goal for these European states in which they could pursue trade ventures. Cuban trade showed a steady shift from the overwhelming dependency on the Soviet bloc to an unstoppable linkage with the market economies. While in the 1980s only 7 percent of Cuba's trade was with (Western) Europe and about 6 percent with Latin America and Canada, in the mid-1990s these partners accounted for 90 percent of Cuba's total commerce. In 1994, 38 percent of Cuban imports and 29 percent of its exports were with the European market. Europe today occupies about a third of all trade activity with Cuba.[9]

Tourists were again courted by the Cuban government. Figures showed a steady increase, from 300,000 visitors in 1990 to more than 700,000 in 1995. Gross income generated from this source increased five times from 1990 to 1995, from an income of 200 million pesos to about 1 billion.[10] Canada, Italy, Spain, and Germany contributed the greatest number of tourists.[11] In 1997, according to Cuban government sources, income from tourism reached a gross of $850 million, provided by the visits of 1,171,000 tourists. Italy, Canada, and Spain were the main sources. More than half of all joint ventures established in Cuba include European investments. And aid funds from Europe total $64 million since 1993.

European Reactions to U.S. Policy

Individually, each European state showed different approaches to the expanded U.S. embargo owing to their varied degrees of commercial and political links with Cuba and their specific relations with the United States. Nonetheless, as far as attitudes are concerned, European countries showed a remarkable consensus of opposition. "Special relationships" with the United States appeared not to be an obstacle. Indeed, the European reaction to Helms-Burton revealed impressive unity. While in the 1980s the European Community barely had a cohesive "foreign policy" beyond certain commercial and aid arrangements such as the Lomé Convention, in the 1990s the situation changed somewhat. The European Union has provided to date the most effective answer to the U.S. law, and at the same time it has coordinated the machinery for a compromise with the United States to avert a trade war of serious consequences.

The United Kingdom, which has maintained cordial, profitable relations with Cuba, was the first European state to enact a specific mechanism as a shield for damages caused by the U.S. embargo in the form of the Protection of Trading Interests Order (United States–Cuban Assets Regulations).[12] This was the culmination of a steady policy of opposing the U.S. demands.

Although numerous French voices have expressed concern about France's deference to Castro's Cuba, French leaders of all parties have expressed displeasure with U.S. Cuba policy, especially Helms-Burton. President François Mitterrand often called the law "stupid" and in March 1995 gave Castro a warm reception when he visited Paris for a function of the United Nations Educational, Scientific and Cultural Organization (UNESCO).[13] This was not an isolated sign of solidarity but only the continuation of France's long fascination with Cuban culture and products. It also reflected the attraction raised by the Cuban Revolution in leftist French circles in the 1960s, although intellectual fascination with Castro dramatically decreased in recent years.[14] In 1997 the French government crafted a commercial agreement with Cuba to protect investments.[15] Alcatel, Pernod, Pierre Cardin, Rhone-Poulenc, and Total are among the many French companies with substantial interests in Cuba.

The attitude of the Federal Republic of Germany, before the collapse of the Berlin Wall, was reticent and cautious toward Cuba because of its close relations with the communist German Democratic Republic.[16] Cuba and West Germany did not have diplomatic relations between 1963 and 1975. Bonn maintained a wait-and-see attitude. When the cold war ended, with the country united, German policy toward Cuba revealed a sort of double track. Germany became one of the standard trading partners of Cuba by virtue of its industrial power and Germany's strong presence in Latin America. German business people were cautious, but the Investment Promotion and Guarantee Agreement signed in 1996 helped to promote new activities. Today, German companies operating in Cuba include Mercedes-Benz, BASF, Bayer, LTU, and Lufthansa. German tourists in Cuba rank among the top spenders, and German hotel investment is only surpassed by Spain. The German government, however, implemented a policy of restraint concerning human rights and prospects for democratization.[17]

Italians are also leaders in tourism in Cuba, while commercial links between the two countries have been strong. Italian investment has also displayed a certain autonomy when compared with the rest of European involvement in Cuba. A recent example is the deal crafted between ITT and the Italian company STET (since mid-1997, Italy Telecom). Taking over about 30 percent of the shares of the Cuban telephone system that the Mexican company Domos elected to abandon, the Italian company agreed to pay ITT (the former operator of the Cuban telephone network) an undisclosed amount, rumored to be about $300 million.[18] This decision raised eyebrows in Europe as a sign that the Italian company elected to protect its investments in the United States by paying the price demanded by Washington. However, Lamberto Dini became in June 1998 the first EU foreign minister to visit Cuba since the end of the 1980s.

Although it cannot be considered "European" in the narrow sense, the Vatican's perception of Cuba constitutes an important ingredient in this analysis in view of the consequences of the epoch-making visit of Pope John Paul II to Cuba in January 1998. The Catholic Church thought that a policy of engagement was preferable to the pattern of isolation and the pope's attitude is, in political terms, in unison with the European Union's and member states' policy.

Spain: The Globalization of a Bilateral Relationship

The unique link between Spain and Cuba remained undisturbed through the turbulent changes that have occurred in both nations since 1898. At one point, Franco's Spain was Cuba's closest economic and political link with the West.[19] With the rebirth of Spanish democracy, trade and investment between the two nations grew spectacularly, while the cooperation aid package that Cuba received was one of the largest ever bestowed by Spain in Latin America. This decisive engagement implemented by the Social-Democrat administration (1982–96) sustained the hope of contributing to a political transition, perhaps following the Spanish model.[20]

With the arrival of a new conservative government, Spain's policy toward Cuba underwent some noticeable changes. In the Ibero-American summit held in Chile in November 1996, the Spanish premier made a public offer to Castro to renew bilateral cooperation agreements in exchange for political reform. Almost simultaneously, Spain presented to the EU Council of Ministers a new cooperation-aid plan toward Cuba entirely conditioned on the enactment of political reform. In retaliation, Castro withdrew his *placet* for a new Spanish ambassador. Spain took a wait-and-see and ambivalent attitude that lasted until April 1998 when the Spanish premier decided to name the new Spanish ambassador, relaunching a new chapter of warm relations between the two countries, and making the short confrontational period a simple footnote in history. Wisely, Castro elected to maintain correct relations with the Spanish conservative government, instead of hoping for a doubtful (by his calculations) victory of the Social-Democratic Party, the Partido Socialista Obrero Español (PSOE), in 1999.

Spanish investors in Cuba feared lack of protection when the financial guarantees and other incentives (frequently tied to the acquisition of Spanish goods) were withdrawn by Madrid. Other European countries could very well fill the space left by Spanish interests. Business signals were contradictory. Spanish investment for 1996 reached $11.4 million, tripling the figures of 1995. In 1997 Spain was leading foreign investment in Cuba in the number of joint ventures (65 out of 300). Only Canada surpassed Spanish investment in volume. Spain also became the most important trade partner of Cuba (in contrast to its sixth place in 1994). Total commerce figures between the two countries reached $600 million in 1997, with Spanish exports to Cuba increasing 18 percent. Spanish tourism investment reached $1 million in 1996, and the trend continued in 1997.[21] As a sign of the new critical policy of the Spanish government, a line of credit worth $13 million for exports to Cuba was canceled. However, at the end of 1997, Madrid reversed its hard-line attitude, in essence matching the PSOE's policy, making available an overall program of additional loans, humanitarian aid, and scholarships totaling $6.5 million. The result is that Cuba leads the list of countries with debt to Spain exceeding $500 million in unpaid loans. Culminating a series of economic and political visits to Cuba by Spanish representatives, in April 1998 an impressive delegation of more than one hundred Spanish companies under the leadership of José María Cuevas, the president of the Spanish Confederation of Employers, visited Cuba, with the purpose of increasing investment and trade.[22] Josep Piqué, minister of Industry and Energy, became the first member of the conservative cabinet to visit Cuba. He was warmly received by Castro and announced a new program of Spanish investments.[23]

A Triangular Link: Warnings and Obstacles

In the late 1980s and early 1990s, the European Union became more involved in Cuban affairs. Yet Havana continued to be the exception in the Latin American and Caribbean region by lacking a comprehensive aid agreement. The main EU institutions had issued declarations and approved resolutions extremely critical of the policies of the United States. Concurrently, the EU systematically denounced violations of human rights in Cuba.[24] Representative of the official EU attitude toward Cuba and the U.S. embargo are the words issued in 1994 by Gerhard Henze, Germany's representative to the UN General Assembly, acting as president of EU members:

—Because of its choices in economics and politics, the Cuban government is largely responsible for the deterioration of the situation in the country.

—The European Union condemns the repeated violations of human rights in Cuba, in particular in the political field.

—We have opposed U.S. legislative initiatives, including the CDA, designed to tighten further the unilateral trade embargo against Cuba by the extraterritorial application of U.S. jurisdiction. We believe that such measures violate the general principles of international law and sovereignty of independent states.

—The EU believes that the U.S. trade embargo against Cuba is primarily a matter that has to be resolved bilaterally.[25]

This two-pronged approach has been consistent over the years.

Following the recommendation the European Commission made on June 28, 1995, a delegation of the troika (France, Spain, and Italy) traveled to Havana in November 1995 for exploratory conversations. The European Council held in Madrid on December 15, 1995, charged the commission with presenting a draft of a cooperation aid agreement to be ready during the following semester.[26] Manuel Marín, the vice president of the European Commission, visited Havana in early 1996 and met with Fidel Castro, who flatly rejected the conditions.[27] Just days after, Cuban Air Force MiGs shattered all plans. While protesting the approval of Helms-Burton, Europeans condemned the criminal act against the unarmed planes. As a result, the U.S. government hardened the embargo, while the EU placed its cooperation agreement in hibernation.

From the Blocking Statute to a Compromise

The EU decided to denounce the Helms-Burton law in the WTO. During the second half of 1996, the U.S. government made a considerable effort to convince the EU to find an elegant face-saving solution. The Clinton administration consistently presented itself to the Europeans as a reasonable partner, in contrast with the image of the U.S. Congress as the real problem. This message has been interpreted by European governments and the EU as a global tactic that would allow the State Department and White House envoys to return to Congress saying that they had achieved common U.S. goals without giving anything away. Critical European voices of the EU-U.S. agreement of May 18, 1998, point out that the ultimate U.S. objective is to obtain U.S.

economic supremacy through the implementation of a proposed investment code.

However, European governments had their hands tied by the Regulation adopted in November. The Parliament and the commission had already issued sufficient signs of protest.[28] It was now the turn of the council to counteract the consequences derived from the U.S. law. The council's Regulation contained protective measures that prohibit accepting the extraterritorial effects of the Helms-Burton law.[29]

First, the European Council established its justification for opposing this and other laws on the basis that the EU has had as one of its objectives the contribution to "the harmonious development of world trade and to the progressive abolition of restrictions on international trade." The Regulation's main objectives were set as follows:

—The United States has enacted laws [the Torricelli and Helms-Burton laws][30] that purport to regulate activities of persons under the jurisdiction of the member states of the European Union; this extraterritorial application violates international law and has adverse effects on the interest of the European Union.

—Therefore, the Regulation provides protection against the extraterritorial application of these laws and binds the persons and interests affected to inform the Commission.

—No judgment of a court outside the European Union regarding the effects of these U.S. laws will be recognized and no person shall comply with any requirement or prohibition derived from them.

—Any person affected shall be entitled to recover any damages caused by the application of these laws.[31]

With the measures taken by the European institutions, the EU aimed to concentrate on removing what they perceived were the most adverse effects of Title III and Title IV of the Helms-Burton law.[32] The council also adopted a Joint Action as an example of the "second pillar," the EU's common foreign and security policy.

Showdown at the World Trade Organization

As a result of successive warnings demanding a U.S. rectification that never materialized, the path taken by the actions and reactions of Brussels and Washington led to a dead end. On February 3, 1997, a definitive legal initiative against the United States was intended to be debated within the framework of the WTO. The European Union had warned that the temporary suspension of Title III was not sufficient. The rest of the law was still considered a violation of the principles of commercial exchange. The United States countered that the Helms-Burton law was not an issue of concern to the WTO, since the limitations imposed on trade with Cuba were a matter of national security.

This give-and-take gave the appearance that the EU left the sensitive issue of Cuba untouched and seemed not to be concerned with the political and social evolution (or lack of it) of the Cuban regime. Brussels wanted to get the record straight.

The "Common Position"

On December 2, 1996, the Council of Ministers of Economy and Finance approved a Common Position on Cuba. Its objective was "to encourage a process of transition to pluralist democracy and respect of human rights and fundamental freedoms."[33] It was the confirmation of a well-established policy. The European Union also had codified its foreign policy toward Cuba. However, in contrast with the U.S. policy, the EU made it clear that it wanted to continue the dialogue with Cuba. The document included the following main items:

—The EU states that it is encouraging a peaceful transition in Cuba to a pluralist democracy. The EU prefers this to happen through the initiation by the government of Cuba, not by coercion from outside.

—If Cuba wishes to receive a favorable treatment through a cooperation agreement, it must show progress in the democratic process. This progress should be reflected in periodic semester reports submitted by the commission to the council. The reports should include the status of respect for human rights, the release of political prisoners, a reform of the criminal code, and the ending of harassment of dissidents.

—The EU wants to maintain the dialogue not only with the Cuban government but with all sectors of Cuban society.

—The EU recognizes the progress made in economic reforms and is willing to offer economic cooperation through the member states.

—Humanitarian aid will continue through appropriate nongovernmental organizations.

This set of conditions was not well received by the Cuban regime, and, as noted, Spain became the target for Cuban retaliation in retribution for its prominent role in the hardening of the conditions. However, in spite of all this friction, and in compliance with the terms of the "Common Position," the EU has maintained its humanitarian aid to Cuba. This aid is distributed through European nongovernmental organizations (NGOs) but not without difficulties imposed by the resistance of the Cuban government, and sometimes complicated by the additional conditions implemented by the donors.

A more recent development in EU-Cuba relations added a novel dimension. In June 1998, the EU approved observer status for Cuba in the Africa, Caribbean, Pacific (ACP) group of countries, regulated by the Lomé Convention, opening the door for permanent membership in the advantageous trading system composed of former European colonies.[34] The Spanish government took credit for this plan,[35] apparently endorsed by the Caribbean states, but the EU Council of Ministers warned that Cuba would have to show substantial progress in "human rights, good governance, and political freedoms" in order to meet the criteria of the provisions of the Common Position still in effect. The council also inserted two additional conditions: "the obstruction of the Havana Ambassadors (EU) Human Rights Working Group shall cease, and that the four members of the Dissidents' Working Group now in prison shall be released."[36] The European Commission had to issue statements clarifying that the observer status granted to Cuba did not mean a position in the Lomé Convention,[37] while internal assessments used the case of South Africa to predict that Cuba's membership in the ACP group may have to wait for a period of more than six years. Whatever the difficulties and the expected long negotiations, it is a fact that Lomé observer status is a success for the Cuban government and a subtle, effective mechanism for receiving preferential treatment and political recognition.

The Making of a Truce: The First Understanding

In an effort to defuse transatlantic tensions and as an apparent counter gesture for the European concessions as expressed by the Common Position on Cuba, on January 3, 1997, President Clinton suspended, for the second time, the controversial Title III of the law. This second step, coupled with renewed European emphasis on human rights and support for a democratic transition, defused tensions between the United States and Europe.

The early 1997 postelectoral honeymoon between Brussels and Washington had replaced the rocky 1996 relationship. However, an important roadblock remained. Part of the quarrel was left untouched. U.S.-European links were still tense as the "drop-dead date" of April 12, 1997—the deadline for the European Union to formalize its first complaint about Helms-Burton in the WTO—approached. After hours of negotiation, the United States and European Union reached an agreement to avert the transatlantic trade dispute, at least until the following October 15, 1997 (a six-month truce), which was renewed. Under the accord, the White House committed itself to pressure Congress to water down portions of the law, especially Title III, and remove Title IV. The EU agreed to take action to discourage individuals and firms from dealing in property confiscated by Havana, and the EU would drop its WTO complaint against the United States.[38] In addition, the EU crafted another compromise with the United States. At the 1997 annual meeting of the Human Rights Commission of the United Nations held in Geneva, EU members sided with a resolution against the U.S. economic sanctions[39] but endorsed U.S. claims against Cuba for human rights violations.[40]

Common Sense: Damage Control

Amidst this tension between Brussels and Washington, a limit has been set: avoiding irreparable damage to the WTO. Both parties understood each other because "mutual assured destruction" would not benefit anyone. Josef Joffe summarized this well: "Today, Europe and America threaten each other with economic warfare when negotiations stall. But threats are where the conflict usually stops because everyone is deadly afraid of destroying the global trading system."[41] Common sense comes into action and presses for responsibility and the choosing of priorities. Battles fought with an exchange of threats to unleash commercial wars in the theaters of the World Trade Organization and the North American Free Trade Agreement are not unlike old-time nuclear threats made during the cold war. Both parties know that the unthinkable (firing intercontinental missiles or wrecking the free-trade networks) will never happen—one hopes. The repercussions caused by Cuba may be disproportionate to the objective value and impact of this nation in the global arena. No party would dream of saying it in public, but the reality is that Cuba is not worth a commercial or political war between Washington and Brussels.

Conclusion

U.S.-European relations involving Cuba are very much a work in progress. But in view of the May 18, 1998, understanding between the EU and the United States, the following recommendations should be entertained:

—With regard to its economic relations with the United States, the EU should continue to make every effort to convince Washington that a serious confrontation over trade and investment in Cuba should be avoided given the relative importance (or lack of it) of the case. Iran, Iraq, and Libya are far more important for European interests than Cuba. Irreparable damage to global relationships should be avoided.

—A willingness to meet some U.S. concerns should not be ruled out, especially if the goal is to make the Cuban transition as painless and peaceful as possible. Due but careful consideration should be given to the proposed Multilateral Agreement on Investment (MAI), even if the end result is to allow President Clinton an additional excuse to keep waiving the application of Title III of the Helms-Burton law. European policy toward Cuba should continue to be implemented with a high degree of transparency, both for domestic purposes and to reduce any adverse impact on the United States.

—While maintaining all the previously approved measures (Regulation, Common Position, Joint Action) enacted, a wait-and-see attitude (both toward Cuba and U.S. policies) may not be the most ambitious policy but it is the most advisable in view of the unpredictable course that the Cuban regime might take as well as uncertain U.S. policies.[42]

—European interests would be ill-served if they contribute to the exacerbation of the extreme hardships of the Cuban people by unnecessarily limiting current engagement. European governments should maintain the policies that have been implemented until now. However, while economically engaging the Cuban society, careful consideration should be given to the possible permanent labeling of European investments as contributing to the formation of a drastic dual economy in Cuba. Only history will confirm or correct the present resentment toward European investors expressed by the sectors of the Cuban society unable to receive the economic benefits of payments in hard currency. The making of an "ugly European" image (with total disregard for the development of democracy and labor issues) should be an item of concern in the future. Due consideration should be given to the implementation of the Arcos Principles, a set of guidelines designed to promote liberalization and workers' rights, crafted with the pressure of dissident Cuban organizations.[43]

—Spain has a special historical role to play in Cuba. This should be pursued with a high sense of responsibility—and deserves both the full cooperation of its European partners and a certain understanding by the United States.

—Linking aid to the improvement of human rights conditions should be an aim but not a fixed precondition. Although it is not free of obstacles and manipulations inserted by the Cuban regime and donors, aid distribution through NGOs may be the most effective path.

—Coordination of member state policies should be a priority so that U.S. and Cuban protagonists do not exploit divisions in Europe.

European opposition to the U.S. embargo, together with coordinated policy toward Cuba regarding human rights, will ultimately be seen as doing more good than harm. The goal of bringing democracy to Cuba is a widely held objective in Europe, despite the perception in certain U.S. circles that European aims do not include explicit designs for democratic change. However, the use of legislation with explicit extraterritorial impact has produced counterproductive results, giving partners and competitors an excuse to "stand up" to U.S. hegemony, especially when this is an exercise with few political risks (as it is in the case of Cuba). Pressure and negotiation may render more effective results for U.S. interests if implemented in a rather more subtle way than with the use of legal instruments that may be a violation of international law and constitutional principles—especially as using extraterritorial approaches holds little hope of realizing the stated political results: the end or the reform of "difficult" regimes. As a consequence, the Helms-Burton law (as a classic example of a policy of secondary sanctions) may be an unfortunate footnote worthy of being forgotten.

Notes

1. "Understanding with Respect to Disciplines for the Strengthening of Investment Protection," *European Union News*, May 18, 1998. For a detailed analysis of the evolution of the content and language of the agreement, see *Inside U.S. Trade*, May 1, 1998, pp. 1–6, and May 15, 1998; and *Americas Trade*, May 15, 1998, pp. 1–6.

2. For EU members: AFP, "Francia y España obstacularizaron trato," *El Nuevo Herald*, May 18, 1998; *Inside U.S. Trade*, "Member States Poised in Fight to Accept U.S.-EU Agreement on Helms-Burton," May 22, 1998; José Miguel Larraya, "Duro ataque de los socios del gobierno al acuerdo UE-EE.UU. sobre Cuba," *El País*, June 4, 1998. For different commentator: Hermenegildo Altozano, "España, la ley Helms-Burton y el Acuerdo Multilateral de Inversiones," *Expansión*, May 14, 1998. For U.S. sources: Thomas W. Lippman, "Politicians at Odds on Sanctions as Policy," *Washington Post*, May 19, 1998; and Jonathan Miller, "How Europe Forced Cuba Deal," *Miami Herald*, May 24, 1998. For Cuba: "Castro insta a la UE a rechazar el acuerdo sobre la ley Helms-Burton," *Expansión*, May 20, 1998; AP, "Castro Condemns Agreement," *Miami Herald*, May 20, 1998; AFP, "Castro califica el acuerdo entre EE.UU. y la UE de 'amenazante y no ético,'" May 20, 1998; Mauricio Vicent, "Castro advierte que ningún entendimiento entre la UE y EE.UU. puede realizarse a costa de Cuba," *El País*, May 25, 1998.

3. "Helms Tells European Union: 'No Deal'" statement released by U.S. Senate Committee on Foreign Relations, May, 18, 1998; "Helms Aide Tells EU to 'Drop Dead' on Request for Helms-Burton Fix," *Inside U.S. Trade*, May 29, 1998, pp. 1, 16; "Member States Poised to Accept U.S.-EU Agreement on H-B," *Inside U.S. Trade*, May 22, 1998, pp. 1, 21; "Gingrich critica acuerdo de Clinton con Europa," *El Nuevo Herald*, May 23, 1998; and "Senators Urge Albright Not to Grant ILSA Waivers for Libya Projects," *Inside U.S. Trade*, May 29, 1998.

4. Decreto Legislativo, no. 50, February 15, 1982.

5. See IRELA, *Economic Transformation and Cooperation with the European Union*, Conference Report (Havana, December 1995), p. 8, draft of the 1995 Cuban Law on Foreign Investment (http://www.cubaweb.cu/invertir/flaim.html).

6. U.S.-Cuba Trade and Economic Council, N.Y. (http://www.cubatrade.org).

7. P.L. 102-484, sec. 1701–1712, October 23, 1992.

8. Alistair Hennessy and George Lambie, eds. *The Fractured Blockade: West European-Cuban Relations during the Revolution* (London: Macmillan Press, 1993), p. iii.

9. Ministry of Commerce, Spain.

10. *Banco Nacional de Cuba, Annual Report 1994* (Havana).

11. S. Consultores Asociados, S.A. (CONAS), *Inversiones y Negocios, 1995–96* (Havana, 1997).

12. For a comprehensive treatment of this relationship between the United Kingdom and Cuba, see George Lambie, "Anglo-Cuban Commercial Relations in

the 1960s: A Case Study of the Leyland Motor Company Contracts with Cuba," in Hennessy and Lambie, *The Fractured Blockade,* pp. 163–97. For a shorter view on the same topic, see Gareth Jenkins, "Trade Relations between Britain and Cuba," in Donna Rich Kaplowitz, *Cuba's Ties to a Changing World* (Lynne Rienner Publishers, 1993), pp. 117–27. See "Protection of Trading Interests (U.S.-Cuban Assets Control Regulations) Order," no. 2449, October 14, 1992.

13. Craig R. Whitney, "Castro Given Big Welcome by Mitterrand," *New York Times,* March 14, 1995, p. A9.

14. George Lambie, "De Gaulle's France and the Cuban Revolution," in Hennessy and Lambie, *The Fractured Blockade,* pp. 197–233.

15. AFP and other news agencies, April 25; and Octavi Martí, "Francia reta a EE.UU," *El País,* April 26, 1997 (Internet edition).

16. For a commentary on this relationship, see the section on Germany included in the article by Wolf Grabendorff, "The Relationship between the European Community and Cuba," in Kaplowitz, *Cuba's Ties to a Changing World,* pp. 89–116.

17. From a Cuban perspective, see Francisco R. Graupera, "Cuba and Germany: Towards a New Opening?" *Revista de Estudios Europeos,* La Habana, January-March 1997, pp. 19–51; and Wolf Grabendorff, "Germany and Latin America," in Susan Kaufman Purcell and Françoise Simon, *Europe and Latin America in the World Economy* (Lynne Rienner, 1994).

18. Juan O. Tamayo, "Firma italiana se burla de ley Helms," *El Nuevo Herald,* March 6, 1997; Christopher Marquis, "New Test Looms in Wrangle over Property Cuba Seized," *Miami Herald,* April 26, 1997; and "Empresa podría evitar efecto de ley Helms," *El Nuevo Herald,* April 26, 1997 (Internet editions).

19. For a review of that era, see George Lambie, "Franco's Spain and the Cuban Revolution," in Hennessy and Lambie, *The Fractured Blockade,* pp. 234–75.

20. For a selection of my previous publications on the relationship between Spain and Cuba, see the following: *Cuba y España: relaciones y percepciones* (Madrid: Biblioteca Cubana Contemporánea, 1988); "Las relaciones actuales entre Cuba y España," *Afers Internacionals* (Barcelona), no. 12-13 (1988), pp. 5–19; "Las relaciones actuales entre Cuba y España," *Política Exterior,* vol. 1 (Verano 1987), pp. 282–86; "Las relaciones Madrid-La Habana," *Política Exterior,* vol. 2 (Primavera 1988), pp. 275–79; "Relaciones y percepciones entre España y Cuba: Trasfondo de la 'Crisis de las embajadas,'" in Carlos Robles Piquer, ed., *Cuba 1990: Realidad y futuro* (Santiago de Compostela: Fundación Alfredo Brañas, 1991), pp. 27–47; "España, la Unión Europea y Cuba: la evolución de una relación especial a una política de gestos y de presión, "Occasional Paper (University of Miami, Cuban Studies Association, 1996); "España y Cuba: una relación *muy especial,*" *Afers Internacionals,* no. 31 (1996), pp. 147–66, "España y Cuba: Una relación muy especial," and "Posdata," in Joaquín Roy and Juan Antonio March, eds., *El espacio iberoamericano: dimensiones y percepciones de la relación especial entre España y América Latina* (Miami/Barcelona: Instituto de Estudios Ibéricos/Centro de Estudios

Internacionales, 1996). For English edition, see "Spain and Cuba" and "Postscript," in Joaquín Roy and Juan Antonio March, eds., *The Ibero-American Space: Dimensions and Perceptions of the Special Relationship between Spain and Latin America* (Miami/Lleida: Iberian Studies Institute, University of Miami/Jean Monnet Chair, University of Lleida, 1997).

21. Ministry of Foreign Affairs and Ministry of Trade, Spain.

22. News wires. "De visita numerosa delegación española," EFE, *El Nuevo Herald*, April 15, 1998 (Internet edition).

23. *Cinco días*, June 19, 1998; and Mauricio Vicent, "Piqué viaja a Cuba," *El País*, June 21, 1998; and "Josep Piqué, recibido por Fidel Castro," *ABC*, June 23, 1998.

24. See resolutions of the European Parliament for 1987, 1988, 1990, 1992, 1993, and 1996 in the compilation published by IRELA, *Europa-América Latina: veinte años de documentos oficiales* (Madrid, 1996), pp. 769–803.

25. Agenda Item 24, "Necessity of ending the economic, commercial and financial embargo imposed by the United States of America against Cuba," "Explanation of Vote" (New York, October 26, 1994).

26. See Angel Viñas, "La Unión Europea y Cuba: historia de una acción de estrategia exterior en la post guerra fría," in *Temas de economía internacional* (Bilbao: Universidad del País Vasco, 1996), pp. 311–59.

27. For an insider's perspective of the events, see the interpretation offered by Richard A. Nuccio in this volume.

28. See texts of resolutions of the European Parliament of 1992, 1993, and 1996, and the declarations of the council and the presidency of the European Union of 1995 in the compilation by IRELA, *Europa-América Latina.*

29. Council Regulation (EC), no. 2271/96; and *Official Journal of the European Communities* (European Union, November 29, 1997).

30. The annex specifically listed all U.S. legal measures that the European Union considers unacceptable. It also includes the Iran and Libya Sanctions Act of 1996.

31. Council Regulation (EC) 2271/96, November 22, 1996.

32. Jürgen Huber, "The Blocking Statute of the European Union," *Fordham International Law Journal*, vol. 20 (1997), pp. 699–716.

33. "Common Position Defined by the Council on the Basis of Article J.2 of the Treaty on European Union, on Cuba," December 2, 1996. For a detailed analysis of the evolution of this measure, see *The EU's Common Position on Cuba: Internal Debate, Reactions and Impact* (Madrid: IRELA, 1996). For a detailed review of the wider context, see *Cuba y la Unión Europea: las dificultades del diálogo* (Madrid: IRELA, 1996).

34. News wires, June 30, 1998.

35. Spanish minister of Foreign Affairs Abel Matutes included this accomplishment in his detailed summary of recent international activities, along with

Spain's opposition to Helms-Burton, as an answer to the criticism from the PSOE. See "Un poco de sosiego, por favor," *El País*, July 17, 1998.

36. General Affairs Council, press communiqué, June 29, 1998.

37. Agence France-Presse, June 29, 1998.

38. *Washington Post*, April 12, 1997; Christopher Marquis, "Europe, U.S. Make Cuba Deal," *Miami Herald*, April 12, 1997; and Cynthia Corzo, "EU y Europa pactan sobre Ley Helms," *El Nuevo Herald*, April 12, 1997 (Internet editions).

39. AFP, April 3, 1997. The resolution was passed by thirty-seven votes in favor and eight against.

40. Robert Evans, *Reuters*, April 17, 1997. Out of fifty-three members, nineteen voted for, twenty-four abstained (as opposed to twenty-eight the year before), and ten voted against (five more than in 1996). In 1998 the EU states and candidates for membership backed the U.S. initiative, but it was rejected by a combination of abstentions and negative votes.

41. Josef Joffe, "How America Does It," *Foreign Affairs*, vol. 76 (September-October 1997), p. 25.

42. As an illustration of the resistance to change expressed by the backers of the Helms-Burton law on its second anniversary, see the report compiled by the staff of the U.S. Senate Committee on Foreign Relations and the Committee on International Relations of the U.S. House of Representatives, *Cuba at the Crossroads: The Visit of Pope John Paul II and Opportunities for U.S. Policy* (Government Printing Office, March 1998). Along the same lines, see the content of the hearing before the Subcommittee on International Economic Policy and Trade of the House International Relations Committee, presided over by Congresswoman Ileana Ros-Lehtinen, especially statements by Claudio Benedí of the Junta Patriótica Cubana, Francisco Hernández of the Cuban American National Foundation, and Ralph Galliano, editor of the *U.S.-Cuba Policy Report*. See *Interfering with U.S. National Security Interests: The World Trade Organization and the European Union Challenge to the Helms-Burton Law*, March 19, 1997, 105 Cong. 1 sess. (Government Printing Office, 1997). In contrast, see the moderate declaration by the State Department's Michael E. Ranneberger in a statement before the Subcommittee on International Economic Policy and Trade of the House International Relations Committee, March 12, 1998. Jorge Hernández of the U.S. Chamber of Commerce explicitly opposed the U.S. embargo.

43. On July 17, 1998, Concilio Cubano, a coordinating body of dissident organizations in Cuba, denounced the violation of World Labor Organization legislation in the foreign investment practices.

GEOFFREY KEMP

4 | *The Challenge of Iran for U.S. and European Policy*

F or most Americans the mental image of Iran remains that of self-flagellating mobs screaming
"Death to the Great Satan" and holding blindfolded diplomats hostage.
Recently the imagery has begun to change. In February 1998, American wrestlers in Tehran were given a hero's welcome. The American flag
was raised, and the crowd delighted in cheering the U.S. team in both
victory and defeat. Still, it will be a long time before Iran becomes a
popular country in the United States. In contrast to the VIP treatment
given the U.S. wrestlers during their competition in Tehran less than
two months earlier, when the U.S. wrestling team hosted the Iranians
at the World Cup championship in Oklahoma, the Iranians were detained at the airport and fingerprinted and photographed by U.S. officials. Iranians, including many who want to improve relations with the
United States, also still harbor resentment about the past. They cite the
1953 CIA-orchestrated coup d'etat against Mohammed Mossadeq; support for Shah Mohammed Reza Pahlavi's regime; the support for Saddam
Hussein during the Iran-Iraq war, including the imposition of an effective arms embargo on Iran and the shooting down of an Iranian
civilian airliner; and the continued high-level military presence in the
Persian Gulf.

To break down these mental barriers will require time and constructive diplomacy. One positive fact is that most Iranians like Americans and are intrigued by the United States. This reality generates angst on the part of Iran's conservative mullahs. They realize that opening the doors to Americans will inevitably mean a diminution, if not end, to their power and prestige.

To address the challenge of Iran for U.S. and European policy, this chapter first examines the problems the Iranian regime faces and the evolution of U.S. policy toward Iran since 1991. It then considers U.S. objectives toward Iran, differences with Europe over policy, and prescriptions for improving relations with the Islamic Republic of Iran.

Iran's Problems

The United States and Europe are concerned about Iran's support for terrorism, rejection of Israel and the peace process, its interests in weapons of mass destruction, and its bad human rights record. The Clinton administration has labeled Iran as a "rogue" or "outlaw" state, along with Iraq, North Korea, Libya, Cuba, and Sudan.[1] (Interestingly, Syria is not formally certified as a "rogue.") Nevertheless, in view of its size, geography, and wealth, Iran is an extremely important player in the strategic stakes in the Persian Gulf and Caspian Basin.

Iran's revolution in 1979 established a new model of government in which Islam would play the central role. It has not worked out as originally conceived by Ayatollah Ruhollah Khomeini. Not only has the Iranian model had extremely limited success outside Iran, it now finds itself defending Khomeini's legacy among its own people. The regime has become defensive, and many of its leaders are widely disliked by ordinary Iranians. The dramatic presidential election on May 23, 1997, which witnessed the runaway victory of a "moderate" mullah, Mohammed Khatami, over the choice of the conservative hierarchy, Ali Akbar Nateq-Nouri, was a vote of "no confidence" in the domestic policies of the regime and has caused both Iranians and outsiders to reassess the nature and future of the regime.

An underlying fear of the regime remains that the United States seeks to undermine the Islamic Republic. However, the U.S. administration has reassured the regime in its more recent statements that U.S.

policy does not seek to overthrow the Iranian government.[2] Nonetheless, until the recent thaw in U.S.-Iran relations, Iran had good cause to be wary. In 1993 the Clinton administration announced its policy of "dual containment" of both Iran and Iraq. It was derived from an assessment that the current Iraqi and Iranian regimes are hostile to American interests in the region. Clinton's policy was distinguished from previous ones, which consigned American interests in the Middle East to a local balance of power among the key regional countries. America's interests in the Gulf were considered too important to be left to the regional powers to manage. Dual containment entails an enhanced American military commitment to the Gulf with closer military ties to such key powers as Israel, Saudi Arabia, and Turkey.[3]

U.S. military power poses a direct military challenge to Iran and dilutes potential Iranian influence in the Gulf. With its ally Israel, U.S. military hegemony is a key manifestation of alien (foreign) intervention in the region. The American naval vessels in the Gulf, defense cooperation agreements and prepositioned equipment in Arab Gulf states, and allied aircraft enforcing the no-fly zones over Iraq are a disconcerting presence. The regime's leadership remembers past U.S. discrimination against Iran, particularly during the Iran-Iraq war when the United States sided with Iraq and led an arms embargo and conducted military operations against Iran. Then, after being defeated by Iraq, Iran had to watch with humiliation as the United States and its allies trounced Iraq in Operation Desert Storm. Furthermore, Iran is well aware of Israel's formidable strategic reach, including long-range aircraft, ballistic missiles, and nuclear weapons. Israel's close military relations with Turkey pose another threat. Iran is further humbled by the global American campaign to stop any cooperation or sales of commercial and research nuclear reactors to Iran, while at the same time the United States studiously avoids any veto efforts to curb Israel's nuclear program. In addition, although the U.S. government has formally stated that it accepts the legitimacy of the Iranian revolution, Iran is troubled by statements from some Republicans in the U.S. House of Representatives calling for the overthrow of the Iranian government.

The mullahs' obsession with America—matched, it must be said, by a parallel U.S. preoccupation with the "rogue" state—obscures other security issues of concern to any Iranian regime. Iran faces a number of potential security threats, many of which have little to do with the United States or the West. Coupled with Iran's economic difficulties, these issues help foster long-term insecurities in Iran.

Located in a zone of conflict and unrest, Iran faces strategic threats on all sides with the most obvious, significant threat—aside from the United States—emanating from Iraq. The two countries fought an eight-year war that cost at least 200,000 Iranian lives and did significant damage to the infrastructure and to the Iranian regime's standing. Fear of Iraq and a desire for revenge coexist for the Iranians, most of whom were affected by the war. The "War of the Cities," heavy casualties, prisoners of war, Iraq's use of chemical weapons, and brutal fighting on the frontlines all took their toll.

Gulf relations are a second area of concern, and Iran has pursued a seemingly contradictory policy. This strategy has led to mixed results. On the one hand, the regime is making efforts to lessen Iran's isolation and build stronger ties with its Arab Gulf neighbors. To be sure, Iranians are particularly gratified that they hosted the Organization of the Islamic Conference in December 1997 and are heartened by their growing cooperation with Saudi Arabia. On the other hand, Iran's assertive, hegemonic tendencies appear especially strong while Iraq has been contained, thus undermining its efforts to strengthen relations with the Arab Gulf states. Animosity between Iran and its Arab neighbors persists. The Saudis were the principal host of U.S. military forces during the 1990–91 Gulf crisis, and Saudi influence in the Organization of Petroleum Exporting Countries (OPEC) and ability to keep Iran out of Gulf security talks have frustrated Iranian policymakers. Moreover, the Islamic rivalry pits Iran's Shi'ites against Saudi Arabia's Wahhabis. Furthermore, Iran has differed with the United Arab Emirates over the control and sovereignty of the islands of Abu Musa and Greater and Lesser Tunbs and has occupied them, refusing to submit the dispute to international arbitration. The Arab Gulf countries see Iran's tactics on the islands as evidence of its hegemonic aspirations. On their own, the Arab Gulf states pose no military threat to Iran, but their agreements with the United States enable them to act more brazenly toward the Islamic Republic.

Iran is also threatened by unrest and civil war in several of its neighboring states. Iraq is fragmented, and until recently, Iraqi Kurds operated in an autonomous safe haven in northern Iraq. The Caucasus is also a hotbed of civil strife, with unresolved conflicts between Armenia and Azerbaijan over Nagorno-Karabakh, the conflict in Georgia over Abkhazia, and Russia's continuing tensions with Chechnya. Afghanistan, long torn apart by a seemingly endless civil war, is now increasingly under the control of the hostile Taliban. Further to the east, Iran has become embroiled in the chaos and fighting in Tajikistan, the one central Asian country whose population is predominantly Persian speaking and of Shi'ite faith. Furthermore, Iran currently hosts the world's largest refugee population, accommodating more than 2 million, mainly from Afghanistan (estimated at 1.4 million) and Iraq (580,000).[4]

Furthermore, Iran's current economic troubles provide little comfort for the regime. The oil price collapse and the Asian financial crisis resulted in decreased revenue in 1998. Oil sales provide approximately 80 percent of Iran's export revenues. Iran needs to rebuild its deteriorating oil fields, which suffer from serious production and maintenance problems. Attempts to be part of deals in the Caspian Sea and its unresolved disputes with Qatar over the latter's offshore North Field gas reserves can be seen as part of Iran's effort to get a larger share of the resource pie.[5] Yet natural gas development requires huge amounts of up-front capital investment and secure, long-term contracts with consumers. In this regard, the U.S. policy of trying to limit international investment in the Iranian energy sector has been partially successful and therefore costly for the regime.[6]

Nevertheless, while the Islamic Republic faces a long list of internal and external problems, many of its own making, the regime is fairly strong. The Iranian leadership is not monolithic and is readily contrasted with Iraq; different factions openly and fiercely compete with one another for public support. Although there is consensus that Saddam Hussein runs a tyranny, reviews of the mullahs are more mixed, with some observers arguing that the regime, though thoroughly repressive, has become less brutal and totalitarian since the death of Ayatollah Khomeini in 1989. Even the United States has refrained from calling for the overthrow of the Iranian regime; rather, Washington requires that the regime change specific policies. The debate among the United States and its chief allies concerns the most appropriate ways to bring about these changes.

Evolution of U.S. Policy since 1991

In his inaugural address on January 20, 1989, President George Bush seemed to reach out to Iran when, in reference to the American hostages held in Lebanon by pro-Iranian groups, he said, "There are today Americans who are held against their will in foreign lands, and Americans who are unaccounted for. Assistance can be shown here, and will be long remembered. Goodwill begets goodwill."[7] Iran's subsequent felicitous behavior toward the allies during the Gulf War and its intervention in the release of the hostages by the end of December 1991 raised the possibility that some rapprochement with the Islamic Republic might be possible. However, no major U.S. gestures were forthcoming during the Bush administration, and U.S.-Iranian relations remained frozen. No effort was made to consult with Iran after the Gulf victory in early 1991 even though Iran had remained neutral during the war. When the Middle East peace conference was convened in Madrid in November 1991 as a result of a U.S. initiative, Iran hosted a gathering of radicals opposed to the conference.

When the Clinton administration assumed office in January 1993, the United States undertook a reappraisal of policy in the Persian Gulf. The administration was critical of the Reagan-Bush legacy, which had decisively tilted toward Iraq during the Iran-Iraq war (1980–88), and it continued to pursue friendly relations with Baghdad until August 1990.

Clinton administration policy toward Iran can be broken down into three phases. Phase one of this policy, lasting from May 1993 to May 1995, saw the enunciation of the dual containment strategy as an effort to keep both Iraq and Iran weak. The United States would guarantee Gulf security, act as the "balancer" in the region, and deploy sufficient military power to deter, or, if necessary, defeat both Iraq and Iran in a future confrontation.[8]

However, it was clear from the beginning that a differentiated policy of containment toward the two countries would be pursued. Iraq was subject to UN-mandated international sanctions resulting from the invasion and occupation of Kuwait in August 1990. U.S. policy was (and still is) to remove the Saddam Hussein regime. In the case of Iran, U.S. policy was initially more benign, the focus being to change key elements of Iranian policy, namely, support for international terrorism, rejection of the Arab-Israeli peace process (including Israel's right to exist), development of weapons of mass destruction, and violations of human rights and international law. These objectives have remained consistent since 1993.

During the period 1993–95, although the import of all Iranian products into the United States was banned by executive order, U.S. oil companies, through their foreign affiliates, were Iran's largest purchaser of oil. In 1994 U.S. companies purchased 30 percent of Iran's oil exports.[9] In parallel, various efforts were made to establish a dialogue between the United States and Iran, but they were stymied, primarily because of preconditions that the Iranians insisted precede any discussion, such as the return of Iranian financial assets seized by the United States in 1979 at the time of the hostage crisis. The Clinton administration has refused to release these assets as a precondition, and major differences remain between the two countries about their value.

For its first two years of office the Clinton administration made prolonged efforts to elicit cooperation from U.S. allies, particularly in Europe, to isolate Iran. These included attempts to persuade Europeans not to export dual-use items to Iran, not to reschedule any credits they had issued to Iran or to issue any new credits, and not to support loans to Iran by international or multilateral banks.[10] The Europeans were lukewarm to the U.S. administration and refused to consider economic sanctions as part of the effort to pressure Iran to change its behavior. By the spring of 1995, in response to criticism from Europe that the United States was selling large quantities of Iranian oil on the international market, pressure from Congress, and external developments, that is, the finalization of a major nuclear reactor deal in January 1995 between Russia and Iran and the agreement between Iran and an American oil company, Conoco, to develop the South Pars gas field in the Persian Gulf, the Clinton administration was convinced that additional unilateral steps needed to be taken to isolate Iran. On April 30, 1995, President Clinton announced in a speech to the World Jewish Congress that he would ban all U.S. trade with and investment in Iran.[11] This more confrontational policy launched phase two of the Clinton administration policy toward Iran and remained in place until May 1997.

During this second phase of policy, the debate in Washington was between hawks and superhawks. Few, if any, decisionmakers were in favor of offering Iran an "olive branch." The hawks were those who wished to further isolate Iran economically, while trying to find ways to

cooperate with Europe in order to increase pressure on the Iranian government to change its behavior. The superhawks were those who saw no
possibility of negotiating with or moderating the actions of the Iranian
regime. What was necessary was a counterrevolution.

This second phase saw increased tension between the U.S. administration and Congress on the one hand, and the European Union (EU)
on the other hand. Frustration in Congress with Europe's refusal to join
sanctions against Iran led to the drafting of legislation that would impose U.S. penalties on foreign companies that conducted business in
Iran's energy sector. The administration did not initially support the
proposed legislation for a host of reasons including worries about a backlash from the Europeans. However, the administration eventually supported a compromise law whose purpose was to reduce Iran's potential
to acquire weapons and technology and fund terrorism. Under the law
the United States would penalize those foreign companies who invest
more than $40 million in Iran's energy sector. As a result of intense
negotiations with the executive branch, the draft legislation was revised
and passed in August 1996 as the Iran and Libya Sanctions Act of 1996
(ILSA).[12] (In August 1997, one year after ILSA's enactment, because the
EU countries did not impose economic sanctions on Iran, the investment threshold required to trigger sanctions under ILSA dropped to
$20 million.) There was no debate in the United States about the impli-
cations of the extraterritoriality imposed by the ILSA, even though the
European Union had already initiated a World Trade Organization dispute settlement procedure in May 1996 regarding the extraterritoriality
of the Cuban Liberty and Democratic Solidarity (LIBERTAD) Act of
1996 (or Helms-Burton) concerning foreign investment in Cuba.[13]

The United States continued to press its case with Europe to support economic sanctions against Iran. The pressure peaked between April
and May 1997 when German courts found the Iranian government
culpable in the assassinations of Iranian dissidents in a Berlin restaurant
(Mykonos) in 1992. During this period, a resolute effort was made to
persuade the Europeans that their decision to abandon the policy of
critical dialogue with Iran and withdraw their ambassadors should
be followed by economic sanctions. However, this initiative was short-
lived owing to the unexpected and resounding victory of the "moderate" cleric Mohammed Khatami on May 23, 1997, in the Iranian
presidential elections.

Khatami's election significantly changed the landscape in Washington, and, as a result, phase three of the Clinton administration policy toward Iran emerged. It is once more fashionable for members of the policymaking community to discuss the possibility of opening a new relationship with the Islamic Republic.[14] Despite continued objection to Iran's more contentious policies, the administration decided to extend an olive branch to President Khatami. This change in policy was most clearly demonstrated by Secretary of State Madeleine K. Albright's speech to the Asia Society in June 1998. The speech was paralleled by a similar video message taped by President Clinton to the Iranian people on June 21 before the World Cup soccer match between the United States and Iran, in which he said, "As we cheer today's game between American and Iranian athletes, I hope it can be another step toward ending the estrangement between our nations. I am pleased that over the last year, President Khatami and I have both worked to encourage more people-to-people exchanges, and to help our citizens develop a better understanding of each other's rich civilizations."[15]

Another instance of the administration's goodwill toward the new Iranian regime includes the State Department's announcement on October 8, 1997, that the premier opposition group to the Iranian regime, the Mojahedeen e-Khalq, was to be placed on the terrorist list, making it susceptible to a law that freezes its financial assets in the United States, denies U.S. visas to its members, and subjects Americans who assist the group financially, or with weaponry, to ten years in prison.[16] This gesture to the new Iranian leadership reportedly was partly because of President Khatami's decision to replace the former Intelligence Minister Ali Fallahian, an architect of terror campaigns, as well as other controversial personnel in the old Iranian cabinet.

However, in parallel with these positive developments, recent U.S. policy decisions may jeopardize any sort of rapprochement with the regime. Of concern to the Iranians are several issues, including the creation of Radio Free Iran; the State Department listing of Iran as the most active state sponsor of terrorism in 1997; continued U.S. efforts to block a proposed Caspian pipeline through Iran; refusing to certify Iran's antinarcotics program; and, detaining, fingerprinting, and photographing Iranian visitors to the United States.[17] Furthermore, several factors still condition Washington's negative attitude toward the Iranian regime. First, the decision by the French company Total (together with Russia's Gazprom and Malaysia's Petronas) to sign a $2 billion deal with the Iranian government to develop gas fields in South Pars that had originally been granted to Conoco angered many in Congress, provoking members to pressure the administration to enforce ILSA. Fortunately, this issue was in part resolved in May 1998 when the Clinton administration waived the penalties on Total, Gazprom, and Petronas in return for supposedly greater cooperation from the EU and Russia on halting military technology transfers to Iran and combating the threat of terrorism.[18] According to the White House "Fact Sheet on Cooperation on Non-Proliferation and Counterterrorism," enhanced cooperation between the United States and the European Union includes the following:

—An EU commitment to give high priority to proliferation concerns regarding Iran;

—A clear public undertaking to prevent dual use technology transfers where there is a risk of diversion to WMD [weapons of mass destruction] purposes;

—Strengthen information sharing on nonproliferation issues and threats with the United States;

—Agreement to pursue development of new and better controls on "intangible" technology transfers (for example, via electronic transmission);

—Closer coordination of export control assistance to third countries;

—Closer coordination of diplomatic efforts to stem technology exports by other countries to proliferators, including Iran;

—Agreement to work together and with others to ensure ratification of all eleven counterterrorism conventions. The EU will give particular attention to obtaining adherence by Central and Eastern European states that are seeking EU membership.[19]

In addition, Russia's commitment to control sensitive technology transfers includes the following:

—Establish[ing] supervisory bodies in all enterprises dealing with missile or nuclear technologies, to ensure compliance with relevant regulations;

—Set[ting] procedures for exporting enterprises to ensure proper controls, and outlin[ing] "red flags" which indicate that a proposed purchaser is not legitimate;

—Giv[ing] the Russian Space Agency responsibility for oversight of the space rocket industry;

—Establish[ing] a range of measures for licensing military exports.[20]

Furthermore, when Secretary Albright announced the U.S. waiver for Total, Gazprom, and Petronas, she said she expected that any future cases involving EU companies "would result in like decisions with regard to waivers for EU companies." She went on to say that the United States remained strongly opposed to oil and gas pipelines that transit Iran, and, "We will carefully examine any proposals for trans-Iranian pipeline construction across Iran for possible implications under ILSA and take whatever action is appropriate."[21] The ambiguity over future implementation of ILSA remains a serious problem. Administration officials have privately stated that what they think it means is that as long as Iran is merely the transit route for a pipeline linking two other parties, that is, Turkmenistan and Turkey via Iran, the pipeline would not be subject to ILSA. However, if it became part of the Iranian gas network, then ILSA would apply.

The second major unresolved issue concerns the Khobar Towers bombing, which occurred in June 1996 killing nineteen American airmen in a terrorist attack outside Dhahran, Saudi Arabia. There is a strong suspicion that the Iranian intelligence agencies were culpable or involved in this activity. Although there is no clear proof—no smoking gun as yet—if it is ever proven definitively that Iran was behind the attack, any prospect for improving U.S. bilateral relations with Iran would be suspended. There would be great pressure on President Clinton to respond with much more stringent action, possibly including military operations, against Iran irrespective of the newly elected leadership. However, while terrorism remains one of the most divisive issues in U.S.-Iranian relations, several positive developments allow the administration to build upon them, including the public statement by the Saudis that the Khobar Towers bombing was an internal affair (although they insist that the investigation is ongoing); Khatami's replacement of the minister of intelligence thought to be responsible for the Mykonos operation; Iran's public condemnation of terrorism during the Organization of the Islamic Conference meeting in Tehran, including attacks against Israeli civilians; and the Iranian government's announcement that it would no longer pursue Salman Rushdie on September 24, 1998.

A third factor to consider is the Iranian leadership led by President Khatami. On January 7, 1998, President Khatami addressed the American people during a remarkable interview on CNN. He encouraged more dialogue between American citizens and Iranians and recommended "the exchange of professors, writers, scholars, artists, journalists, and tourists." Khatami went on to say, "When I speak of a dialogue, I intend dialogue between civilizations and cultures. Such discourse should be centered around thinkers and intellectuals. I believe that all doors should now be opened for such dialogue . . . [so that] a better future for both countries and nations may be forged." However, Khatami categorically ruled out any direct government-to-government negotiations at this time, and he continued to speak in very hostile terms about Israel and the American-backed Middle East peace process. According to many Iranian specialists, he rejected a dialogue between the governments because of discord within Tehran. Since Khatami's overwhelming election victory, he has faced strong opposition from the conservative factions led by Supreme Leader Ayatollah Khamenei. (It is Khamenei's harsh rhetoric that continues to poison relations with the United States. However, some suggest that he is prepared for better relations but wishes to proceed much more cautiously than Khatami.) The outstanding issues that divide the United States and Iran are sufficiently serious and far reaching that it may be a long time before a substantive dialogue can produce concrete results. Although there has been contact between Iranian and American diplomats in multinational forums, primarily at the United Nations, it cannot substitute for direct bilateral talks.

The possibilities for a dialogue will be moot if anything dramatic happens to Khatami, such as assassination or ouster. Without such a scenario, most people believe that Iran's decision to open up to the West in general and the United States in particular is part of a new approach aimed at solidifying and strengthening its regional position while at the same time finding ways to expand and develop its economy. Whether the Iranians like to admit it or not, U.S. sanctions have had an impact on their economy, particularly in the energy sector.[22] The Iranians are anxious to participate in both the vast opportunities posed by growing demand for natural gas and the possibility of hosting routes for oil and gas pipelines through their territory from the Caspian region. In the long run many of Iran's interests coincide with American interests in the region; thus pressure is growing for both governments to develop a less confrontational relationship.

From the U.S. perspective, continuing confrontation with Iran risks a divisive and public dispute with Europe, particularly if ILSA remains in effect and the United States sanctions European companies. Aside from questions about the legality of ILSA, if invoked it would not only further damage relations between the United States and Iran and the United States and Europe but would provide Russia and other countries a golden opportunity to make mischief in the region.

Against this backdrop, track II (nongovernment) diplomacy could play an important role in opening up a government-to-government dialogue, particularly in the early stages when it would be difficult for either President Khatami or President Clinton to make any overt gestures toward the other given the hostility and opposition to the normalization of relations that still exists in both countries. Although the Clinton administration continues to emphasize that no substitute exists for an open, official dialogue, it is believed that the U.S. government would support such diplomacy.[23]

U.S. Political, Economic, and Strategic Objectives toward Iran

The United States understands that Iran is an important country that occupies a critical piece of real estate in one of the most important strategic regions in the world. Thus the political objectives of American policy both in the medium and the long term are clear: to use a variety of methods to persuade the Iranian regime to change its policies toward the overall dynamics of Middle East peace and security.

The commitment to Israel's security is a primary ingredient of U.S. policy in the Middle East. Iran's objection to Israel's right to exist and its belligerent actions toward the Arab-Israeli peace process are perhaps the most important obstacles to any significant change in U.S.-Iranian relations. Although there have been some more moderate statements by Iranians toward Israel, namely, refraining from referring to Israel as the "Zionist entity," Iran continues to condemn Israel's right to exist. Although Khatami condemned the killing of innocent Israelis in his interview on CNN in January 1998, he went on to refer to Israel as an "expansionist, racist, terrorist regime—which does not even have the backing of the Jewish people." Nonetheless, although there are some hardliners in Iran who truly believe in the evils of Zionism, most sophisticated Iranians know that this posture is primarily political and, given the right conditions, Iran's leaders will quietly adjust to the realities of the Jewish state. American strategy throughout the region is critically dependent on a successful resolution of the Arab-Israeli conflict. Arab-Israeli peace will not be ensured until a broader security regime, including reducing or eliminating the unconventional weapons threat to Israel from Iraq and Iran, is achieved.

The Clinton administration believes that there is a strong connection between the success of the Arab-Israeli peace process and the ability of the United States to sustain a credible deterrent in the Persian Gulf, including protecting the Arab Gulf countries along with their vast oil resources from potential hegemons such as Iraq and Iran. If the peace process is in jeopardy, the United States will find it more difficult to operate openly and in concert with its Arab allies in defending the Gulf. Although some dispute that this connection is as strong as the Clinton administration claims, it is generally accepted that a successful outcome of the peace process, that is, a resolution of the Palestinian issue and peace treaties between Israel, Syria, and Lebanon, would significantly increase American power and prestige throughout the region since it would likely lead to peace treaties between Israel and most of the Arab world (the exceptions at this time being Libya, Sudan, and Iraq). With the Palestinian issue resolved and Israel at peace with its neighbors, isolating the "rogue" regimes and stabilizing the Gulf would be easier to pursue.

Political objectives are also linked to the overarching economic reality that, in the medium and long term, Persian Gulf oil—and, to a lesser extent, the potential of the Caspian Basin to contribute to world energy supplies—remains the most important factor in the global oil market. With growing demand for petroleum and natural gas in Asia, expansion of Western economies, and the eventual improvement of Russian and eastern European economies, world demand for energy is likely to grow significantly in the next century. Even if alternative sources are further developed, Persian Gulf resources remain the ultimate strategic prize.[24]

American dependency on Persian Gulf oil has declined in the last year owing to new resources developed in the Western Hemisphere and Africa. However, the American economy, like most advanced economies, is intimately linked to the price of oil. Since oil is a fungible commodity with a universal benchmark price, any major disruption in Persian Gulf supplies will lead to a short-term spike in oil prices that could have a serious impact on world markets and, in turn, affect economic prosperity and growth. Thus continued access to reasonably priced Persian Gulf energy remains a top priority for American economic planning.

A second economic concern with huge political and strategic consequences relates to the possibility that Persian Gulf oil wealth could fall under the control of Saddam Hussein or the Islamic Republic, that is, if Saudi Arabia were to capitulate to Iraqi or Iranian hegemony. Leaders hostile to the West could manipulate the world oil market and at the same time accrue vast amounts of wealth from oil sales. These lucrative earnings would allow these regimes to develop weapons of mass destruction and their associated delivery systems much more readily than they are currently able to under existing restraints and sanctions. Thus a third element of American mid- to long-term policy is to deny Iran and Iraq the economic wherewithal to rebuild their military forces and pose a military threat to the United States and its allies in the Gulf. Although the impact of hindering both Iran and Iraq from developing their oil and gas resources may contribute marginally to higher oil prices, it is a policy the United States is still willing to pursue since oil prices have generally remained stable over the past few years, and the absence of Iraq from the oil market (aside from the amounts it can sell under UN Security Council Resolutions 986 and 1153) has not yet caused serious shortages. If shortages become apparent in the coming years, pressure to change sanctions policy toward Iraq and Iran may increase, thus presenting further challenges to American policy.

Since the United States regards the Persian Gulf and the Caspian Basin as critical factors in the world geopolitical equation, the long-term U.S. strategic objective in the region is military stability. This can only be achieved by reintegrating Iraq and Iran into the political structure of the Gulf and the Middle East. Very few in the United States believe this is possible in Iraq as long as Saddam Hussein remains in power. However, there is more optimism that Iran could be brought into the process if fundamental changes occur in its policy. The ultimate objective would be to establish a security regime throughout the Middle East that would rely less or not at all on a major American forward military deployment, which is both costly and potentially risky. Military stability can only be ensured if there is a comprehensive Middle East settlement. The strategic objective of U.S. policy, therefore, is to bring about a reconciliation among Israel, Iran, and Iraq in tandem with the Arab countries. Only under these circumstances would it be possible to establish a security regime in the region that could address the contentious issue of Israel's weapons of mass destruction, as well as the potential of Iraq and Iran to violate current treaties and develop their own weapons of mass destruction capabilities. An additional issue that will have to be addressed is whether this security regime would ultimately include India and Pakistan. South Asia's importance cannot be underestimated given its proximity to the Gulf, India and Pakistan's May 1998 nuclear tests, and the longer range of new missile systems that these countries are developing.

In the medium term, the United States will continue to maintain a formidable forward military presence in conjunction with access rights and prepositioning agreements with the countries in the region. The overarching dimensions of American military strategy involve continued close military ties with Turkey, Egypt, and the Gulf Cooperation Council countries. The United States will continue to be dependent on access to Diego Garcia and its forward basing structure in Eastern Asia, which could be used in any surge contingency similar to that which was experienced in the Gulf War.[25]

The Sanctions Debate in the United States

The current debate over U.S. sanctions and Iran occurs on several levels. First, Iran is one of many countries to which the United States has applied unilateral sanctions. Thus U.S.-Iran policy is part of the larger debate in Washington about the effectiveness of sanctions as an instrument of foreign policy.[26] By and large, there is a growing consensus that the blunt instrument of unilateral sanctions has rarely been effective. However, the administration has not won congressional support for waiving ILSA, and many members of Congress have threatened to amend the legislation to prevent the president from waiving sanctions without a congressional review.[27] The divisiveness over sanctions between Congress and the administration was demonstrated by President Clinton's June 23, 1998, veto of the Iran Missile Proliferation Sanctions Act, a bill designed to end Russian transfers of missile technology to Iran. Congress has not yet voted to override the veto, since the Clinton administration said it would use its own authority to sanction Russian companies. A vote to override the veto or resuscitate a bill seems likely in 1999, since the bill initially passed by a wide margin in both the House of Representatives and the Senate.

Second, discussion over the limitations and selectiveness of American policy toward Iran has been heightened by reference to U.S.-China policy. It is noted that the United States has a vast trade relationship with China despite its human rights record. The administration has called for "constructive engagement" rather than sanctions as the best way to modify unacceptable Chinese policies. Third, criticism of U.S. sanctions policy, especially Helms-Burton and ILSA, has surfaced within the American diplomatic community, who for years fought strongly against the Arab secondary boycott of Israel on the grounds that it was against the norms of international behavior and the free market. The Arabs were in a technical state of war with Israel and argued, just as the proponents of Iran sanctions do, that sanctions were implemented as an issue of national security. The diplomatic community now finds itself having to defend Helms-Burton and ILSA, which in many ways resemble the boycott they so strongly and eloquently opposed. Fourth, the most Eurocentric decisionmakers and activists argue that a serious confrontation between the United States and the European Union over Iranian sanctions must be avoided at all costs. They believe a confrontation will merely strengthen the Iranian regime at the expense of the NATO alliance, which has other, more important, issues to resolve.

Supporters of an American compromise on this issue contend that the world's superpower can make a concession on ILSA with manageable consequences. Although it might encourage some radicals to take a more aggressive stance toward America on the grounds that the United States had conceded to the Europeans, these advocates would argue that opening up the region, particularly relations with Iran and possibly Iraq at some point, threatens the regimes themselves far more than it does the United States and its security commitment to its allies.

On the other side of the debate are those such as Representative

Benjamin A. Gilman (R-N.Y.) and Senator Jesse Helms (R-N.C.), who are prepared to be tougher on the Europeans. They believe that if the United States acquiesces to Europe on the issue of sanctions that it will undermine the overall American security umbrella in the Gulf. However, the advocates of using sanctions and enforcing U.S. laws are not completely intractable. They understand that once the ILSA legislation is implemented, it may lose a lot of its purpose.

U.S. versus European Policy

It is clear that U.S. policy toward Iran is gradually changing. The election of Mohammed Khatami has prompted a new examination of the wisdom of the dual containment strategy. Although the administration still holds to the original goals of the policy, there is no doubt that the winds of change coming from Tehran have been felt in Washington. Mutual, hostile rhetoric is way down, and the administration now says many positive things about Khatami and his utterances. The administration is encouraging Americans to visit Iran, and there is talk of streamlining the visa process. In fact, the administration is openly in favor of a political dialogue with the Iranian government—as indeed it has been for some years. Iran, on the other hand, while unwilling at this point to consider such direct contact, is promoting track II diplomacy.[28] The reasons for this are clear: the Iranians feel that any official dialogue at this point in time would in fact be a monologue, with the United States laying down the list of changes that Iran must undertake in order to get back into America's good graces. The Iranian government will not do this. It wishes to lay the groundwork for a more equal relationship and there will be, as the Iranians put it, "no going back to the status quo ante."

In this limbo what one can anticipate—absent violent reactions against the Khatami initiatives by radicals and conservatives in Iran—is a slow process of reconciliation beginning with public diplomacy and culminating with a limited restoration of diplomatic relations. However, it will be a long time before an American ambassador is back in Tehran. The United States is too much a magnet for Iranians and others at this point in time, and the regime would feel threatened by such high-level representation.

In contrasting the American policy with that of Europe, it is important to note that for now on most issues there is a concurrence of opinion, including the status of Iran's compliance with international treaties such as the Nuclear Non-Proliferation Treaty and the Chemical Weapons Convention. The only real major difference concerns sanctions, particularly ILSA, which the Europeans regard as illegitimate. The Europeans share American concerns about Iran's weapons of mass destruction, its opposition to the Arab-Israeli peace process, its support of terrorism, and its human rights record. They do not believe, however, that sanctions will help ameliorate these downsides. Quite to the contrary. Europeans argue very forcibly that sanctions have the reverse impact. As British Foreign Secretary Robin Cook said in a speech to the European Institute in Washington on January 15, 1998:

> We must respond to the dangers posed by Iran as well as the opportunities. But isolating Iran is not the right response. Isolating Iran politically won't help the advocates of change in Iran or advance our concerns about human rights—isolating Iran economically won't hit the target we want—economic measures will not have any serious affects on Iran's attempts to acquire weapons of mass destruction. To do that we need to prevent Iran from getting hold of the materials to make those weapons, and it is on that goal that we all need to focus our energies.

Aside from ILSA there seems to be a narrowing of the differences of opinion between the United States and Europe, particularly since Khatami's election. The Europeans have reaffirmed that they will now conduct ministerial-level dialogues with the Iranian regime and will continue to pursue a policy of "critical engagement" with the regime, though what their agenda will be is not yet clear. This obviously is not the case in the United States.

The differences between the American and European approaches have opened an avenue for the Iranians to exploit, which they are capable of doing very adroitly. The fact that there is a major European diplomatic presence in Tehran gives the Europeans a much more hands-on policy toward the Iranian government and positions them for better economic access if and when U.S. sanctions are removed. Furthermore, it is not only on Iran that the Europeans take issue with the United

States. There is strong criticism of the low-key U.S. response to the stalled Middle East peace process, including many of the actions taken by the Netanyahu government, particularly on territorial withdrawal and Israeli settlements.

Nevertheless, U.S. and European policy toward Iran has begun a process of reconciliation, with overtures such as President Clinton's remarks before the U.S.-Iran World Cup soccer match in June 1998, Secretary Albright's speech to the Asia Society, and the administration's announcement at the May 1998 G-8 Summit in England. Whether this reconciliation will last if more European companies now start to do business with Iran's energy sector remains to be seen. The Republican-led Congress could introduce even tougher legislation if Iran's actions do not change. Ultimately, the best way to consolidate this reconciliation is for all friends of the United States, particularly the Europeans, to tell the Iranians at every possible occasion that until their policy toward Israel changes in both an existential and practical manner, it will be very difficult to persuade the U.S. Congress to fundamentally change its sanctions policy.

Clearly, sanctions alone will not contain the Iranian missile program (as the test of the Shahab-3 in July 1998 demonstrated), impede options for other weapons of mass destruction, or make the Iranians more reconciled to Israel's policies toward the Palestinians. The best course for the United States is to use the opportunity created by the continuing confrontation with Iraq to reassess its overall policy and help nurture more friendly contacts with Iranians, in hopes that at some point in the future it will lead to formal dialogue. In the meantime, a priority must be to work closely with the Europeans to examine ways to reduce Iran's desire for a large-scale nuclear energy program. This will not be easy in view of commitments Iran has made to the Bushehr project, the high level of Russian support it has received, and amid the psychological impact of the India and Pakistan nuclear tests. The one carrot the United States can offer both Iran and Europe concerns energy investment and pipeline routes. A grand bargain among Iran, the United States, and the EU would be for Iran to restrict its nuclear program to the Bushehr project in exchange for support for its oil and natural gas program and the removal of sanctions. Alas, such a bargain is far easier to imagine than it will be to bring about.

Notes

1. See, for example, Secretary of State Warren Christopher's statements that the Clinton team has a "stronger policy of isolating Iran than the prior administration did. We think Iran is an international outlaw . . . and we're trying to persuade other nations of the world to feel as we do, to treat Iran as an outlaw," in an interview on *Larry King Live*, June 28, 1993. See also President Clinton's remarks at the "Multinational Audience of Future Leaders of Europe" (Brussels: January 9, 1994), where he stated, "Growing missile capabilities are bringing more of Europe into the range of *rogue* states such as Iran and Libya."

2. See Secretary of State Madeleine K. Albright's speech before the Asia Society dinner, New York, June 17, 1998: "We fully respect Iran's sovereignty. We understand and respect its fierce desire to maintain its independence. We do not seek to overthrow its government." See remarks by Assistant Secretary of State for Near Eastern Affairs Martin Indyk, "U.S. Policy in the Middle East," *Program Brief,* vol. 4 (Washington: Nixon Center for Peace and Freedom, August 5, 1998).

3. Geoffrey Kemp, *Forever Enemies? American Policy and the Islamic Republic of Iran* (Washington: Carnegie Endowment for International Peace, 1994), p. 7.

4. UN High Commission on Refugees, "Country Profiles: Islamic Republic of Iran," www.unhcr.ch/world/mide/iran.htm, last updated May 1997.

5. Geoffrey Kemp and Jeremy Pressman, *Point of No Return: The Deadly Struggle for Middle East Peace* (Washington: Carnegie Endowment for International Peace, 1997), p. 168.

6. For more on Iran's energy sector, see Julia Nanay, "The Outlook for Iran's Oil and Gas Sector," paper prepared for the Nixon Center for Peace and Freedom, May 13, 1998; and Jahangir Amuzegar, "Iran's Economy and the U.S. Sanctions," *Middle East Journal*, vol. 51 (Spring 1997), p. 191.

7. George Bush, Inaugural Address of the President of the United States, January 20, 1989.

8. The rationale for the dual containment policy is discussed in Anthony Lake, "Confronting Backlash States," *Foreign Affairs*, vol. 73 (March-April 1994), pp. 45-55; and "Symposium on Dual Containment: U.S. Policy toward Iran and Iraq," *Middle East Policy*, vol. 3, no. 1 (1994), pp. 1–26.

9. Kenneth Katzman and Lawrence Kumins, "Iran: U.S. Trade Regulation and Legislation" (Washington: Library of Congress, Congressional Research Service, March 24, 1995).

10. Kenneth Katzman, "Iran: U.S. Policy and Options," (Washington: Library of Congress, Congressional Research Service, August 13, 1997), p. 7.

11. Ibid., p. 9.

12. Because of the intervention of Senator Kennedy and pressure from the Pan-Am 103 victims' lobby, Libya was added to the D'Amato legislation as an amendment at the last minute.

13. European Commission, *1997 Report on United States Barriers to Trade and Investment* (Brussels, July 1997).

14. See Zbigniew Brzezinski, Richard Murphy, and Brent Scowcroft, "Differentiated Containment," *Foreign Affairs*, vol. 76 (May–June 1997), pp. 20–30; Jahangir Amuzegar, "Adjusting to Sanctions," *Foreign Affairs*, vol. 76 (May–June 1997), pp. 31–41; Shaul Bakhash and Robin Wright, "The U.S. and Iran: An Offer They Can't Refuse?" *Foreign Policy*, no. 108 (Fall 1997), pp. 124–37; and Robert Pelletreau, "The United States and Iran: We Should Be Talking," *Al-Hayat*, August 29, 1997.

15. Videotaped remarks of President Clinton on Univision Video before the U.S.-Iran World Cup Game, June 21, 1998.

16. Norman Kempster, "U.S. Designates 30 Groups as Terrorists," *Los Angeles Times*, October 9, 1997, p. A4.

17. See Robin Wright, "Iran Says U.S. Is Imperiling Move toward Reconciliation," *Los Angeles Times*, May 5, 1998, pp. A1, A4; Robin Wright, "Iran Wrestlers Try to Pin Down Détente at U.S. Meet," *Los Angeles Times*, April 6, 1998, pp. A1, A3; and Department of State, "Patterns of Global Terrorism: 1997" (Washington, 1998).

18. U.S. Department of State, *Report to the Congress on the Iran-Libya Sanctions Act* (Washington, May 18, 1998). In this report the secretary of state decided that although the three foreign companies (Total, Gazprom, and Petronas) were engaged in activities covered by ILSA, it was in the U.S. national interest to waive sanctions against these companies.

19. White House Office of the Press Secretary, "Fact Sheet on Cooperation on Non-Proliferation and Counterterrorism," May 18, 1998.

20. Ibid.

21. Secretary Albright's remarks to the 1998 Asia Society dinner, June 17, 1998.

22. See Eliyahu Kanovsky, *Iran's Economic Morass: Mismanagement and Decline under the Islamic Republic* (Washington: Washington Institute for Near East Policy, 1997), app. 4.

23. See Secretary Albright's remarks to the 1998 Asia Society dinner, June 17, 1998: "In his interview with CNN in January, President Khatami called for a dialogue between civilizations, something which President Clinton welcomed because of our strongly-held view that there is much common ground between Islam and the West, and much that we can do to enrich each other's societies"; President Clinton's remarks before the U.S.-Iran World Cup Game, June 21, 1998; and remarks by Assistant Secretary of State for Near Eastern Affairs Martin Indyk, "U.S. Policy in the Middle East."

24. For additional analysis of Persian Gulf and Caspian Basin energy geopolitics, see Geoffrey Kemp, *Energy Superbowl: Strategic Politics and the Persian Gulf and Caspian Basin* (Washington: Nixon Center for Peace and Freedom, October 1997).

25. For a more in-depth strategic assessment, see Geoffrey Kemp and Robert E. Harkavy, *Strategic Geography and the Changing Middle East* (Brookings, 1997), especially part 3, "Military Options and Planning."

26. See remarks by Congressman Lee Hamilton, "Sanctions, Congress and the National Interest" (Washington: Nixon Center for Peace and Freedom, July 20, 1998); and James Schlesinger, "Fragmentation and Hubris: A Shaky Basis for American Leadership," *National Interest*, no. 49 (Fall 1997), pp. 3–9.

27. Michael Lelyveld and Leo Abruzzese, "Lawmakers Eye Leash on Clinton over Waivers," *Journal of Commerce*, May 22, 1998, p. A1.

28. President Mohammed Khatami, interview on Cable News Network, January 7, 1998; Iran also promoted track II diplomacy by inviting Americans to participate in meetings in Iran (that is, the eighth annual Persian Gulf seminar, "Regional Approaches in the Persian Gulf," February 1998).

PETER RUDOLF

5

Critical Engagement: The European Union and Iran

In Germany, the policy of "critical dialogue" with Iran was occasionally seen as a typical example of a common European foreign policy toward an important country in a crucial region. It is indeed typical: it highlights the limits and problems of foreign policy coordination in the European Union.[1] The intergovernmental nature of foreign policymaking by consensus has not changed substantially even after the refinements of the Common Foreign and Security Policy at the Amsterdam summit in June 1997. European interests and European approaches in foreign policy are defined by the European Council of Heads of State or Government and the Council of Ministers; the European Commission participates in all debates and has a right of initiative. The European Parliament is consulted and kept informed but has no formal, substantial powers. Thus occasional debates and critical resolutions in the European Parliament on policy toward Iran are nothing more than expressions of sentiment.[2]

I wish to thank Johannes Reissner and Roscoe S. Suddarth for their helpful comments and Jürgen Rogalski for his support in collecting sources for this article.

The European approach toward Iran is a mixture of widely shared political dispositions, distinctive national approaches, and limited efforts at coordinating national policies at the intergovernmental level. Beneath the surface of coordination, there is unregulated economic and political competition. Policy toward Iran at the European level shares the general dilemma of European Middle East policy, which is "caught between lofty ambitions and good intentions on the one hand and incapacity to shape these into coherent policy approaches on the other hand."[3] Critical dialogue remains largely a common declaratory policy with limited operational implications.

To understand European policy toward Iran, one has to move below the level of European Union declaratory policy and occasional actions and take the interests and perspectives of the major European countries into account. These major players—Germany, France, Great Britain—have had rather special relationships with Iran. The convergence of their interests led to the launch of the critical dialogue in December 1992. This policy of engagement was suspended after, on April 10, 1997, a German court concluded as part of its verdict that the September 1992 assassination of exiled Iranian Kurdish dissidents at the Mykonos restaurant in Berlin had been ordered by the highest levels of Iran's government. Already before this verdict, the label "critical dialogue" was dropped and, in Germany, replaced by a "policy of active influence."[4] But the European Union still clings to its traditional instincts in dealing with Iran. From the prevailing perspective in Europe, the election of President Mohammed Khatami and recent developments in Iran have vindicated the basic assumptions of the critical dialogue.

The following analysis proceeds in five steps. First, the origins of Europe's policy of critical dialogue will be explained by the convergence of interests among the major European players. Second, the strategic assumptions, the national agendas, and the perceived results of critical engagement will be analyzed. Third, a closer look at German policy toward Iran and its domestic context will show how deeply engagement is rooted in the case of the country that has been most closely identified with this approach. Fourth, an analysis of recent policy coordination at the European level, its limits, and its changing dynamics helps explain the persistence of engagement. Fifth, the paper ends with a rather sobering evaluation of proposals for coordinated transatlantic policies toward Iran.

Origins of Engagement

Iran's importance for Western Europe after 1945 stems mainly from one factor—oil. The drastic increase in oil prices after the 1973 Yom Kippur War transformed the economic relationship, since Iran developed into a highly attractive market for European exports and into a financial source for investments.[5] The Islamic revolution did not sever this beneficial economic relationship. But political relations deteriorated in the aftermath of the revolution and in the wake of the Iran-Iraq war and the taking of European hostages by Iranian-backed forces in Lebanon. European attempts at improving political relations in the late 1980s suffered a setback when the Iranian clergy imposed the *fatwa* on British citizen Salman Rushdie and Iranian exiles were murdered in Europe. But with the release of Western hostages in Lebanon, Iranian overtures toward Europe and permission to borrow foreign money, the stage was set for what became known as critical dialogue.

This concept directly grew out of the German approach toward Iran after the Islamic revolution. Whereas Great Britain and France had their particular problems with Iran, pursuing an anti-Iranian policy during the Iran-Iraq War, Germany, looking back on a long, good relationship with Iran, stuck to a position of neutrality. It even tried to moderate between the warring parties. Between 1978 and 1987, Germany increased its share in the Iranian market from 21.9 percent to 26.2 percent. It regained and secured its position as the leading source of Iranian imports after the United States had almost vanished from the Iranian market.[6]

Critical dialogue was a genuine German approach and at the same time a successful initiative to shape a common European approach in an area where Europe could take the lead.[7] The approach was endorsed by the European Community at the meeting of the European Council in Edinburgh in December 1992. Because of Iran's importance in the region, Europe would enter into a dialogue with the Iranian government.[8] In the view of the European heads of states and governments assembled in Edinburgh, this should be a critical dialogue,[9] in which concerns about Iranian behavior would be raised and improvements demanded on various issues, especially human rights, the death sentence against Salman Rushdie, and terrorism. Improvements in these areas were considered pivotal for building closer relations.

This agenda—human rights, Salman Rushdie, terrorism—reflected the main concerns of the three major European powers: Germany, Great Britain, and France. For Germany, critical dialogue had always been mostly about human rights. The distinctive German contribution to the policy consisted of four "German-Iranian Human Rights Seminars," which took place between 1988 and 1994. With German urging, these seminars moved from rather abstract discussions to concrete judicial and legal questions, which were debated in the last of these seminars in November 1994.[10] It is not by chance that in Germany critical dialogue was mainly about human rights issues. Critical dialogue was the brand name for German policy toward Iran under Foreign Minister Klaus Kinkel, who entered office in May 1992 with a strong rhetorical attachment to human rights. To some extent though, the human rights orientation of the critical dialogue can be interpreted as political cover for booming business relations with Iran in the early 1990s.

Within the European Union, Great Britain had the most troublesome relationship with Iran, for years being the only Western European country represented in Tehran below the ambassadorial level.[11] After a stormy relationship in the 1980s and a failed normalization of relations, Britain had particular problems with Iran in the 1990s: first, alleged Iranian financial and arms support for the IRA, which, of course, was denied by Tehran;[12] second, the *fatwa* against Salman Rushdie. For more than four years, the British government pursued an intentionally quiet policy on this issue, hoping that the *fatwa* would "wither on the vine." But when Salman Rushdie effectively internationalized his case by establishing contacts with other Western countries (for example, he was received by German Foreign Minister Kinkel in October 1992) and a last-ditch effort to come to a solution failed, the British government had no choice but to confront the Iranian government.[13] The situation has improved significantly since Iran's government officially revoked the *fatwa* in September 1998.[14] Despite this positive development, Rushdie's life remains threatened by a *fatwa*, supported by private citizens.

France's relationship with Iran was heavily strained in the 1980s. From 1987 to 1988 diplomatic relations were broken off. France supported Iraq during the war between Iran and Iraq. At the same time, France suffered from terrorist activities linked to Iran. This included a streak of seven bomb attacks in the Paris area between February and September 1986, which left 10 people killed and 152 wounded. All of these terrorist actions were accompanied by demands to release the five Iranians who were serving a prison sentence in France for killing two people in the failed 1980 attempt to assassinate Shapour Bakhtiar, the last prime minister of the shah. In July 1990 President François Mitterand pardoned these terrorists—a decision heavily criticized at home. The French government wanted to break the cycle of violence and to pave the way for a normalization of relations with Iran. A further hurdle was removed in December 1991 when agreement was reached on a twelve-year-old financial dispute over Iranian investment in the French Eurodif Uranium Enrichment Facility.[15] Iran now emerged as an export market for French industry, which could compensate for the loss of the Iraqi market. Recurring hints at the geostrategic importance of Iran accompanied this process of rapprochement. The trial of the three Iranians accused of killing Bakhtiar and his secretary did not impede this process. The French prosecution had argued that all three men acted on direct orders from Iran, basing its claim mainly on the involvement of an employee at the Iranian embassy in Bern.[16] But this suspect was acquitted.[17] Fear of terrorist attacks in France and French institutions in Iran led to the decision in late 1993 not to extradite two Iranians to Switzerland, who were wanted there for involvement in the assassination of two political exiles.[18] The two suspects were allowed to leave for Iran, a decision the French government justified by "national interest."

The adaptation of critical dialogue as the European version of engaging Iran, exemplified by Germany, Great Britain, France, and their individual relationships with Iran can be explained by the convergence of national interests. These countries generally shared the view of Iran as an important power in a crucial and volatile region. In practice, the adaptation of the critical dialogue led to EU-Iranian talks twice a year at the state secretarial level. Critical dialogue remained largely a common declaratory policy, free of costs and flexible enough to accommodate national policies.

Critical Engagement: Assumptions and Agendas

The main stated objective of "critical engagement"[19] was to induce changes in Iranian behavior—to move Iran toward "responsible and constructive cooperation."[20] The policy was based on two closely related assumptions. First, Western policy should reckon with different political forces in Iran. For supporters of critical dialogue, this policy aims at persuading moderates in Iran that a change in policy is in Iran's basic self-interest.[21] Supporters of critical dialogue also argue that keeping open lines of communication forces the Iranian political elite to face the issues unacceptable to the West.[22]

Second, European policy has rested upon the assumption that Iranian behavior can be influenced through communication and incentives within an approach that can be characterized as diffuse linkage. The further improvement of European-Iranian relations is linked with Tehran's living up to European expectations, not only in word but in deeds. This linkage may be termed diffuse because the incentives have not been—at least publicly—explained or tied to specific changes in Iranian behavior. Iran has to fulfill as many expectations as possible, before progress is offered. The time frame for Iranian concessions remains open. The most specific public linkage between Iranian behavior and the deepening of relations was made by the German government. No bilateral cultural agreement and no treaty with the EU would be made without progress on the case of Salman Rushdie.[23]

Despite setbacks, a thorough reevaluation of this very "soft" or "implicit" form of conditional engagement seems to have never occurred.[24] The most specific European demand—a reliable, satisfactory agreement on the death threat against Salman Rushdie—remained elusive until September 1998. Although the Iranian government assured the European Union that it would not send out anybody to kill the author, it stuck to its line that the *fatwa* as an expression of Islamic law could not be revoked. This position was orally stated in response to a demarche of the European Union from April 19, 1995. But a written pledge was never obtained from the Iranian government. Despite this unsatisfactory solution, the foreign ministers of European Union states repeated that there was no alternative to the critical dialogue in policy toward Iran.[25] This also meant that alternatives to the implicit concept of diffuse linkage probably never received serious attention.[26]

The EU has not tired of repeating what it expects from Iran. Probably the most specific list of expectations was presented by German Foreign Minister Kinkel to the Bundestag in May 1996:

—First, a positive attitude towards the Middle East peace process;

—Second, recognition of the democratically elected Palestinian national authority;

—Third, implementation of the commitment made to the EU not to sponsor terrorism in the Middle East, neither financially nor logistically;

—Fourth, a concrete contribution to a peaceful solution in Lebanon by exerting a moderating influence upon the Hezbollah;

—Fifth, a pledge to assist in cooperative and peaceful solutions in the Near East;

—Sixth, improvements in the human rights situation, especially full freedom of press, speech, and religion;

—Seventh, effective control of compliance with the Chemical Weapons Convention; and

—Eighth, an end of all intelligence activities that threaten Iranians living abroad.[27]

Diffuse linkage has never been extended to economic relations. The common European approach was confined to the political relationship with Iran. It did not affect the evolution of economic relations between Iran and individual European countries. EU member states did not try to coordinate those elements of their foreign economic policies toward Iran that are left in the realm of member states, such as the granting of official export credits and credit guarantees.[28]

With respect to economic relations, EU member states share a core consensus that no economic sanctions should be applied beyond export controls for dual-use technologies. When the Clinton administration imposed comprehensive sanctions in May 1995, the major European countries were quick to denounce the effectiveness of economic sanctions and to stress the value of political dialogue.[29] This position did not change after the policy of dialogue came under severe stress in the wake of the Mykonos verdict and some cracks in the common European position emerged.[30] This consensus among European governments against economic sanctions is mirrored within EU nations, where there are no politically relevant calls for economic sanctions, only the occasional reminder by business corporations and trade organizations that trade sanctions would cost jobs.[31]

On the basis of a shared preference for engagement and the rejection of containment and isolation, every EU member state was free to pursue its particular version of critical dialogue. The EU obviously did not define the limits of generally acceptable political cooperation with Iran. In the case of Germany, State Minister Bernd Schmidbauer, responsible in the Chancellor's Office for the German Federal Intelligence Service, developed contacts with the Iranian chief of intelligence Ali Fallahain. They were, as the German government claimed, instrumental in achieving the release of hostages in Lebanon and a prisoner exchange between Israel and the Hezbollah.[32] Other European countries, especially Great Britain, considered these contacts beyond the acceptable limits of critical dialogue.[33]

France also put its spin on the common policy. In spring 1996, Foreign Minister Hervé de Charette sought Iranian cooperation in bringing about a cease-fire between Israel and the Hezbollah in Lebanon. Iran's role in this successful effort was taken as proof that critical dialogue could produce positive results.[34]

With respect to its distinctive political agenda in relations with Iran, Greece clearly stood out among EU members. In summer 1996, the Greek government proposed a quadrilateral session of Iran, Bosnia, Greece, and Serbia for dealing with problems in the Balkans, and it invited Iran as mediator between Ankara and Athens on the Cyprus question.[35] At a December 1997 meeting in Athens, the foreign ministers of Greece, Iran, and Armenia signed a tripartite letter of understanding to promote economic cooperation, building upon the basis for trilateral initiatives established in summer 1995.[36]

While Greece is at one extreme, Denmark is at the other. In August 1996, Denmark withdrew participation in the critical dialogue.[37] The Danish Foreign Minister Niels Helveg Petersen flatly stated that critical dialogue had not achieved any results and would not lead to any results.[38] The Danish government and especially its foreign minister drew these conclusions from the fact that they had been duped in the case of Salman Rushdie.[39] Disillusionment about the official European approach and the Iranian human rights record ran even deeper in the Danish Parliament.[40]

As the Danish example shows, the results of critical engagement are open to conflicting interpretations. To some extent, they are a reflection of vested interests in this policy.[41] But even most supporters of critical engagement will concede that the policy has not led to substantial results. They would add that the same holds true for the very different American approach.

The Deep Roots of Engagement: The German Case

In the American debate, European policy is widely seen as relentlessly driven by economic interests, with critical dialogue being the ideological legitimization. Indeed, economic interests are important (especially in times of high unemployment and strict monetary policy criteria). European exports to Iran declined after Iran cut back its imports in order to ensure repayment of its debts accumulated in the early 1990s and mostly held by creditors in Europe and Japan (about $20 billion in mid-1997).[42] Although Iran is still seen as a potentially interesting market, the major European economic interest has been to secure Iran's debt service. To this end, Germany took the lead in a series of bilateral rescheduling agreements with creditor countries after the United States blocked rescheduling arrangements within the Paris Club. Thus Iran has been able to service its debt—and was saved from severe financial problems.[43]

As a closer look at Germany's policy toward Iran shows, the cooperative approach has deeper institutional and ideological roots than just mere economic interest. Economic interests and historically shaped strategic preferences are inseparably interwoven, reinforcing one another.[44] Germany can still be characterized as a "trading state" with its security outlook traditionally focused on Europe. Nevertheless, it drastically reformed its export control policies under American pressure and now applies rather tight controls on items that can be used for the development and production of weapons of mass destruction and missiles.[45] Apart from the willingness to control exports, there is a widely shared belief that trade contributes to reducing international tensions and that trade embargoes are ineffective and only hurt the population. In this respect, nothing has tarnished the view of comprehensive economic sanctions more than their morally problematic effects upon the civilian population in Iraq. In addition, different lessons have been drawn from the end of the East-West conflict in the United States and in Germany. In the prevailing view in Germany, the end of the conflict was rather a result of *Ostpolitik* and détente than of containment and a hard-line approach.

Even if Germany had few economic interests in Iran, its approach would be different from the American one. Economic interests have certainly contributed to Germany's inclination toward a "soft" approach, but they can hardly explain why the German government has hung on to its old policy. Economic interests are not paramount, but they do play a role despite the fact that the trade relationship has reached a low point.[46] From DM 8 billion in 1992, German exports to Iran fell to DM 2.34 billion in 1995, and DM 2.2 billion in 1996. Imports from Iran amounted to DM 1.1 billion in 1996. Among the 200 countries having a trade relationship with Germany, Iran ranks 45 in exports, and 49 in imports. Gone are the days when Iran was one of Germany's major trading partners outside Europe. But for Iran, Germany is still among the most important trading partners; 15 percent of Iranian imports stem from Germany.

During the first half of 1997, exports amounted to DM 1.528 billion, indicating a slight upward trend. German industry is pushing for new public ("Hermes") export credit guarantees.[47] It remains to be seen whether the German government will risk provoking the United States again as in February 1995 when—for the first time after the war between Iran and Iraq—Hermes extended credits up to DM 150 million. Total risks from Hermes credit guarantees amounted to DM 6 to 7 billion in fall 1996, for which the German government would have to compensate German banks and firms if Iran stopped paying off its debts. The number went down to DM 5.15 billion in spring 1997 and DM 3.3 billion by the end of 1997. In spring 1997, between DM 1 and 2 billion in outstanding bank credits were not covered by official credit guarantees. However, Iran has gone to great lengths to repay its debts. And occasionally it tries to lure German firms with the promise of attractive deals, which so far have not yet materialized. But from German industry's view, Iran remains a potentially attractive market. About 170 German firms are represented in Iran and direct investment is quite low (according to official figures, DM 31 million in 1994), actually much lower than Iranian investment in Germany (in early 1995, DM 1.378 billion, up from DM 645 million in 1992).

There is an important economic dimension to the German-Iranian relationship. But economic interests cannot fully account for why Germany has adhered to a policy so much criticized in the United States. And economic interests do not explain why engagement is the widely preferred approach in the German debate about dealing with Iran. The domestic consensus in favor of engagement has not covered the full spectrum of official relations with Iran, especially not the close relationship with the Iranian intelligence service. These contacts became extremely controversial when, in March 1996, a federal court issued an arrest warrant for the chief of Iranian intelligence, implicating him in the Mykonos case. But despite some occasional calls in the Bundestag to break off diplomatic relations during the course of the Mykonos trial and death threats against German prosecutors by the Iranian clergy, even many German critics believe in the potential value of engaging Iran. They have not called for joining the United States in imposing economic sanctions.[48]

The role of human rights in German-Iranian relations is controversial, views on intelligence relations differ, and bipartisan unease in the Bundestag about the government's version of critical engagement has grown.[49] But the principal consensus in favor of some sort of engagement has remained broad. For example, Social Democratic members of the Bundestag put off a long-planned trip to Tehran in February 1997 as a reaction to the persecution of the Iranian literary editor Faradsch Sarkuhi, who seemed to have become victim of a plot when he was accused of spying for Germany and France. But in general, the SPD representatives wanted to keep talking to the Iranian government. Even the Green Party, which has been for quite some time critical of German policy toward Iran, does not favor an American-style policy of isolation.

The reaction in Germany to the Mykonos verdict reflected these basic attitudes. Members of Parliament called for suspending the critical dialogue and for reviewing current policy but spoke against breaking off diplomatic relations.[50] The first debate in the Bundestag on policy toward Iran after the Mykonos verdict clearly showed broad bipartisan sentiment that critical dialogue had failed—in contrast to the position of Foreign Minister Klaus Kinkel, whose resignation was demanded by the spokesman of the Green Party.[51] The majority of the Parliament asked the government to review relations with Iran and to develop a new concept together with the other members of the EU. The Bundestag supported maintaining relations with Iran but at a minimum level as long as Iran did not change its behavior.

Crisis and Persistence of Engagement

In the aftermath of the Mykonos verdict, the EU struggled to preserve a fragile capacity for common action and a minimum of Euro-

pean solidarity. This inward-looking aspect of foreign policy cooperation dominated the European debates and action, when the German
government had to react and expected European solidarity. From the
beginning, diverging interests among member states blocked any strong
reaction.

After the verdict on April 10, 1997, the European Union, represented by the presidency, immediately condemned the involvement of
Iranian authorities in the Mykonos murders, making clear that it regarded "such behavior as totally unacceptable in the conduct of international affairs." While affirming its interest in a "constructive relationship
with Iran," it stated that "no progress can be possible while Iran flouts
international norms, and indulges in acts of terrorism" and that "under
present circumstances there is no basis for the continuation of the critical dialogue." The first crack in the European common reaction appeared when not all member states followed through on the invitation
of the presidency of the European Union "to recall their Ambassadors
for coordinated consultation on the future relationship of the European
Union with Iran."[52] Greece did not recall its ambassador, officially arguing that isolation of Iran would not be the best instrument to condemn terrorism.[53] When the European foreign ministers met on April
29, 1997, the split among member states foreclosed any substantial reaction. It is not clear whether some member states, especially Great
Britain, really considered imposing some sanctions. Reportedly, Great
Britain and Germany, supported by Denmark, the Netherlands, Swe-
den, and Austria, pushed for more than symbolic reactions, while France,
Italy, and Greece rejected any discussion of sanctions. They were eager
to guarantee that a ban on official visits would not foreclose informal
contacts with Iranian officials. France reportedly wanted to secure "technical" exceptions to permit senior trade officials to visit Iran.[54]

The result of the internal deliberations seemed to confirm what an
unnamed EU diplomat expected: "There is a lot of noise about the
need for action, but in the end the economic relationship is what
counts."[55] The European Council affirmed that under present circumstances the continuation of the critical dialogue did not have a basis,
which basically meant the "suspension of official ministerial visits to or
from Iran under the present circumstances." The only common steps
the European foreign ministers could agree upon in principle were related to the Iranian intelligence infrastructure in Europe: "cooperation

to ensure that visas are not granted to Iranians with intelligence and security functions" and "concertation in excluding Iranian intelligence personnel from European Union States."[56] Apart from that, the European foreign ministers agreed to send their ambassadors back.

This decision revealed, as Josef Joffe rightly observed, that the European Union was incapable of moving beyond a business-as-usual approach in dealing with Iran.[57] The quick return to normal relations was only hindered by Iran, making bluntly clear that the German and the Danish ambassadors would not be welcomed back in Tehran. Again, European solidarity in the face of discrimination was at stake, and the inward-looking aspect of European policy remained dominant. In Germany, it was even considered a success that Europe did not completely cave in to the Iranian demand that the German ambassador would have to return as the last of all European ambassadors.[58]

In the end, the German ambassador returned later but accompanied by his French colleague. This French-made compromise demonstrated how eager France was to go forward with its business dealings. Germany accepted this compromise because European solidarity was under severe stress and about to crack. The return of the European ambassadors, including a British chargé d'affaires, in November 1997 after seven months of absence was not accompanied by a substantially new approach toward Tehran. Europe had not found a new diplomatic formula replacing the discredited label "critical dialogue." In Tehran the return to normalcy was heralded as a victory in the struggle against the U.S. policy of isolation.[59] And it was rightly taken as proof that in dealing with Europe bilateral relations with individual EU members are what counts.[60] Among the European countries, Germany, once Iran's most important trading partner, had "now been reduced to quite a very ordinary country."[61]

France had became Europe's driving force in relations with Iran. The French government was ready to challenge the United States over the Iran and Libya Sanctions Act of 1996 (ILSA), which probably would not have gained its impetus without the fact that the French firm Total stepped in when the American corporation Conoco was blocked from developing oil fields off Sirri Island in the Persian Gulf. Total's move was part of a long-term strategy to establish its presence in Iran. Since 1990 negotiations had been under way, with a memorandum of understanding signed with Iran in 1991.[62] The threat of American sanctions did not help to deter Total from further pursuing this business strategy that so far culminated in the $2 billion contract to explore and exploit the South Pars gas field in the Persian Gulf. Prime Minister Lionel Jospin commented on the deal, which was signed in September 1997, with the words: "Personally I rejoice in it."[63] This undertaking fully fit into French policy toward the Middle East as well as toward the United States. Since coming to office in early 1995, Gaullist President Jacques Chirac had tried to reassert French influence in the Middle East, staking out an independent role largely at odds with the United States.[64]

The common European approach provided cover for an independent French policy that aimed at deepening France's trade relationship with Iran at a time when German-Iranian relations had deteriorated over the Mykonos trial.[65] Whereas in Germany policy toward Iran led to stormy debates in the Bundestag, criticism in the French national assembly was confined to a small minority on the left.[66] Whether other European countries agreed with the French version of policy toward Iran or might have preferred not to challenge the United States on the sensitive question of new investment in the Iranian petroleum sector remains an open question.[67] The German government (which was as silent on the French deal as the British) certainly would rather have avoided a situation that it always has feared—having to choose between Paris and Washington. But once the question of American extraterritorial sanctions under ILSA was raised with the Total deal, France could count on European support against American sanctions. The threat of sanctions had the effect of uniting the European countries in their opposition against the extraterritorial outreach of American policy. Even Great Britain, otherwise the United States' most solid partner in Middle East policy, did not stray from the common European position.[68]

The Iranian government explicitly welcomed France's active role in the Middle East as counteracting American hegemony.[69] France had become Iran's preferred partner in Europe. French companies were buoyed by the popularity France gained in the wake of the Total deal. In November 1997, the French Foreign Trade Center held a seminar on business with Iran.[70] The French Insurance Company for External Trade (COFACE) also was ready to underwrite business dealings with Iran.

The rush to Tehran was not confined to France.[71] Other EU countries—such as Spain—also wanted to capitalize on the renormalization of relations with Iran.[72] Italy, which buys about 15 percent of its imported crude oil from Iran and whose export-oriented machine tool industry has a considerable interest in the Iranian market, was at the forefront of returning to business as usual.[73] This occurred despite the fact that in the summer of 1997, 326 members of the Chamber of Deputies—more than half the members—and 115 senators signed a resolution heavily critical of the critical dialogue, which stated: "to pursue the current approach means to encourage the mullahs to continue with their policies of repression and of exporting terrorism."[74] This cross-party coalition against traditional policy mainly consisted of left-of-center parliamentarians. Italian policy kept more in line with the views of those deputies and senators, some of them politically important, who at the same time urged the government to restore normal relations with Iran as soon as possible.[75] The Italian government did not want to leave the leading role in the Middle East to France.[76] In this way, political and economic competition among European countries accelerated the return to normalcy in relations with Iran.

Managing Transatlantic Tensions

As the preceding analysis indicates, it is doubtful whether a window of opportunity ever existed for forging a more coordinated Western approach in the wake of the Mykonos trial.[77] Various policy proposals were made about the procedural setting as well as the substance of policy coordination.[78] These proposals suffered from two problems. First, domestic opposition to critical engagement within European countries was overestimated.[79] Frustration with the critical dialogue was not accompanied by a readiness to resort to economic sanctions. Thus any proposal that entailed a European commitment to economic sanctions was doomed to lead nowhere. Second, contrary to widespread perception, transatlantic conflict over policy toward Iran does not stem only from preferences for different instruments. Although the United States and Europe share basic goals in their policies toward Iran, the importance the United States and European countries attach to these goals is not the same, something that makes for policy differences. Iranian international behavior is not considered an urgent threat to vital European interests. It is inconceivable that a European policymaker or diplomat would say that "no nation's behavior poses a greater threat" to European political and security interests than Iran.[80] Or consider the issue of terrorism. At least in the French view, the United States has singled out Iran as an "ideal scapegoat," although other countries also have supported Middle Eastern terrorism.[81] Despite the concern about Iranian support for terrorist activities, Iran is not singled out in Europe as belonging to a special class of countries. This kind of moral stigmatization is largely alien to the foreign policy discourse in Europe (with South Africa under apartheid being the exception). Even the British government, which had "a particularly strong grievance with Iran," considers this country an "important regional player"—and not a "rogue regime" or a "backlash state."[82]

European governments and experts never became convinced of the argument that engagement is the appropriate policy toward some "difficult states," but that in other cases "engagement would simply feed the regime's appetite for inappropriate or dangerous behavior."[83] American policy toward Iran is widely perceived as largely irrational, driven more by a traumatic fixation with Iran and domestic politics than by long-term strategic interests, which nevertheless will eventually prevail. European policymakers and experts have never been convinced that Iran is the rare case, perhaps the only case where multilateral economic sanctions will really do the job.[84] Since the shift toward a strict policy of containment and sanctions is perceived as the result of domestic politics in the United States, the underlying strategic logic of U.S. policy has never received the serious consideration in Europe it might deserve. If even the Central Intelligence Agency seems not to believe in the success of sanctions,[85] why should the Europeans join a policy doomed from the start?

In Europe, the election of Khatami and other developments in Iran, including the ratification of the Chemical Weapons Convention in November 1997 and revocation of the *fatwa* by the Iranian government in September 1998, are taken as proof that, despite all setbacks, a policy of keeping up lines of communication and not isolating Iran is perhaps more than ever the appropriate one.[86] From the European perspective, the obvious power struggle in Iran has verified the working hypothesis of European policy. Thus British Foreign Minister Robin Cook, representing the EU presidency, urged the United States to take a more flexible approach, thereby supporting moderates in Iran.[87] Europe has already moved to closer ties with Iran, including the resumption of high-level contacts, which started with Italian Foreign Minister Lamberto Dini's visit to Tehran in early March 1998 and with the return of a British ambassador to Iran. The EU no longer talks about critical dialogue, but the approach has basically remained the same.[88] The EU will try to balance the upgrading of contacts with a renewed commitment to oppose terrorism and to strengthen efforts at blocking Iran from obtaining weapons of mass destruction. The tightened controls over Iranian embassies though will be maintained.

In the view of the Clinton administration, these steps obviously do not add up to the "substantial measures" to inhibit Iran's efforts to threaten international peace and security that Congress set as precondition for a general waiver of the application of sanctions under sec. 4(c) of ILSA.[89] The EU had insisted on a general waiver of the application of sanctions for EU nationals. The prospect of this solution was part of the fragile truce the EU and the United States reached in April 1997 in the WTO conflict over the extraterritorial aspects of ILSA and the Cuban Liberty and Democratic Solidarity (LIBERTAD) Act of 1996.[90] Pressured by Congress to impose sanctions against Total and its partners and torn between competing interests, the Clinton administration decided not to grant this blanket waiver but to exercise the national interest waiver under sec. 9(c) of ILSA.[91] The announcement of this decision on May 18, 1998, was accompanied by Secretary of State Madeleine K. Albright's statement indicating that EU companies making investments similar to South Pars could also expect this "national interest waiver."[92] But parts of Congress will certainly continue to put pressure on the administration and the European allies if other firms follow Total in investing in Iran.[93] Although the new renewed transatlantic armistice on the threat of American sanctions does not satisfy all European expectations, transatlantic tensions over policy toward Iran have eased.

But policies toward Iran do not yet converge. The Clinton administration is cautiously ready to engage the new Iranian leadership in a process of "parallel steps," addressing the main concerns of both sides.[94] However, as long as U.S.-Iranian rapprochement remains more potential than real, the United States and the EU will have to manage their strategic divergence.[95] Without attempts at coordinating policies, tensions over Iran will not disappear and might even become more acrimonious if new evidence comes out linking Tehran to the Khobar Towers bombing or revealing a more developed Iranian nuclear capability.

But the scope for transatlantic policy coordination within a broader strategic framework is small. Although the "benchmark approach" suggested by Geoffrey Kemp is widely debated in transatlantic policy circles as a highly plausible framework, it has not persuaded staunch supporters of Europe's traditional approach.[96] In their view, a set of explicit benchmarks for changes in Iranian behavior coupled with a deadline for compliance and the threat of political and economic sanctions might lead down a slippery slope and end with a containment approach if Tehran does not fulfill the expectations within a given time frame.

Another strategic framework for transatlantic policy coordination could be the strategy of "conditional reciprocity," as it was developed in general by Alexander L. George.[97] In contrast to the benchmark approach, such a strategy would rely more strongly on the prospect of incentives than on the threat of sanctions. Economic incentives and other concessions would be linked to specific changes in Iranian policy, which would be made clear in advance. Benefits would only be granted in response to an actual change in behavior. And they would be designed in such a way that they could be withdrawn if the other side does not comply with agreements (if this is not possible, other ways of sanctioning noncompliance would be necessary). The incentives must be important enough so that at least some groups in Iran gain from this process of conditional reciprocity. Specific and crucial tests of whether Iran is willing to play along with internationally accepted norms could be built into this process.

Both approaches entail serious risk. They could provide hard-liners in Tehran with veto power over improvements in relations with the West. Given the fragmented, multipolar structure of political power in Iran, it would probably be impossible or at least extremely risky for any Iranian president to control all disturbing activities, foremost the support of terrorist movements abroad by the powerful revolutionary guards. They are probably beyond the control of the political leadership, and they are—independent of the Iranian army—in the weapons procurement business.[98]

A less ambitious, but more realistic, approach for transatlantic policy coordination would be to identify the scope for common action on the nuclear question, which is of utmost importance to the United States but of less concern in Europe. Although concerns about the Iranian nuclear program have often been articulated in Europe, at least from the official German point of view, there is no concrete evidence that Iran is engaged in nuclear activities that run counter to its obligations under the Nonproliferation Treaty.[99] In a narrow sense, this might still be true since the Iranian nuclear program seems to be in an early phase, with no secret or unsafeguarded installations already in the stage of pilot projects, at least according to publicly available information.[100] Nevertheless, the U.S. government is convinced of Iran's ambition to develop nuclear weapons and extremely concerned about the nuclear infrastructure and expertise Russia is providing. But proponents of engagement in Europe remain skeptical of American intelligence estimates about Iran's nuclear program. They do not share alarmist interpretations of available data, mostly provided by the United States, which seem to be colored by the general negative view of Iran as a country driven by Islamist ideology.[101] They would not deny that Iran, situated in a region with nuclear weapon states (Israel, Pakistan, India) and given the uncertainty about the future of Iraq's weapons of mass destruction program, does have an interest in pursuing a nuclear weapons program. But the motives are seen less rooted in an expansionist radical ideology than in the "normal" behavior of a proud national state and important regional power. For proponents of engagement in Europe, the early stage of Iran's nuclear weapons program provides time in which Iranian intentions and behavior might change.[102] Although estimates of Iran's nuclear intentions and the priority it attaches to the nuclear program vary both in the United States and in Europe, the issue remains of far greater importance and salience to the United States. Thus any initiative would probably have to originate from the United States.

Transatlantic coordination of policies on this issue could combine a short-term and a long-term perspective. First, Iranian nuclear intentions could be tested by a common U.S.-EU initiative—preferably put forward together with Russia—that would probe Tehran's willingness to accept more intrusive inspections by the International Atomic Energy Agency (IAEA), including the application of new monitoring techniques and "no notice" inspections in declared and undeclared facilities.[103] Ideally, Germany and other EU members should be willing to link the prospects of new export credits and guarantees (which seem to have a considerable symbolic value for Iran) with cooperation on the nuclear issue. But economic competition among EU members will make the necessary policy coordination rather unlikely.

Second, cooperative avenues to nudge Iran away from its path toward nuclear weapons could be explored. Since Iran has a stated need for nuclear power plants as a source of energy, the West could help Iran develop its gas resources to meet the rising domestic demand for energy.[104] This, of course, would presuppose a profound shift in American policy, making any initiative in this field unlikely under current conditions.[105] This also holds true for another more far-reaching proposal for coping with Iran's nuclear intentions on the premise that they are nurtured by security needs: "Any effective resolution of Iran's nuclear ambitions would therefore need to be part of a concrete regional security arrangement that addresses these concerns."[106] All this promises to be daunting, as would be the task of reconciling U.S. and European approaches should Iran choose to develop nuclear weapons despite the international community's preference that it not.

Notes

1. In general on foreign policymaking in the European Union, see Martin Holland, *European Union Common Foreign Policy* (St. Martin's Press, 1995); Matthias Dembinski, *Langer Anlauf-kurzer Sprung. Die Außenpolitik der Europäischen Union nach der Reform von Amsterdam* (Frankfurt am Main: Frankfurt Peace Research Institute, 1997); and Philip H. Gordon, "Europe's Uncommon Foreign Policy," *International Security*, vol. 22 (Winter 1997–98), pp. 74–100.

2. For example, in May 1997, the European Parliament passed a resolution demanding that the member states should end the policy of critical dialogue and adopt a common approach with respect to their diplomatic missions in Tehran. See "EP fordert Beendigung des kritischen Dialogs," *Europe*, no. 6976 (May 17, 1997), p. 3.

3. Eberhard Rhein, "Europe and the Greater Middle East," in Robert D. Blackwill and Michael Stürmer, eds., *Allies Divided: Transatlantic Policies for the Greater Middle East* (Cambridge, Massachusetts/London: MIT Press, 1997), pp. 41–59, quotation on p. 43.

4. The notion "Politik der aktiven Einwirkung" was first used in a speech given by German Foreign Minister Kinkel before the American Jewish Committee on May, 8 1996, in *Bulletin* (Presse- und Informationsamt der Bundesregierung), no. 38 (May 13, 1996), p. 419.

5. On the evolution of relations between Iran and Western Europe, see Anthony Parsons, "Iran and Western Europe," *Middle East Journal*, vol. 43 (Spring 1989), pp. 218–29; and Fred Halliday, "An Elusive Normalization: Western Eu-

rope and the Iranian Revolution," *Middle East Journal,* vol. 48 (Spring 1994), pp. 309–26.

6. For these figures, see Parsons, "Iran and Western Europe," p. 228.

7. On the origins and the rationale of the critical dialogue, see Udo Steinbach, "Ist der Iran das Reich des Bösen? Die Vereinigten Staaten und Europa streiten über die Politik gegenüber Teheran," *Der Überblick,* vol. 32 (June 1996), pp. 30–32.

8. Europäischer Rat, Schlußfolgerungen des Vorsitzes, *Bulletin* (Presse- und Informationsamt der Bundesregierung), no. 140 (December 28, 1992), p. 1300.

9. The term "critical" sets this dialogue apart from the "dialogues" the EU is engaged in with over thirty countries and regional groupings. These "political dialogues" rest upon a formal decision of the Political Committee or the ministers and an agreement with the third state concerned, providing for regular contacts at various levels beyond normal diplomatic relations. The EU has entered into these dialogues mainly as a reaction to the demand of third states or regional groupings. See Jörg Monar, "Political Dialogue with Third Countries and Regional Political Groupings: The Fifteen as an Attractive Interlocutor," in Elfriede Regelsberger, Philippe de Schoutheete de Tervarent, and Wolfgang Wessels, eds., *Foreign Policy of the European Union: From EPC to CFSP and Beyond* (Lynne Rienner Publishers, 1997), pp. 263–74.

10. On the problems and results of this human rights dialogue, see Udo Steinbach, "Der schöne Schein ist längst verblaßt vom Sinn eines Menschenrechtsdialogs mit Teheran," *Frankfurter Allgemeine Zeitung,* March 28, 1995, p. 11; and Jens-Uwe Rahe, "Wertediskussion in Teheran mit Hardlinern," *Die Tageszeitung,* November 17, 1994, p. 12.

11. The British embassy was closed in September 1980 for security reasons and reopened in November 1988. After diplomatic relations were broken off by Iran in March 1989, the restoration of relations at the level of chargé d'affaires followed in September 1990.

12. See Annika Savill and David McKittrick, "Iran Plot to Aid IRA Exposed," *Independent,* April 29, 1994, p. 1; and "Britische Warnungen an die Adresse Teherans," *Neue Zürcher Zeitung,* May 2, 1997, p. 2.

13. See Annika Savill, "UK Pursuing New Policy in Rushdie Affair," *The Independent,* February 25, 1993, p. 10.

14. Barbara Crossette, "Iran Drops Rushdie Death Threat, and Britain Renews Tehran Ties," *New York Times,* September 25, 1998, p. A1.

15. France accepted Iran's claims from a deal which never materialized and was willing to pay back a $1 billion loan granted by Iran in the days of the shah's regime.

16. See "Iran Welcomes Paris Acquittal," *The Independent,* December 8, 1994, p. 13.

17. According to a report in the French news magazine *L'Express,* which was strongly denied by the French government, the French interior minister had arranged the delivery of ship-to-ship missiles or other weapons to Iran to appease the

Iranian leadership before this trial and to buy off terrorist activities. See Joseph Fitchett, "France Denies Selling Missiles to Iran in Exchange for Peace," *International Herald Tribune*, March 24, 1995, p. 10.

18. See Claude Lorieux, "France-Iran: les silences de la raison d'État," *Le Figaro*, January 3, 1994.

19. The term "critical engagement" is taken from Jackson Janes, "Foreword," in Peter Rudolf and Geoffrey Kemp, *The Iranian Dilemma: Challenges for German and American Foreign Policy*, Conference Report (Washington: American Institute for Contemporary German Studies, April 1997), p. IV.

20. Foreign Minister Klaus Kinkel on May 9, 1996, in Deutscher Bundestag, Stenographischer Bericht, Plenarprotokoll 14/104, p. 9217.

21. Steinbach, "Ist der Iran das Reich des Bösen?"

22. As one German expert on Iran summarized the basic element of the critical dialogue: "Its aim is to maintain contact with Iran as an important regional power and to use moral persuasion to convince Iran that it harms its own interests by crossing the limits of internationally recognized civilized behavior." Johannes Reissner, "Europe, the United States, and the Persian Gulf," in Blackwill and Stürmer, *Allies Divided*, pp. 123–42, here p. 138.

23. See Antwort der Bundesregierung auf die Kleine Anfrage der Abgeordneten Freimut Duve, Rudolf Binding, Brigitte Adler, weiterer Abgeordneter und der Fraktion der SPD, "Ergebnisse des 'kritischen Dialogs' mit dem Iran über Menschenrechtsfragen," Deutscher Bundestag, 13. Wahlperiode, Drucksache 13/3485, January 16, 1996, p. 4.

24. For the term "soft" or "implicit" conditional engagement, see the chapter by Kenneth I. Juster in this volume.

25. See "Die Europäische Union und Iran wollen die Rushdie-Debatte beenden," *Frankfurter Allgemeine Zeitung*, June 30, 1995, p. 2; and "EU will Dialog mit Iran pflegen," *Frankfurter Allgemeine Zeitung*, April 23, 1996, p. 2.

26. For example, in a reaction to Iranian verbal support for suicide bombings in Israel, the EU foreign ministers issued a statement in Palermo on March 10, 1996, calling upon Iran to clearly condemn terrorism. Despite the slight toughening of European rhetoric, the foreign ministers again avoided any specific linkage. They demanded that Iran should demonstrate "some progress and convergence of views" on such fundamental issues as the Middle East peace process and terrorism. See Daniel Williams, "EU Ministers Urge Iran to Condemn Terrorism," *Washington Post*, March 11, 1996, p. A12.

27. Foreign Minister Klaus Kinkel on May 9, 1996, in the Bundestag, in Deutscher Bundestag, Stenographischer Bericht, pp. 9217–18.

28. See Antwort der Bundesregierung auf die Große Anfrage der Abgeordneten Amke Dietert-Scheuer, Dr. Helmut Lippelt, Gerd Poppe, weiterer Abgeordneter und der Fraktion BÜNDNIS 90/DIE GRÜNEN, "Iran-Politik der Bundesregierung," Deutscher Bundestag, 13 Wahlperiode, Drucksache 13/3483, January 16, 1996, p. 4.

29. See "EU: Keine Wirtschaftssanktionen gegen den Iran," *Süddeutsche Zeitung*, May 3, 1997, p. 2.

30. Only Great Britain, if at all, seemed to be open to discuss the use of economic sanctions. See Knut Pries, "In Brüssel wird gerechnet, was in Iran zu verlieren ist," *Frankfurter Rundschau*, April 12, 1997, p. 2.

31. As a matter of fact, between September and December 1997, the EU temporarily imposed economic sanctions on Iran: a three-month ban on the import of Iranian pistachios after the Dutch authorities had alerted the European Commission about the contamination of pistachios by a carcinogenic bacterium. The ban was lifted after Iran agreed to comply with European standards, requiring additional tests of these products. Since the import prohibition and its lifting coincided with the crisis in European-Iranian relations and its end, the Iranian press suspected political reasons for this ban. See "Iran Says EU Lifts Pistachio Ban from December 15," *Reuters*, November 17, 1997.

32. See Martin E. Süskind, "Bonns guter Draht nach Teheran zahlt sich aus," *Süddeutsche Zeitung*, July 23, 1996, p. 1.

33. See "Empörung über Kontakt zu Irans Geheimdienst," *Süddeutsche Zeitung*, October 1993, p. 2.

34. See Paul Taylor, "France Warns U.S. against Iran Trade Sanctions," *Reuters*, August 5, 1996.

35. See *Tehran IRIB Television First Program Network* (FBIS-NES-96-163, August 21, 1996).

36. See *Voice of the Islamic Republic of Iran* (FBIS-NES-97-357, December 23, 1997).

37. Observers who interpret European policy mainly in terms of economic interests would note that trade with Iran was of little importance for Denmark at the time. Exports had declined by more than half between 1992 and 1996. The expectation of the early 1990s that Iran might become Denmark's most important market in the Middle East had already vanished with the decrease of feta cheese exports, Denmark's major export product to Iran. It had not been compensated by growth in other areas of trade. See *Berlingske Tidende*, February 8, 1995, p. III 4 (FBIS-NES-95-046, February 8, 1995); *Berlingske Tidende*, April 12, 1997, p. III 4 (FBIS-WEU-97-085, April 12, 1997).

38. See the interview with foreign minister Niels Helveg Petersen in *Die Zeit*, August 30, 1996, p. 5.

39. After a visit of the Iranian Deputy Foreign Minister Mahmud Vaezi in Copenhagen in early 1995, Danish officials declared that Vaezi had assured them that Tehran would not follow through on the death sentence against Salman Rushdie. Some days later, the official Iranian news agency contradicted the Danish statement. Since then, the Danish government unsuccessfully tried to get Vaezi to repeat his promise before representatives of the EU. See "Dänemark beendet 'kritischen Dialog,'" *Süddeutsche Zeitung*, August 17 and 18, 1996.

40. In November 1996 it passed a resolution calling upon the government to

enter into a dialogue with the democratic Iranian opposition. This resolution was part of the reaction of the *Folketing* to the so-called Rushdie affair that erupted when the Danish government, citing security reasons, first refused an entry visa to Salman Rushdie for the award of the European Aristeion literature prize. The government could barely avoid a no-confidence vote in Parliament. But the resolution was probably the most critical a Danish government had ever been exposed to. The reaction of Foreign Minister Petersen, who doubted that there was any credible opposition group, showed that he was not happy about this resolution: "This of course gives the Foreign Ministry the additional task of finding these groups." Quoted in *Politiken*, November 15, 1996, p. 7 (FBIS-WEU-96-224, November 15, 1996). As a direct outgrowth of the human rights focus by the *Folketing*, public funding was provided for the translation of critical UN human rights reports into Farsi. See Kenneth R. Timmerman, "Denmark Takes the Lead on Iran," *Wall Street Journal Europe*, November 27, 1996, p. 8; *Svenska Dagbladet*, November 15, 1996, p. 6 (FBIS-WEU-96-224, November 15, 1996); *Berlingske Tidende*, October 17, 1997, p. 12 (FBIS-WEU-97-293, October 20, 1997).

41. According to French President Chirac, one positive result of the critical dialogue in the field of human rights was that Iran granted pardons to some Iranian Jews who had been sentenced to death. See William Drozdiak, "Europeans Skeptical of Isolating Iran," *Washington Post*, March 15, 1996, p. A23.

42. Apart from Dubai and Japan, Germany, France, Italy, and the United Kingdom are Iran's most important trade partners. In 1995 German exports amounted to $1.658 million, followed by France ($570 million), Italy ($525 million), and the United Kingdom ($520 million). Among European countries the main buyer of Iranian exports, mainly oil and gas, was at that time Italy ($1.782 million), followed by France ($1.388 million), Germany ($822 million), and the United Kingdom ($196 million). See "Iran: Selected Trade Partners, 1992-1996," *Middle East Economic Digest*, February 14, 1997, p. 32; and Kenneth Katzman, *Iran: U.S. Policy and Options* (Washington: Congressional Research Service, 1997), p. 7.

43. See Javad Kooroshy, "Die wirtschaftliche Dimension der deutsch-iranischen Sonderbeziehung," *Blätter für deutsche und internationale Politik*, vol. 42 (January 1997), pp. 66–73.

44. See Michael Brenner, Wolfgang F. Schlör, and Phil Williams, *German and American Security Policies: Strategic Convergence or Divergence* (Sankt Augustin: Konrad-Adenauer-Stiftung, 1994), pp. 65–78; and Charles Lane, "Germany's New Ostpolitik," *Foreign Affairs*, vol. 74 (November–December 1995), pp. 77–89.

45. See Harald Müller and others, *From Black Sheep to White Angel? The New German Export Control Policy* (Frankfurt am Main: Peace Research Institute, Frankfurt, 1994).

46. See Peter Ziller, "Ein mustergültiger Schuldner," *Frankfurter Rundschau*, November 26, 1996, p. 4; Gregor Schmitz, "Milliardenschulden und der 'Mykonos'-Prozess," *Rheinischer Merkur*, November 29, 1996, p. 15; "Teheran lockt mit Milliarden," *Frankfurter Rundschau*, January 30, 1997, p. 1; "Gespannte

Beziehungen," *Frankfurter Rundschau*, November 4, 1997, p. 4; "Mykonos-Urteil wird den Rückzug der Exporteure aus dem Iran beschleunigen," *Süddeutsche Zeitung*, April 12 and 13, 1997; "Irans Handelsüberschuß ist im vergangenen Jahr spürbar gesunken," *Frankfurter Allgemeine Zeitung*, April 14, 1997, p. 15; and for a detailed analysis of economic relations, see Kooroshy, "Die wirtschaftliche Dimension der deutsch-iranischen Sonderbeziehung."

47. See Sabine Haupt, "Teheran wieder im Blickfeld," *Handelsblatt*, December 12, 1997, p. 11.

48. See, for example, the debate in the Bundestag on May 9, 1996 (Deutscher Bundestag, Stenographischer Bericht, Plenarprotokoll 13/104, pp. 9206–18). Even the sharpest and most polemical attack against the critical dialogue in the German debate ended in a rather lukewarm recommendation to heighten pressure on Tehran. See Arthur Heinrich, "Zur Kritik des 'Kritischen Dialogs'. Der Sonderweg Bonn-Teheran," *Blätter für Deutsche und Internationale Politik*, vol. 41 (May 1996), pp. 532–43.

49. In an early outburst of frustration with the way the German foreign ministry handled policy toward Iran, the Bundestag passed a resolution in November 1995 calling upon the government to cancel the invitation of the Iranian foreign minister to a conference on Islam planned by the German foreign ministry. Members of the Bundestag were angry that the Iranian government had justified the killing of Israeli Prime Minister Yitzhak Rabin. After the vote in Parliament, Foreign Minister Kinkel decided to postpone the conference.

50. See "Den 'kritischen Dialog' überprüfen," *Frankfurter Allgemeine Zeitung*, April 11, 1997, p. 3.

51. See the debate on April 17, 1997 (Deutscher Bundestag, Stenographischer Bericht, Plenarprotokoll 13/169, p. 15267); and "Kinkel: Die Politik des kritischen Dialogs mit Iran ist nicht gescheitert," *Frankfurter Allgemeine Zeitung*, April 21, 1997, p. 2.

52. Presidency statement on behalf of the European Union, April 10, 1997, Bulletin EU 4-1997, Common foreign and security policy (12/17).

53. See Knut Pries, "In Brüssel wird gerechnet, was in Iran zu verlieren ist," *Frankfurter Rundschau*, April 12, 1997, p. 2.

54. See Tom Buerkle, "EU and an Angry Iran Turn Up War of Words," *International Herald Tribune*, May 2, 1997, p. 1; "EU/Iran: Rat lehnt kritischen Dialog mit dem Iran sowie jedwede ministeriellen Kontakte ab—Zurücksendung der Botschafter," *Europe*, no. 6965, April 30, 1997, p. 2; "License to Murder," *Times*, April 30, 1997, p. 23; and "'Kritischer Dialog' bleibt suspendiert," *Frankfurter Allgemeine Zeitung*, April 30, 1997, p. 8.

55. Quoted in Lionel Barber, "EU Reviews Iran Options as Envoys Set to Return," *Financial Times*, April 29, 1997, p. 4.

56. See European Union Statement at the Council meeting held in Luxembourg on April 29 and 30, 1997, Bulletin EU 4-1997, Common foreign and security policy (13/17). In the United Kingdom, the last remaining Iranian intelligence

officials were reportedly expelled in 1994. See *London Press Association*, April 11, 1997 (FBIS-WEU-97-101).

57. Josef Joffe, "Mykonos und der Gesichtsverlust der Mächtigen," *Süddeutsche Zeitung*, April 30, 1997.

58. Even the Greek ambassador had in the meantime left Tehran—for a "vacation" back home—the Greek way of straddling between some solidarity with Germany and interest in not antagonizing the Iranians.

59. See Richard Meng, "Den 'kritischen Dialog' lassen die Diplomaten zurück," *Frankfurter Rundschau*, November 15, 1997, p. 2; and "EU-Botschafter wieder in Iran," *Süddeutsche Zeitung*, November 15, 1997, p. 7.

60. See the editorial in *Jomhuri-ye Eslami* (Tehran), November 15, 1997, pp. 1, 15 (FBIS-NES-97-325, November 21, 1997).

61. Commentary in *Kayhan International*, November 23, 1997, p. 2 (FBIS-NES-97-334, November 30, 1997).

62. See "Signing Up When Others Step Aside," *Middle East Economic Digest*, September 15, 1995, pp. 12–13.

63. Quoted in Roger Cohen, "France Scoffs at U.S. Protest over Iran Deal," *New York Times*, September 30, 1997, p. A1.

64. See Robert Satloff, "America, Europe, and the Middle East in the 1990s: Interests and Policies," in Blackwill and Stürmer, *Allies Divided*, pp. 7–39, especially pp. 31–34.

65. After visiting France in November 1996, Iranian Deputy Foreign Minister Mahmud Vaezi stated that France wanted to become Iran's "most important trading partner." Quoted in "Teheran kündigt Ausbau des Handels mit Paris an," *Deutsche Presse-Agentur*, November 8, 1996.

66. In September 1997, thirty socialist, communist, and "green" legislators signed an appeal of the French Human Rights League, warning the government not to resume normal diplomatic relations with Iran too soon. Iran should first officially revoke support of terrorism, refrain from killing dissidents, and end the *fatwa* against Salman Rushdie. See "EU Gesandter sondiert die Lage in Teheran," *Frankfurter Rundschau*, September 8, 1997, p. 2.

67. As a French official, who asked not to be identified, put it: "France has taken a stand on an issue where other Europeans agree but laid low because of U.S. pressure." Quoted in Joseph Fitchett, "France Hopes to Isolate U.S. on Iran Deal," *International Herald Tribune*, October 1, 1997, p. 11.

68. "The UK and its EU partners are opposed in principle to extra-territorial legislation of this kind. Sanctions against an EU company for making what are in my view legitimate investments in Iran's hydrocarbon sector will lead to a transatlantic row which will benefit nobody but the hawks in Iran." "British Policy towards the Middle East," speech by Foreign and Commonwealth Office Minister of State Derek Fatchett to the Washington Institute for Near East Policy, November 26, 1997. Or as a senior British diplomat said about American sanctions policy, "It throws us on the other side of the debate." Quoted in Steven Erlanger, "Isolating

Iran and Iraq: Policy in Tatters," *International Herald Tribune*, November 12, 1997, p. 10.

69. See "Iran Wants French Middle East Role to Counter U.S.," *Reuters*, October 23, 1996.

70. As the representative of Total in Iran was quoted: "Now is the time to come to Iran. The French are well thought of. We should take advantage of this state of grace." Quoted in *Les Echos*, November 21, 1997, p. 2 (FBIS-WEU-97-325, November 21, 1997).

71. In December 1994, the director general for the Middle East and North Africa in the French Foreign Ministry visited Tehran for talks with Iran's deputy foreign minister for Arab and African affairs. Also in December 1997, an agreement was signed about the delivery of one hundred locomotives, including the transfer of French technology to Iran. See *IRNA*, December 22, 1997 (FBIS-NES-97-356, December 22, 1997); *IRNA*, December 24, 1997 (FBIS-NES-97-358, December 24, 1997).

72. In October 1997, Iran announced its intention to buy 335 passenger cars for its railroad from Spain and Denmark. In December 1997, the director general of the Spanish Foreign Ministry visited Tehran to pave the way for strengthening bilateral relations. See *IRIB Television Second Program Network* (FBIS-NES-97-301, October 28, 1997); *IRNA*, December 15, 1997 (FBIS-NES-97-349, December 15, 1997).

73. In November 1997, the director general of the Finance and Economic Affairs Committee at the Foreign Ministry visited Tehran to talk about trade issues. In December 1997, Italian Foreign Ministry Secretary General Umberto Vattani signed an agreement about deepening bilateral relations during his visit in Tehran. See the reports by *IRNA* (Tehran), November 21, 1997 (FBIS-NES-97-325, November 21, 1997), and December 22, 1997 (FBIS-NES-97-356, December 22, 1997). With a share of 4.2 percent of all machine tool exports, Iran ranked fifth among target countries in 1993. In November 1996, the Italian firm Danieli signed a $1 billion contract with National Iranian Steel Company, involving the set-up of two new steel plants. See *Il Giornale dell Macchine & Officina*, February 1995, pp. 9–11 (JPRS-EST-95-014, May 26, 1995); "Iran Says Signs $1 Bln Steel Deal with Italy Firm," *Reuters*, November 9, 1996.

74. The resolution did not only refer to the Mykonos murders, but to the assassination of the representative of the Iranian resistance movement in Italy, Mohammad Hossein Naghdi, in March 1993, which, according to the public prosecutor in Rome, was carried out in all likelihood by an Iranian diplomat. The quote is taken from *Il Giornale*, November 10, 1997, p. 5 (FBIS-WEU-97-314, November 10, 1997). In addition, see *Il Giornale*, July 3, 1997, p. 20 (FBIS-WEU-97-184, July 3, 1997).

75. One of them, Giancarlo Bressa, president of the "Italo-Iranian Friendship Association" and Prime Minister Prodi's adviser on Iranian affairs, hailed Italian-Iranian relations as "excellent, despite the current diplomatic difficulties"

when he was visiting Tehran in summer 1997 for the opening of a steel plant built by Danieli. As quoted by *ANSA* (Rome), July 16, 1997 (FBIS-NES-97-198, July 17, 1997).

76. See *La Stampa*, June 21, 1997, p. 7 (FBIS-WEU-97-174, June 23, 1997).

77. If there was a "window of opportunity," it indeed proved "short-lived." "U.S.-European Policies in the Persian Gulf: Beyond the Friction," sponsored by the Royal Institute of International Affairs and the Stanley Foundation, September 11-12, 1997, Chatham House, London, p. 4.

78. For a procedural proposal, which rightly suggested confining policy coordination to the United States and those European countries with major interests in Iran. See Simon Serfaty, "The States of Europe and the United States in the Persian Gulf," paper prepared for: Workshop on U.S.-European Relations and the Middle East, Wye Plantation, May 8-10, 1997, pp. 30–31. For coordination of policy, some proposals are on the table, one being that senior European and American officials should "seek to identify areas of 'unacceptable' policy and agree what should trigger sanctions." International Institute for Strategic Studies, *Strategic Survey 1996/ 97* (London: Oxford University Press, 1997), p. 50. According to another proposal, the United States should propose to the EU "a U.S.-European agreement on definitive criteria by which to judge the efficacy of any renewed form of critical dialogue, containing a commitment by both sides "to amend each side's policy pending a review of critical dialogue following a twelve to eighteen month testing period." Of course, the author of this proposal hoped that such an approach would "call Europe's bluff on Iran" and vindicate the American approach. Satloff, "America, Europe, and the Middle East," p. 38.

79. See, for example, Satloff, "America, Europe, and the Middle East in the 1990s," pp. 38–39.

80. "I would venture to say that no nation's behavior poses a greater threat to U.S. political and security interests than that of Iran." Stuart Eizenstat, Under Secretary for Economic, Business and Agricultural Affairs, Remarks before the U.S. House of Representatives, Ways and Means Trade Subcommittee, Washington, October 23, 1997, p. 7, 104 Cong. 2 sess. (http:www.state.gov/www/policy_remarks/ 971023_eizen_house.html).

81. As a French diplomat was quoted in the French daily *Liberation*, March 27, 1996, p. 6 (FBIS-TOT-96-013-L, March 27, 1996): "Iran is an ideal scapegoat. Syria cannot be ostracized since it is needed to complete the peace process."

82. "We find it totally unacceptable that in the case of the British author Salman Rushdie, Iran has declared a death sentence against one of our citizens. No country claiming to be part of the international community can wage its own private war against the citizens of another country." See Fatchett, "British Policy towards the Middle East." The recent use of the term "rogue countries" by British Foreign Minister Robin Cook in a *Washington Post* op-ed piece is the rare exception. See Robin Cook, "The Good Fight after the Cold War," *Washington Post*, March 29, 1998, p. C7.

83. Eizenstat, "Remarks before the U.S. House of Representatives," p. 1.

84. The comments of a senior British official probably best express the widespread view of American policy: "U.S. policy on Iran has sounded good but has not worked. This is a situation where the American system forces the United States to act against its own interests." Quoted in Steven Erlanger, "Isolating Iran and Iraq: Policy in Tatters," *International Herald Tribune*, November 12, 1997, p. 10.

85. Asked by Congress whether sanctions are likely to influence Iran's behavior over the next three years, the Central Intelligence Agency responded in May 1996. "Even in the case of broad multilateral support for sanctions against Iran, however, Tehran would not necessarily alter its policies or behavior, in our judgment." *Current and Projected National Security Threats to the United States and Its Interests Abroad*, Hearings before the Senate Select Committee on Intelligence, 104 Cong. 2 sess. (Government Printing Office, 1996), p. 84.

86. See, for example, the response of French Foreign Minister Vedrine to a written question by the National Assembly, *Journal Official*, August 18, 1997, on the web.

87. See "UK's Cook to Urge U.S. to be Flexible with Iran," *Reuters*, January 12, 1998.

88. As the Council of Ministers stated on February 23, 1998, "Iran's willingness to address these concerns [terrorism, weapons of mass destruction, human rights, Middle East process] would greatly enhance the success of the dialogue and Iran's reintegration into the international community." "EU to Resume High Contacts with Iran," *International Herald Tribune*, February 24, 1998, p. 5.

89. Sec. 4(c) says, "The President may waive the application of section 5 (a) [imposition of sanctions] if (1) that country has agreed to undertake substantial measures, including economic sanctions, that will inhibit Iran's efforts to carry out activities described in section 2." In the report of the House Ways and Means Committee the provision was explained in the following way. "The Committee acknowledges that there may be approaches or actions by other countries to inhibit Iran's activities that differ from the current U.S. embargo on Iran, and that measures can be taken individually or collectively, and need not be modeled precisely on U.S. measures. However, the test must be whether measures undertaken by U.S. allies constitute substantial measures to inhibit Iran [sic] efforts to threaten international peace and security." House Committee on Ways and Means, *Iran and Libya Sanctions Act of 1996*, 104 Cong. 2 sess. (Government Printing Office, 1996), part 2 (ftp://ftp.loc.gov/pub/thomas/cp104/hr523p2.txt).

90. Although only the LIBERTAD Act and not ILSA was the subject of the later suspended European WTO complaint, the prospect of a general solution to the threat of ILSA sanctions was one element of the understanding between the United States and the EU, "11 April Understanding between the European Union and the United States on US Extraterritorial Legislation." (http:\\www.eurunion.org).

91. See Dan Balz, "U.S. Eases Stand on Cuba, Iran Sanctions," *Washington Post*, May 19, 1998, p. A15.

92. "We will continue to work with our European allies to broaden our non-proliferation and counterterrorism cooperation even further. In light of their essential cooperation, and as long as this heightened level of cooperation is maintained, we would expect that a review of our national interests in future ILSA cases involving Iran similar to South Pars, involving exploration and production of Iranian oil and gas, would result in like decisions with regard to waivers for EU companies." But after reiterating the strong opposition to oil and gas pipelines, Secretary of State Albright added, "We will carefully examine any proposals for trans-Iranian pipeline construction across Iran for possible implications under ILSA and take whatever action is appropriate." Secretary of State Madeleine K. Albright, Statement on "Iran and Libya Sanctions Act (ILSA): Decision in the South Pars Case," London, United Kingdom, May 18, 1998 (http://secretary.state.gov/www/statements/1998/980518.html).

93. The French company Elf Aquitaine has already indicated its interest in contracts with the Iranian government. The Royal Dutch/Shell Group reportedly plans to participate in the development of the South Pars gas field. See "Following Rival's Lead, Elf May Pursue Iran Deals," *International Herald Tribune*, October 2, 1997; and "Shell to Test U.S. on Iran Sanctions," *International Herald Tribune*, April 28, 1998, p. 5.

94. See the speech by Secretary of State Madeleine K. Albright on June 17, 1998, in New York (http://secretary.state.gov/www/statements/1998/980617a.html).

95. For a recent critical analysis of U.S. policy, see Gary Sick, "Rethinking Dual Containment," *Survival*, vol. 40 (Spring 1998), pp. 5–32.

96. For this proposal, see Geoffrey Kemp, "The United States, Europe, and the Persian Gulf," in Blackwill and Stürmer, *Allies Divided*, pp. 101–22, here pp. 118–21.

97. See Alexander L. George, *Bridging the Gap: Theory and Practice in Foreign Policy* (Washington: U.S. Institute of Peace Press, 1993), pp. 45–60. For the argument to develop a joint policy of "conditional reciprocity" toward Iran, see Peter Rudolf, "Dialog oder Internationales Embargo? Mögliche Leitlinien einer abgestimmten westlichen Iran-Politik," *Frankfurter Allgemeine Zeitung*, November 26, 1996, p. 13.

98. On the power structure in Iran, see Wilfried Buchta, *Politische Machtzentren und Entscheidungsprozesse im Iran* (Sankt Augustin: Konrad-Adenauer-Stiftung, September 1997). In addition, see Al Venter, "Iran Still Exporting Terrorism to Spread Its Islamic Vision," *Jane's Intelligence Review*, vol. 9 (November 1997), pp. 511–16.

99. At least from the official point of view as presented to the Bundestag in 1996. See "Iran-Politik der Bundesregierung," p. 15.

100. See Greg J. Gerardi and Maryam Aharinejad, "An Assessment of Iran's Nuclear Facilities," *Nonproliferation Review*, vol. 2 (Spring-Summer 1995), pp. 207–

13; and Andrew Koch and Jeanette Wolf, "Iran's Nuclear Procurement Program: How Close to the Bomb?" *Nonproliferation Review*, vol. 5 (Fall 1997), pp. 123–35.

101. As an American expert summarized the problem, "In the case of Iran, where the direct evidence of a clandestine Iranian nuclear program appears to be more suggestive than conclusive, there is little doubt that the Clinton administration's interpretation of the available data has been affected by the view that the Iranian theocracy is a fanatical, terrorist-sponsoring regime, implacably hostile to the United States. The prevailing European interpretation of Iran's nuclear program (as well of its sponsorship of terrorism) appears to be based on fairly benign assumptions about the intentions of the Iranian 'moderates,' which fits well with the Europeans' policy of engagement and critical dialogue." Richard A. Falkenrath, "The United States, Europe, and Weapons of Mass Destruction," in Blackwill and Stürmer, *Allies Divided*, pp. 203–30, quotation on p. 223.

102. The revised estimates of Iran's nuclear program by the Arms Control and Disarmament Agency do not support the alarmist view of the mid-1990s. According to the testimony of ACDA Director John Holum before a subcommittee of the House International Relations Committee in March 1997, Iran's program was at least eight years away from a nuclear weapon, since for two years it had made virtually no progress. See Kenneth Katzman, *Iran: Current Developments and U.S. Policy* (Washington: Congressional Research Service, 1997), p. 4.

103. For this proposal, see David Albright, "The Russian-Iranian Reactor Deal," *Nonproliferation Review*, vol. 2 (Spring-Summer 1995), pp. 49–51; Zbigniew Brzezinski, Brent Scowcroft, and Richard Murphy, "Differentiated Containment," *Foreign Affairs*, vol. 76 (May–June 1997), pp. 20–30 (28). See also the call for a "North Korea-Style Solution to the Bushehr Reactor," by Lee H. Hamilton, "Reassessing U.S. Policy toward Iran," speech before the Council on Foreign Relations, New York, April 15, 1998 (http://usaengage.org/legislative/hamilton3.html).

104. For this proposal, see the conference report on "U.S.-European Policies in the Persian Gulf," p. 11.

105. Even an outspoken proponent of continuing containment recently suggested an initiative that would follow the same logic but would leave sanctions against the petroleum sector intact. "Since Iran claims that it pursues nuclear power as a means of generating cheap energy, an offer of low-cost electricity from non-nuclear sources could break the impasse." Specifically, the disbursement of a stalled Japanese loan for a hydroelectric dam was mentioned. Patrick Clawson, "The Continuing Logic of Dual Containment," *Survival*, vol. 40 (Spring 1998), pp. 33–47, quotation on p. 40.

106. Ibid.

KENNETH I. JUSTER

6 | *Iraq: An American Perspective*

When Iraq invaded Kuwait on August 2, 1990, the United States organized and led an international coalition that initially imposed severe economic sanctions on Iraq and then went to war in January 1991 to eject Iraqi forces from Kuwait. This coalition, which began with the United States and the United Kingdom, eventually came to include over thirty countries acting under the auspices of the United Nations Security Council.

After the Gulf War, the United States again led the international community in imposing economic sanctions on Iraq and developing, through the United Nations, an inspections program to discover, dismantle, and destroy Iraq's remaining long-range missiles and weapons of mass destruction. The U.S. government and coalition partners also have enforced no-fly zones in northern and southern Iraq and, on several occasions, the United States has used (limited) military force against Iraq in response to provocative actions by its president, Saddam Hussein.

From the time Iraq invaded Kuwait through the end of the Gulf War, and during the early years of postwar sanctions, there was general

The author thanks Robert Cooper, Aaron Hinojosa, and Nancy Perkins for their assistance with this chapter.

consensus within the international community and widespread cooperation among coalition partners on the overall approach toward Iraq.
Now, eight years after the Gulf War, that consensus and cooperation
have largely dissipated. Although the international coalition continues
to apply sanctions against Iraq, it is divided regarding the value of such
measures. The Russians, the Chinese, and even the French are prepared
to lift the oil embargo against Iraq. The resulting strain in the coalition—and the differing positions of allies—threatens the effectiveness
of international policy toward Iraq and creates increased friction within
the transatlantic alliance. The U.S. government now faces new challenges in pursuing its policy objectives toward Iraq while trying to keep
some semblance of the coalition together.

U.S. Containment Policy toward Iraq

Since 1991, the Bush and Clinton administrations have pursued a
policy of containing Iraq. In the view of the U.S. government, Saddam
Hussein is a ruthless dictator with a "uniquely dangerous regime."[1] Under
Saddam, Iraq has started separate wars against Iran and Kuwait in an
effort to dominate the Persian Gulf; launched ballistic missiles against
the neighboring countries of Iran, Israel, Saudi Arabia, and Bahrain;
and used chemical weapons, both against its own people (the Kurds in
northern Iraq) and against Iranians. From the U.S. perspective, Saddam
remains committed to developing weapons of mass destruction and the
capability to deliver them, becoming the dominant force in the region,
and seeking revenge against the United States, Kuwait, Saudi Arabia,
and other countries. With a certain degree of rhetorical flourish, President Bill Clinton has stated that Saddam "threatens the well-being of
his people, the peace of his region, [and] the security of the world."[2]

To counter the perceived threat of Saddam Hussein's regime, the
major pillars of post–Gulf War U.S. policy have included economic
sanctions to control the financial expenditures of the Iraqi government;
weapons inspections, both to destroy existing arsenals and to monitor
compliance with ongoing restrictions; enforcement of a no-fly zone in
northern Iraq to protect the Kurds and a no-fly zone in southern Iraq,
both to protect the Shi'ites and to create a buffer against an Iraqi military redeployment along the border with Kuwait; and the threat of military action, if necessary, to reinforce each of these undertakings.[3]

There are two principal UN Security Council (UNSC) resolutions that set forth the terms for ending hostilities with Iraq and provide the foundation for these policy objectives: Resolution 686 (adopted on March 2, 1991) and Resolution 687 (April 3, 1991).[4] Resolution 686 demands that Iraq, among other things, rescind its actions purporting to annex Kuwait, accept liability under international law for any loss caused by the invasion and occupation of Kuwait, release all prisoners and return all Kuwaiti property, cease all hostile and provocative actions, and provide information on the location of Iraqi mines. The objective of Resolution 687 is to limit Iraq's ability to reemerge as a regional military threat. To that end, Resolution 687 requires that Iraq unconditionally permit the destruction and removal of all chemical and biological weapons and all ballistic missiles with a range greater than 150 kilometers, as well as all related subsystems and components and all research, development, support, and manufacturing facilities for such weapons and missiles. Resolution 687 also establishes a United Nations Special Commission (UNSCOM) charged with inspection of Iraq's chemical, biological, and long-range missile capabilities. In addition, the resolution requires Iraq to agree unconditionally not to acquire or develop nuclear weapons or to undertake nuclear weapons research, development, support, or manufacturing, with inspections to be made by the International Atomic Energy Agency (IAEA) and UNSCOM, as appropriate.

While imposing these conditions on Iraq, Resolution 687 simultaneously provides for easing the sanctions against Iraq in one important respect, by authorizing the sale or supply of foodstuffs and of materials for "essential civilian needs," with the approval of the UN Sanctions Committee. This authorization became the basis for subsequent resolutions by the Security Council for the provision of humanitarian assistance to Iraq. Indeed, beginning in August 1991, in response to increasing signs of hardship imposed by a deteriorating economic situation in Iraq, the UNSC passed several resolutions to permit Iraq to sell oil to pay for humanitarian supplies, reparations, and operating expenses of various UN oversight bodies involved in Iraq. It took five years of negotiations, however, for Saddam Hussein to agree to the strict monitoring conditions set forth in the various resolutions, culminating in Resolution 986 in April 1995 and, later, Resolution 1153 in February 1998.[5]

With the limited exception for humanitarian assistance, Resolution

687 provides that the sanctions against the *importation from* Iraq of commodities, such as oil, will remain in place until the Security Council agrees that Iraq has complied with all the directives in that resolution related to the destruction of Iraq's weapons of mass destruction and missile delivery systems. The resolution also provides that the Security Council periodically will review Iraqi compliance with *all* relevant UNSC resolutions for purposes of determining whether to reduce or lift sanctions against the *exportation to* Iraq of commodities or products other than medicine, health supplies, and foodstuffs.[6]

The United States and other members of the coalition expected Saddam Hussein to comply promptly with the provisions of Resolution 687 and other relevant resolutions so that all sanctions could be lifted. Not only has Iraq failed to comply, but on repeated occasions it has engaged in provocative actions in violation of UNSC mandates. For example, in October 1994 Saddam Hussein moved two divisions of the Republican Guard (the elite Iraqi troops) to the Kuwaiti border. The United States dispatched a carrier group, warplanes, and more than 50,000 troops to Kuwait. This show of force led Iraq to withdraw its military from the border area with Kuwait—however, Iraq suffered no punishment for having precipitated this incident.[7]

Another troublesome provocation came on August 31, 1996. Until then, the Iraqi Kurds had operated an autonomous safe haven in northern Iraq, established just after the conclusion of the Gulf War. At the end of August 1996, however, the Iraqi army joined forces with troops of the Kurdistan Democratic Party to rout its political rival, the Patriotic Union of Kurdistan. Iraq undertook a full-scale military invasion of the region, with Iraqi forces occupying the city of Irbil and reportedly executing several hundred Kurdish and Turkoman opposition figures.

The U.S. government did not challenge the Iraqi activities in the north, but instead, on September 2, 1996, U.S. forces fired missiles at Iraqi radar sites and air defense capabilities in southern Iraq. The United States also extended the southern no-fly zone from the 32d to the 33d parallel in an effort to restrict Iraq's ability to conduct offensive operations there. Notwithstanding this U.S. response, which the Clinton administration termed a "success," skirmishes between Iraqi-backed Kurdish forces and opposition Kurdish forces continued in northern Iraq.[8] Moreover, European allies expressed irritation at the apparent absence of consultation by the U.S. government before the missile attacks in southern Iraq and concern that the United States appeared to feel increasingly unconstrained in acting unilaterally.[9]

Europeans (and others) also have been irritated that U.S. containment policy appears to go beyond the strict letter of UNSC Resolution 687. First, U.S. policy provides that oil sanctions against Iraq will be lifted only when there is "a high degree of confidence that Iraq has not only complied fully with the technical requirements of the WMD [weapons of mass destruction] provisions but will continue to comply indefinitely."[10] Second, U.S. policy ties the lifting of the oil sanctions—which involve the *importation* of oil from Iraq, as distinguished from sanctions on the *exportation* of items to Iraq—to compliance with *all* UNSC resolutions, rather than just to compliance with Resolution 687 provisions related to weapons of mass destruction, as stated in paragraph 22 of that resolution. Indeed, in March 1997, Secretary of State Madeleine K. Albright reiterated the administration's policy that Saddam Hussein would have to comply with *all* UNSC resolutions before the United States would support the lifting of sanctions.[11] President Clinton reaffirmed that position in February 1998 when he spoke from the Pentagon to the American people, stating that the "economic sanctions will remain in place until Saddam complies fully with *all* U.N. resolutions."[12]

Positions of European Allies and Other Countries

Other members of the international coalition have not adopted the Clinton administration's expansive view of the conditions related to the possible lifting of the oil sanctions and have been much less enthusiastic about the long-term imposition of such sanctions against Iraq. Although coalition partners have generally agreed that Iraq must comply with the UNSC resolutions adopted after the Gulf War, some European countries (led by France), along with Russia, China, and some of the Arab countries, have favored a relaxation of the sanctions in the years since the war. The positions of France, Russia, and China, along with the United Kingdom, are especially important because these countries, together with the United States, constitute the permanent members of the UNSC. They oversee the sanctions program against Iraq, and each can veto any effort either to tighten or to loosen the sanctions.

As time has passed since the Gulf War, the European countries have begun to split in their views toward Iraq. The British generally have remained steadfast in supporting the United States on a tough posture toward Iraq—requiring full compliance with UNSCOM inspections and being prepared to use force against Iraq if Saddam Hussein obstructs such inspections. The French, however, have been much more willing to express their disagreements with Washington, including their view that Iraq is not currently a genuine threat to regional security. The French prefer that diplomacy rather than force be used with Iraq and argue that it is time to end the sanctions and begin the process of reintegrating Iraq (even with Saddam in power) into the international community. France objected to the U.S. retaliation against Iraq after Saddam's August 1996 invasion of the Kurdish area in northern Iraq and subsequently refused to participate in allied air patrols over that territory.

The French policy reflects France's historical, cultural, and commercial ties to the region.[13] France has been actively involved in Middle East politics since the late 1960s. Current French President Jacques Chirac traveled to Baghdad in 1974, when he was prime minister, and had friendly meetings with Saddam Hussein. Indeed, France enjoyed a very profitable commercial relationship with Iraq in the 1970s and 1980s. The French now have significant economic interests tied to a rehabilitated Iraq, including an estimated $7.5 billion in debt owed by Iraq to France, and major opportunities for profitable commercial deals in the oil and construction sectors. There also are more than 3 million Arabs and Muslims living in France, and the French are quite sensitive about any use of force against countries populated with members of these ethnic groups.

At this point, the French feel that eight years of UN sanctions and occasional military action, while failing to change or oust Saddam Hussein, have inflicted great suffering on the Iraqi people. France (and other European countries) also generally dislike the use of sanctions and are more inclined than the United States to try to reach out diplomatically (and commercially) to the Iraqis.[14] Moreover, in its tradition of being an independent voice against bigger powers, France displays a degree of resentment at the indication that coalition policy toward Iraq is dictated primarily by the United States.

Russia, for its part, would like to rebuild its political influence and economic relations both with the Middle East generally and with Iraq in particular—which owes it $8 billion—and thus favors the end of sanctions and strongly opposes any further use of force. China, which historically opposes meddling by outsiders in another country's internal affairs, also would like to create a firm schedule leading to the end of UN sanctions against Iraq. And many of the Gulf states fear that continued sanctions could lead to the fragmentation of Iraq, including the possibility of an Iranian-dominated Shi'ite entity in southern Iraq.[15] The gradual erosion of coalition support for the sanctions has enabled Saddam Hussein on several occasions in recent years to isolate the United States as the main adversary of Iraq.

Recent Developments

Saddam Hussein appeared emboldened by the mild response to his incursion into northern Iraq in August 1996 (and to his other provocations), and by the signs of splintering within the coalition. He precipitated a series of crises in the fall of 1997 and throughout much of 1998. The mixed responses by the coalition demonstrated the policy gap that had by then developed among the permanent members of the Security Council, including between the United States and France.

In October 1997, Saddam Hussein denied entry into Iraq of two U.S. members of the UNSCOM team, refused unrestricted access by the team to certain sites for inspection, and demanded a timetable for the lifting of the sanctions. In response, the United States sought to impose additional sanctions on Iraq, but France, Russia, and China refused to support such measures. Iraq continued with further provocative actions, including threatening the safety of reconnaissance aircraft operating on behalf of UNSCOM, moving significant pieces of dual use equipment from observation areas, and tampering with monitoring cameras. The Security Council's only response was to issue Resolution 1137 (November 12, 1997), which condemned the Iraqi violations, demanded full cooperation with UNSCOM and relevant UNSC resolutions, and, as warned earlier, banned Iraqi officials responsible for interfering with UNSCOM from traveling outside of Iraq. When the United States began to deploy additional military forces to the region, Russian Foreign Minister Yevgeny Primakov undertook a diplomatic initiative (fully supported by French President Chirac) and apparently brokered a deal with the Iraqis that permitted the UNSCOM teams to resume inspections.[16]

Iraq nonetheless continued to deny UNSCOM inspectors full access to critical areas designated for inspection, particularly the so-called presidential palaces, and stated that if UNSCOM did not complete its work in six months, Iraq would no longer permit inspectors in the country. In late January 1998, the U.S. government responded to this second crisis by indicating publicly that military action—a sustained bombing campaign against Iraq—could be expected.

Most members of the coalition were resigned to accepting U.S. military action against Iraq, but few were enthusiastic about such measures. Among the five permanent members of the UN Security Council, only the United Kingdom stood firmly with the United States on the readiness to use force. France refused to participate in any military action (although the French did agree that such action was a viable option if the Iraqis refused to permit UNSCOM inspections).[17] Russia and China firmly opposed the use of force. Except for Kuwait, no Arab country publicly endorsed military action against Iraq, though privately Saudi Arabia and the Gulf states were prepared to accept the use of force.

The ambivalence about military action, along with a concerted effort by France, Russia, and others to reach a diplomatic solution, laid the groundwork for a mission to Baghdad by UN Secretary General Kofi Annan in late February 1998. After three days of negotiations, Secretary General Annan signed a memorandum of understanding (MOU) with Iraqi Deputy Prime Minister Tariq Aziz on February 23, 1998. Under the agreement, Iraq confirmed its acceptance of all relevant UNSC resolutions, including Resolution 687 (on UNSCOM inspections related to Iraq's biological and chemical weapons and long-range missile capabilities) and Resolution 715 (on IAEA inspections related to Iraq's nuclear weapons capability); its willingness to cooperate fully with all inspections; and its granting of unconditional and unrestricted access to requested inspection sites. In return, the secretary general agreed that UNSCOM would "respect the legitimate concerns of Iraq relating to national security, sovereignty and dignity"; that there would be "special procedures" regarding inspections of eight "presidential sites" (including a "Special Group" of "Senior Diplomats" who would accompany inspectors and report directly to the secretary general); and that the "lifting of sanctions is obviously of paramount importance."

The Annan-Aziz MOU elicited a range of reactions—from relief in some quarters that confrontation had been averted, to outrage in others that Saddam Hussein was being "rewarded" merely for abiding by UNSC resolutions that he already was obliged to follow. The European Union (EU) gave its blessing to the accord. The French, in particular, hailed the agreement as a victory for (their) diplomacy and a sign of the limits of U.S. unilateralism (though acknowledging the importance of the threat of military action). The Clinton administration's reaction was ambivalent. Initially, senior members of the administration expressed a degree of skepticism about the agreement and whether it met the U.S. objectives of no control by Iraq over the composition of inspection teams, unconditional and unrestricted access to all inspection sites, and no fixed date for the lifting of sanctions. This skepticism, however, did not prevent U.S. endorsement of the agreement, with President Clinton adding that implementation of the agreement would be crucial and Secretary of State Albright emphasizing that "[i]f Iraq interferes with the inspections or tries to undermine UNSCOM's efforts in any way, we will act firmly and forcefully and without delay."[18]

Directly prior to Secretary General Annan's mission to Baghdad, the UN Security Council had passed Resolution 1153 (February 20, 1998), which expanded the existing oil-for-food program for Iraq by authorizing an increase in oil sales from $2 billion to $5.26 billion every 180 days to fund the humanitarian needs of the Iraqi people and provide repairs to Iraq's degraded petroleum, health, education, and sanitation infrastructure, all under UN supervision. The annualized value of oil that Iraq is now permitted to export under Resolution 1153 ($10.66 billion) is substantially equivalent to the average annual value of Iraq's oil exports from 1981–89 ($9.54 billion), before the Gulf War. Although Resolution 1153 provides that Iraq's expenditures from oil revenues are to be tightly controlled by the UN Sanctions Committee, one analyst has argued that Resolution 1153 goes "a long way towards [Saddam Hussein's] goal of the lifting of sanctions," because Iraq "is now authorized to export oil effectively without limit and to import nearly all types of civilian goods at about half the pre-war level, which is about all [Saddam's] war-ravaged country could absorb in any case."[19]

Despite the Annan-Aziz MOU, both UNSCOM and IAEA inspectors reported a lack of progress with Iraq on the inspections process, and an UNSCOM team discovered that Iraq had previously loaded the nerve gas VX in artillery shells. Yet, in the aftermath of the Annan visit to Baghdad, the Clinton administration appeared to have little appetite for engaging in military action against Iraq. Although the U.S. government previously had stated publicly that "UNSCOM will be testing Iraq's commitments thoroughly and comprehensively,"[20] the United States and the United Kingdom privately had adopted a more cautious, go slow policy—seeking to avoid a new crisis with Iraq—by intervening secretly on several occasions from April through August 1998 to dissuade UNSCOM teams from mounting surprise inspections.

Saddam Hussein already had been able to halt the inspections process—and hide any evidence of Iraq's capabilities for weapons of mass destruction—from November 1997 through February 1998 without incurring any penalty for such action. Disturbed with the recent UNSCOM and IAEA reports and determined not to permit inspectors to get close to secret weapon sites, Saddam again rejected the continued scrutiny imposed by the inspections. On August 5, 1998, Iraq announced that it was suspending cooperation with UNSCOM and the IAEA and was restricting ongoing monitoring and verification activities at declared sites.

In light of its (unannounced) shift in policy, the United States did not promptly threaten the use of force to back up the inspections, choosing instead simply to condemn Iraq's action for the time being, in the belief that the political stage had not been set for stronger action. In the face of this policy shift, which signaled a willingness to sacrifice the efficacy of the inspections process as a means to preserve a consensus for continued sanctions, American Scott Ritter, the chief of UNSCOM's Concealment Investigations Unit, tendered a highly visible resignation. Shortly thereafter, media reports disclosed that UNSCOM inspectors had been obtaining information on Iraq from the intelligence services of several countries, including the United States and Israel. Although such information gathering apparently was consistent with UNSCOM's mandate, the public revelation of these facts—later supplemented by reports that U.S. intelligence services had infiltrated UNSCOM to eavesdrop on the Iraqi military—inflamed Iraqi charges that Ritter and other UNSCOM inspectors had been acting as spies for the Americans and the Israelis.

The standoff with Iraq further deteriorated: the UN Security Council decided in Resolution 1194 (September 9, 1998) to suspend semi-annual reviews of the sanctions program against Iraq until Iraq resumed full cooperation with UNSCOM and IAEA inspectors, thus leaving the sanctions in place indefinitely; and Iraq decided on October 31, 1998, to cease all forms of cooperation with UNSCOM, including the eventual long-term surveillance program scheduled to begin (and last indefinitely) after the accounting for all weapons of mass destruction had been completed. This complete defiance by Iraq of UNSC resolutions finally galvanized international condemnation against Saddam Hussein.

Once again, the Clinton administration, along with the United Kingdom, mobilized for the use of force against Saddam, threatening a sustained military campaign to degrade his weapons capability and weaken his regime. Other UNSC members, including France, Russia, and China, were left with little choice but to denounce Iraq's flagrant violation of UNSC resolutions, and they did not maneuver publicly to oppose military action. Even eight Arab states, including Egypt, Saudi Arabia, and Syria, issued a statement placing responsibility on Saddam if the United States took military action against Iraq.

On November 14, 1998, the United States, together with the United Kingdom, ordered the launch of air strikes against Iraq, only to recall bombers from this mission when Iraq, through a series of last-minute letters to UN Secretary General Annan, rescinded its decisions of August and October to end cooperation with inspectors and promised (again) unfettered access to all sites with no restrictions or qualifications. However, within one week of this military stand-down, Iraq again was not cooperating fully with inspectors and, in mid-December, UNSCOM's executive chairman reported to UNSC members that Iraq was not in compliance with its obligations. The U.S. government finally responded with military force, launching a seventy-hour air campaign against Iraq designed "to degrade Saddam's weapons of mass destruction program and related delivery systems, as well as his capacity to attack his neighbors."[21]

The bombing raid, in which the United Kingdom participated, was limited in time and scope to minimize civilian deaths and collateral damage and to avoid military action during the Muslim holy month of Ramadan. The raid, therefore, did not fully achieve its objective of destroying a circumscribed list of targets, leading some critics to refer to the air attacks as a "pinprick-plus."[22] Nevertheless, the list of targets chosen reflected a strategy designed to weaken Saddam Hussein's control, disrupt communications, and undermine Iraqi propaganda efforts. The raid drew supportive responses from a number of allies in Europe and Asia. However, Russia and China strongly opposed it, and France, though acknowledging that Iraq bore primary responsibility for the situation, deplored the recourse to bombing. Arab leaders muted their criticism of the United States because of their own deep dislike of Saddam, but Arab public opinion was seething in its attitude toward the air strikes.

In the aftermath, the United States reiterated its commitment to a policy of containment in the short and medium term and an effort to replace Saddam Hussein over the long term.[23] In an effort to allay humanitarian concerns, the United States also proposed that Iraq be allowed to pump as much oil as necessary under the oil-for-food program, with strict control of Iraqi expenditures through the use of an escrow account. France and others spoke of developing a new system for limited monitoring of Iraq's arms programs and called for a lifting of the oil embargo, though with continued restrictions (but without using an escrow account) on Iraq's expenditure of oil revenues. And Arab leaders increasingly exhibited a hardened attitude toward Saddam and a willingness to support strong measures directed against him, while remaining deeply concerned about the plight of the Iraqi people. All of this left the UNSC struggling to rebuild the fragile unity that had existed among coalition members, while expecting more confrontations with Iraq in the future.

Lessons of Containment

U.S. policy toward Iraq is at a crossroads. Saddam Hussein's own clumsiness has prevented, at least temporarily, complete disintegration of the international coalition against him. But the likelihood of unified coalition action, including further use of force, is in doubt. Even if some form of inspections were to resume, it is unlikely that they would be effective in ferreting out further weapons of mass destruction, as Iraq again would shut down the inspections if they got close to secret weapons sites. Of equal significance, Iraq has emerged from the crises it precipitated in 1997–98 in a relatively strong position, at times even being rewarded for its intransigence—both by Kofi Annan's involvement and by calls from several members of the UNSC for an end to the oil embargo.

One lesson that emerges from dealing with Iraq relates to the substantial effort required to sustain multilateral sanctions over time. Even in a case as compelling as that of Iraq, without the discipline imposed by the cold war, with differing perceptions of prospective international threats, and with major commercial opportunities at stake, Western allies have gradually felt less inhibited about pursuing narrowly defined interests. Moreover, the longer sanctions have remained in place without causing a perceptible change in Iraq's conduct or toppling its leader, the more "sanctions fatigue" has set in. Many members of the coalition have concluded that they must learn to live with Saddam Hussein and rebuild relations with him. Under these circumstances, it is noteworthy that the coalition and its sanctions regime have persisted for so long and accomplished so much. The UN inspections program to date (aided by information from Iraqi defectors) has prevented Iraq from rebuilding much of its capability for weapons of mass destruction, and the economic sanctions have denied Iraq between $100 billion and $150 billion in oil revenue since the Gulf War—financial resources that would have enabled Saddam to restock destroyed military equipment with significant new purchases.

A second lesson involves the role of the UN Security Council in imposing sanctions. It is usually quite difficult to obtain consensus within the UN Security Council, and the process of doing so inevitably leads to compromises and imposes certain constraints, not the least of which is granting Russia and China a veto over U.S. and European action. In this case, however, the involvement of the UN Security Council has generally been beneficial to U.S. national interests—though less so over time. Despite recent fissures in the coalition, the Security Council has provided enormous legitimacy, first for the Gulf War and then for the imposition of economic sanctions. The enactment of UNSC resolutions has imposed a framework and order on the sanctions regime and the inspections process that almost certainly would not have otherwise existed. Although in recent years U.S. policy has moved from shaping UN consensus to being a captive of the consensus building process, now, with sanctions in place, the United States retains the right to veto any effort by other UNSC members to modify or relax existing measures (though, in practice, enforceability of the sanctions has eroded significantly).

A third lesson is that sanctions (and, in this case, the inspections process) are most effective when backed by the credible use of force—that is, when they are understood by a target state such as Iraq to be part of an overall strategy that has progressed beyond diplomatic protests and includes as its next step some form of substantial military action.[24] The dilemma of this situation is that, if military force is in fact required, then in some sense diplomacy and sanctions may be viewed as having failed, which invests coalition partners with a strong stake in exhausting diplomatic and other nonmilitary options and may impose a reluctance to use military force. But in the Iraqi case, the coalition must be prepared to use such force if necessary, and to use it in substantial quantity, to lessen the likelihood of having to take further action in the future. In this respect, the United States and its coalition partners made the mistake over several years of not responding with significant military force when provoked by Iraq, which progressively eroded U.S. credibility and undermined Iraqi compliance with the inspections process.

Most observers expected that Iraq would eventually comply with the UNSC resolutions, in part to enable it to resume exporting oil. But that has not happened, underscoring the enormous value that Saddam Hussein places on possessing weapons of mass destruction. Since the end of the Gulf War, the more that the United States and other governments warned Iraq about the use of force in response to provocations without actually taking substantial action, the more difficult it became to generate support for such action at a later date. This made the threat to use force less credible over time, progressively raised the threshold for an international consensus on the use of force, and made it more likely that when the United States and the United Kingdom did use force, they appeared to some as the aggressors.

A fourth lesson relates to the overall scope of multilateral sanctions. When the UNSC imposed sanctions against Iraq, it appeared to mark a watershed in world affairs, with the members of the Security Council increasingly expected to act in unison in the aftermath of the cold war and to utilize broad multilateral sanctions as an effective policy instrument. In fact, however, the long duration and sweeping nature of the Iraqi sanctions have produced the opposite result. Other countries now appear much more reluctant than the United States to endorse the imposition of economic sanctions. In the future, such countries may be inclined to support sanctions only if they are subject to explicit sunset provisions, waivers for pre-existing contracts, or other conditions that target and limit them.

A final lesson relates to any possible modus operandi for relaxing the sanctions regime against Iraq. Given Saddam Hussein's track record, other coalition members, including European allies, will be hard-pressed to persuade the United States to move in this direction as long as Saddam remains in power. Once before, in the years directly prior to Iraq's invasion of Kuwait, the United States attempted, with the encouragement of Arab countries and European allies, to pursue a policy of limited engagement with Iraq. That effort to develop a mutually beneficial relationship clearly did not succeed. The legacy of that experience suggests that it will be extremely difficult for the United States to agree to ease the economic sanctions against Iraq or make other positive gestures without prior affirmative action by Iraq to comply with an explicit set of mandatory steps. The UNSC resolutions provide the guidelines for those actions required of Iraq if it is to start down the road of gradual reintegration into the international community.[25]

A Policy Framework for Going Forward

As this chapter goes to press, there is a strong likelihood that Saddam Hussein will remain in power for some period of time and persist in his desire to possess weapons of mass destruction. The United States is committed to trying to stop Saddam from rebuilding his military capability, including his acquisition of such weapons.[26] But other countries—including not only Russia and China, but also France—differ in their perception of this threat from Iraq as well as in their assessment of their own national interests. Given these policy differences, the coalition against Iraq has virtually eroded. In light of U.S. views of Saddam's aggressive intentions and the threat he poses to regional stability, any effort to bridge the significant policy differences between the United States and the other permanent members of the UN Security Council (with the exception of the United Kingdom) will be extremely difficult.

Before the events of 1998, there may have been room for bargaining among UNSC members on Iraq policy. It now appears, however, that the United States and the United Kingdom, on the one hand, and France, Russia, and China, on the other, are locked into positions based on fundamentally different assessments by each of its national interests and the threat posed by Iraq. If the U.S. government had been able to reach an understanding with the French on actions toward Iraq, there might have been a positive spillover effect on the conduct of other Security Council and coalition members, making them less likely to be critical of U.S. policy preferences. But at this point, the best possible outcome may be for the United States and France to agree to disagree and thereby attempt to manage issues related to Iraq so as to minimize the negative fallout on transatlantic relations.

Even in this context, there is no clear consensus within the United States on a single preferred approach to Iraq, with U.S. analysts split among at least three major camps.[27] One camp believes that the best policy toward Iraq remains a long-term strategy of containment. A second camp favors substantial use of force now, including ground troops if necessary, to rid Iraq of Saddam Hussein. The third camp lies somewhere between the other two—favoring a strategy that would promote change in Iraq through a series of political and military measures designed to make Saddam's survival in power increasingly unlikely.

In general, the logic and salient features of these three options are mutually exclusive (though some elements of the different options can be combined). The military invasion policy certainly is at odds with the other two options for more limited action and also appears at this time to be the least realistic of the three. Without an act of overt aggression by Iraq, or clear evidence of the imminent use of weapons of mass destruction, there is virtually no public or political support for invasion, either among U.S. allies or within the public in the United States.

A policy of containment alone, however, leaves the United States (and its partners) primarily in a reactive posture, as has been the case for much of the past eight years. Containment permits Saddam Hussein to continue to orchestrate provocations as and when he sees fit, with the United States and any coalition partners having to respond under increasingly less favorable conditions. But a robust containment policy, which is complemented by political-military measures—a "containment-plus" approach—could shift the initiative back to the United States and its partners, thereby enhancing the ability of the coalition (rather than Saddam) to set the agenda.

A central component of any containment-plus strategy must continue to be the principle enunciated in UNSC Resolution 687 and reaffirmed in the Annan-Aziz MOU of February 1998—sanctions on imports from Iraq will not be lifted until there is UNSC agreement that Iraq's weapons of mass destruction and missile delivery systems have been destroyed. Adherence to this principle would mean that, even though Iraq is now able to sell oil under the oil-for-food program, the UN Sanctions Committee would continue to monitor and control *all* expenditures by Iraq from oil revenues.[28] Of course, if there are no further inspections by UNSCOM or some other group under UNSC auspices, then Iraq will be unable to meet the weapons-destruction prerequisite for lifting import sanctions. But that is the dilemma that Saddam Hussein has created for himself and his country. There is no good reason for the United States or others to alleviate that burden and, thereby, reward Saddam for his intransigence.

To date, U.S. policy has actually gone beyond the terms of Resolution 687, by providing that sanctions on imports from Iraq will not be lifted until Iraq complies with *all* UNSC resolutions (including, for example, resolutions regarding relations with Kuwait, the return of stolen property, a full accounting for prisoners of war and the missing, an end to repression of the Kurds, and the renouncing of terrorism). Indeed, the U.S. government also has asserted on occasion that no sanctions will be lifted as long as Saddam Hussein remains in power. Although the United States has, in effect, "moved the goalposts" on Iraq, that posture is now warranted in light of Iraq's obstruction of UNSCOM inspections, its defiant conduct, and its repeated provocations. A number of Arab leaders currently agree with the U.S. assessment that, ultimately, Saddam must go.

The U.S. government (and whatever coalition partners it can muster) should therefore continue to look for opportunities to maintain pressure on Saddam Hussein and foster conditions that will increase the likelihood of some form of internal coup. A low-grade air campaign against a wide range of Iraqi military assets—as implemented in early 1999 by the United States and the United Kingdom in response to Iraqi challenges to the no-fly zones—is consistent with an overall strategy of trying to unsettle and unseat Saddam, though by itself is not sufficient to accomplish that objective.

The U.S. government also should pressure the French and other Europeans to consider an escalating series of other political-military measures regarding Iraq. Immediate measures, which would be aimed only indirectly at Saddam Hussein but certainly could hasten his downfall, might include a more active effort to end illicit trade with Iraq by smugglers, direct provision of humanitarian assistance to Iraqis living in regions of Iraq outside of Saddam's control, economic support for Iraqi dissidents, and high-powered radio transmissions into Iraq and surrounding Arab countries as part of a public diplomacy campaign (discussed further below).[29] In addition, the United States could urge the Security Council to assess against Iraq the costs related to any show or use of military force required in response to Iraqi provocations— approximately $2 billion in 1998—with such costs perhaps to be forgiven upon the installation of a successor regime in Iraq. The United States also could indicate openly its intention, one hopes with the agreement of other coalition members, to implement more confrontational measures (for example, indicting Saddam, recognizing a government-in-exile, challenging Baghdad's credentials in international organizations, and extending the no-fly zone throughout the country) if Saddam continues to disregard commitments to the Security Council.

Further, the United States (and its coalition partners) should retake the moral high ground relative to Saddam Hussein by launching a vigorous public diplomacy campaign. As one commentator has stated, the U.S. government "has been unable to communicate a credible policy that distinguishes between a positive future for the Iraqi people and the need to eliminate various real threats from Saddam."[30] The United States should be able to reverse this trend in light of the Security Council's expanded oil-for-food program. Iraq is now able to pump a significant quantity of oil—largely negating the oil sanctions—provided that Saddam Hussein complies with the Security Council's guidelines for Iraq's expenditures of such oil revenues on humanitarian and related needs. Through Radio Free Iraq and by other means, the United States and other countries should repeatedly communicate this message to the Iraqi people and those of Iraq's Arab neighbors, making clear that any suffering within Iraq is primarily attributable to the decisions of Saddam and his regime not to take advantage of the oil-for-food program, which has been available since 1991. Such a sustained public diplomacy initiative could meaningfully enhance the coalition's position in the propaganda war of images and messages being waged by Saddam and could go far toward preserving UNSC consensus on how Baghdad is able to spend its oil revenues.

Finally, if there is a further provocation by Iraq, the United States— it is hoped with coalition support—should be prepared to use substantial military force against Iraq's command and control sites, suspected locations of weapons of mass destruction, and the Republican Guard. At the same time, the United States and others should indicate that there is a "light at the end of the tunnel" for the Iraqi people if there is in fact a successful regime change in Baghdad, by offering to lift sanctions, resume commercial relations, and even provide economic assistance under such circumstances.

Conclusion

There may well be no good choices regarding policy toward Iraq, and there certainly are no immediate solutions. Under any scenario, it will take time and require vigilance to advance the goal of a coherent and united Iraq oriented toward the Arab mainstream. Moreover, for reasons involving differing perceptions and interests on each side of the Atlantic, it is now unlikely that the United States and France will be able to reach agreement on the parameters of a joint policy toward Iraq, thus straining transatlantic relations. Nonetheless, from the U.S. perspective, permitting anything less than full compliance by Iraq with its current obligations under the UNSC resolutions would be an unacceptable outcome, signaling to other rogue states that they too can ignore the will of the international community and threaten neighboring countries.

Notes

1. See Bruce O. Reidel, special assistant to the president and National Security Council senior director for Near East and South Asian affairs, "U.S. Policy in the Gulf: Five Years of Dual Containment," remarks at the Washington Institute for Near East Policy, May 6, 1998, pp. 1–2.

2. William J. Clinton, "Statement by the President," White House, December 16, 1998, p. 3. See also William J. Clinton, "Statement by the President," White House, November 15, 1998, p. 2; and William J. Clinton, "Remarks by the President on Iraq to Pentagon Personnel," Pentagon, February 17, 1998, p. 2.

3. See Madeleine K. Albright, secretary of state, "The U.S. Will Stand Firm on Iraq, No Matter What," *New York Times*, August 17, 1998, p. A17; and Samuel R. Berger, national security adviser, "Iraq: Securing America's Interests," *Washington Post*, March 1, 1998, p. C7.

4. For a comprehensive discussion of the impact of economic sanctions on Iraq, see Eric D. K. Melby, "Iraq," in Richard N. Haass, ed., *Economic Sanctions and American Diplomacy* (New York: Council on Foreign Relations, 1998), pp. 107–28.

5. The UNSC has increased over time the authorized level of Iraqi oil sales from $1.6 billion of oil every 180 days in Resolution 706 (August 15, 1991) and Resolution 712 (September 19, 1991), to $2 billion in Resolution 986 (April 14, 1995), to $5.26 billion in Resolution 1153 (February 20, 1998).

6. Resolution 687 also requires Iraq to make a commitment to return seized Kuwaiti property, return prisoners of war, honor its international debts and obligations (which it had renounced in August 1990), and pay compensation for various claims lodged against it. These commitments have yet to be fulfilled, though some of the receipts from oil sales are being allocated for compensation claims.

7. The UN Security Council did issue Resolution 949 (October 15, 1994), condemning the Iraqi deployment, calling for an immediate withdrawal, and demanding that Iraq not take any other action to enhance its military capability in southern Iraq.

8. See, for example, Wire Reports, "Two Raids a Success, Clinton Declares," *Baltimore Sun*, September 5, 1996, p. 1A.

9. See Johannes Reissner, "Europe, the United States, and the Persian Gulf," in Robert D. Blackwill and Michael Stürmer, eds., *Allies Divided: Transatlantic Policies for the Greater Middle East* (MIT Press, 1997), p. 129.

10. Anthony Lake, "Confronting Backlash States," *Foreign Affairs*, vol. 73 (March-April 1994), p. 51 (Lake was President Clinton's national security adviser at the time he wrote this article). UNSC Resolution 715 provides for the long-term monitoring of Iraq's weapons of mass destruction programs, which could involve, among other things, the installation of a permanent surveillance system.

11. Madeleine K. Albright, secretary of state, "Preserving Principle and Safeguarding Stability: United States Policy toward Iraq," Remarks at Georgetown University, March 26, 1997, p. 5.

12. Clinton, "Remarks by the President on Iraq to Pentagon Personnel," p. 4. Emphasis added.

13. See the chapter by Dominique Moïsi in this volume for a full discussion of French policy toward Iraq and the motivating forces behind that policy.

14. The German position has been somewhere between that of Britain and France. The Germans politically support the United States when the Americans deem the use of force against Iraq to be necessary, but for their own historical reasons, the Germans remain on the sidelines in any such military activity. Notably, Germany had significant economic relations with Iraq and anticipates major commercial deals with Iraq if and when sanctions are lifted.

15. See Geoffrey Kemp, "The United States, Europe, and the Persian Gulf," in Blackwill and Stürmer, *Allies Divided*, p. 111.

16. It is unclear what Russia offered or promised the Iraqis in return for Iraq's temporary resumption of UNSCOM inspections.

17. Other European allies, including Germany, Spain, Portugal, Denmark, the Netherlands, Iceland, Hungary, Poland, and the Czech Republic, eventually agreed to provide forces, bases, or logistical support for military action. Outside of Europe, Canada, Argentina, Australia, and New Zealand also agreed to provide such support.

18. Madeleine K. Albright, secretary of state, "NATO Enlargement," Hearings before the Foreign Relations Committee, Senate, 105 Cong. 2 sess., February 24, 1998, p. 10. In addition, UNSC Resolution 1154 (March 2, 1994), which was voted under Chapter VII of the UN Charter (providing legal grounds for use of military force), warned Iraq of "the severest consequences" if it blocked UNSCOM inspectors.

19. Patrick Clawson, "'Oil for Food' or the End of Sanctions?" *Policywatch,* no. 303 (Washington: Washington Institute for Near East Policy, February 1998), pp. 1–2.

20. Madeleine K. Albright, secretary of state, "Departments of Commerce, Justice, and State, the Judiciary, and Related Agencies Appropriations for 1999," Hearings before the Subcommittee on the Departments of Commerce, Justice, and State, the Judiciary, and Related Agencies of the Committee on Appropriations, House of Representatives, 105 Cong. 2 sess., February 25, 1998 (Government Printing Office, 1998), p. 6.

21. William J. Clinton, "Remarks of the President on Iraq," White House, December 19, 1998, p. 1.

22. See, for example, Rick Atkinson, "Is Mission 'Pinpricks' or Punitive?" *Washington Post,* December 18, 1998, p. A55.

23. Clinton, "Remarks of the President on Iraq," White House, December 19, 1998, pp. 1–2.

24. See Jeffrey P. Bialos and Kenneth I. Juster, "The Libyan Sanctions: A Rational Response to State-Sponsored Terrorism?" *Virginia Journal of International Law,* vol. 26 (Summer 1986), pp. 849–55; and Gary Hufbauer, "The Snake Oil of Diplomacy," *Washington Post,* July 12, 1998, p. C1 (referring to the "escalating 'force curve'—a steady progression from diplomatic protest, to economic sanctions, to military intervention").

25. Theoretically, there are at least three forms of engagement: unconditional engagement (indicative of strong relations between two countries); "implicit" or "soft" conditional engagement (indicative of good relations, but where there are still positive and negative aspects to a relationship that is not fully normalized); and "explicit" or "hard" conditional engagement (indicative of poor relations, where a step-by-step road map is required for progress toward better relations). The situation with Iraq falls, at best, into the third category.

26. Samuel R. Berger, assistant to the president for national security affairs, "Remarks on Iraq," National Press Club, December 23, 1998, p. 3.

27. See Patrick L. Clawson, ed., *Iraq Strategy Review: Options for U.S. Policy* (Washington: Washington Institute for Near East Policy, 1998) for an analysis of

six alternative policies: contain broadly, contain narrowly, undermine, overthrow, deter, and invade.

28. Under UNSC Resolution 1153, the UN Sanctions Committee monitors and controls all expenditures by Iraq under the oil-for-food program. UNSC Resolution 687 does not provide for such control of expenditures from revenues Iraq would receive if sanctions were lifted on the purchase of imports (such as oil) from Iraq; in that event, Resolution 687 would continue only to provide sanctions on the export of certain items to Iraq. However, in light of repeated, material violations by Iraq of the inspections provisions of Resolution 687, the United States should insist that any potential lifting of sanctions so as to permit Iraq to obtain revenues from the sale of oil and other goods be accompanied by a continued UN monitoring and control process regarding Iraqi expenditures.

29. The U.S. government already is beginning to undertake some of these measures. See White House Office of the Press Secretary, "Text of a Letter from the President to Congress: Status of Efforts to Obtain Iraq's Compliance with UN Resolutions," June 24, 1998, pp. 1–2.

30. Jean AbiNader, "The Gulf between the Arabs and America," *Washington Post*, March 1, 1998, p. C1.

7 | *Iraq*

F rance's approach to Iraq cannot be understood fully if one does not take into account a complex array of factors, ranging from historical to domestic political considerations and from regional policy toward the Middle East to global foreign policy considerations. To these factors one must add the fact that France's policy toward Iraq reflects the French urge to be different in what is France's unique and quasi-obsessive relationship with the United States. To be "different" does not mean to oppose systematically the policy of Washington. It is in fact the reverse, since Paris is increasingly careful to demonstrate in words if not in deeds how much French diplomacy takes into account the need to find a common ground or at least some compromise between the two capitals. Thus France's judgment is that inevitable differences of visions, priorities, and interests on the subject of Iraq should not be allowed to jeopardize a relationship deemed essential for obvious strategic, political, and economic considerations.

Yet it must be said at the same time that the current state of U.S.-French relations is more than ever a mirror reflecting France's confidence in itself. The less secure France is about itself, the more antagonistic its policy compared with that of the United States. If any meaning remains to the word "Gaullist" today, it is France's enduring ability and propensity to say no to the United States. During 1998, the French progressively regained more confidence in themselves at a time when the American presidency, in part paralyzed by scandal, was less able than usual to demonstrate authority and continuity.

Despite such a complex political background, relations between Washington and Paris (and Europe) on how best to deal with Iraq have been consistent. The February 1998 crisis involving Iraq should not create false illusions. France's diplomatic influence appeared to have been decisive in February 1998 only because of the credibility of the American military deterrent and thanks to Washington's uncertain strategic vision. The November 1998 crisis played out differently, with French tacit, if not explicit, approval of U.S. sword wielding in the Gulf. Yet the basic problem caused by conflicting U.S. and European approaches toward Iraq, and other difficult states, remains.

France and Iraq: The Recent Past and the Special Relationship

To understand and analyze France's policy toward Iraq, one must start with the historical and political background of the so-called Arab policy of France, initiated by Charles de Gaulle.

Asked in the late 1970s how he perceived the international role of a middle-sized power like France, Jean François-Poncet, the former foreign minister, replied: "The expression middle-size does not satisfy me: it contains an element of resignation that is not part of our national character. There are in the world two super-powers and just after, great traditional powers like France."[1] Today, France's perception of itself and of its role in the world is much more realistic and much less bombastic. Hubert Védrine, the present foreign minister, acknowledges the uniqueness of the position of the United States in the world, a country he describes as a "hyper-power."[2] For Védrine, France has to adjust to the realities of a largely unipolar world, something that does not mean that France cannot make a difference in global affairs nor does it rule out striving for a more multipolar world.

Since the end of World War II, and more specifically since the beginning of the Fifth Republic, the Middle East has been for France an essential piece of a global political project characterized by the attempt to transcend a purely regional, that is, European, role for itself. In a world divided by blocs, France saw itself as a potential mediator between East and West and between North and South. For France, the Middle East represented an ideal region for implementing this aim. Strategically it was East-West, while economically it was more North-South. Of course, these rather rhetorical concepts did not hide the more "concrete" interests such as oil and influence.[3]

To the American accusation in the 1970s that France "stoops for oil" and that French diplomacy was purely mercantilistic, French spokesmen were quick to answer that France had traditional interests in the Middle East.[4] After liberating itself from the entanglement in Algeria by granting it independence in 1962, France sought to reestablish its traditional influence in the Arab world as a prerequisite to achieving broader influence in the third world. Such a move implied curtailing the overly close relationship with Israel, based on the anti-Arab position that had been dominant during most of the Fourth Republic. Neglecting the sentiment of public opinion of the time and most members of the political class, France, after 1967, became the first European country to establish a special relationship with the Arab world—providing it with military assistance and giving it political and diplomatic support at the United Nations. While defending the principle of Israel's right to exist, France went as far as possible in the direction of the Arab consensus.[5]

France's relations with Iraq were a central element in France's Arab policy. Iraq was perceived as a special, if not an ideal, partner for France. At that time Iraq was perceived as a useful balancing force and not as either a regional or international danger. It had the right size in its regional context—neither too big nor too small. It seemed to have the right leader, a young modern secular "enlightened" ruler, Saddam Hussein, who fully seduced his equally young French counterpart, the newly appointed prime minister of France, Jacques Chirac. Chirac's trip to Baghdad in 1974, one of his first diplomatic activities, was perceived as a success by both sides.[6] In some ways, as in the Treaty of Rapallo between the Soviet Union and Germany in 1922, the two men—Chirac and Saddam Hussein—like the two countries they represented gave each other added legitimacy, even a reciprocal "anointment." The political orientation of the Iraqi regime, instead of being a deterrent, was an absolute plus for France. While the Soviet Union was the main purveyor of arms to Iraq, the French presence could be seen as a moderating influence on this potentially radical state.

The United States appreciated this implicit division of labor. Paris was a welcome Western presence in Baghdad, while Washington was the principal actor in Tehran.[7] France could therefore at the same time indulge in its tendency to deal with nearly radical states and still be a useful actor in the Western world. The Jacobin spirit largely prevalent in some key segments of the French establishment felt in tune with the "strong and dynamic" personality of Saddam Hussein. He seemed to be the perfect example of what a modern secular Arab leader should be. France, which had experienced the frustration of defeat in the Algerian war of independence and whose Muslim population was already significant, viewed this secular dimension as a highly significant consideration for a model of the Arab future.[8] For a man like Jean-Pierre Chevènement, an important and well-respected figure of the French left, Saddam Hussein was the very incarnation of what an Arab leader should be: strong, charismatic, and capable of successfully resisting the negative influence of an intolerant and dogmatic Islam.

These personal, diplomatic, even ideological, considerations merely reinforced more down-to-earth calculations. Iraq was above all a country that offered virtually unlimited energy resources, and in the short term, a secure if not necessarily cheap source of oil, an important consideration in the wake of the October 1973 Yom Kippur War. Furthermore, this rich, dynamic, ambitious country was willing and capable of buying expensive and sophisticated French weapons, including Dassault fighter bombers, Matra missiles, and Thomson electronic devices. For French firms the Iraqi market represented an absolute bonanza. Moreover, a French-Iraqi military and commercial relationship could be seen as the best way to balance Iraq's sole dependency on Soviet war matériel, thereby frustrating Soviet ambitions in the region. For France the ability to export weapons systems was essential to the effort to maintain and develop a credible independent arms industry. There was also another, even less benign, contribution of France to the "modernity" of Iraq, namely, the sale of a nuclear reactor, intended of course for strictly civilian use but with the potential to become far more dangerous despite the involvement of the International Atomic Energy Agency (IAEA).[9]

France's special links with Iraq, and the unique relationship of the

United States with Iran, worked smoothly and efficiently as long as the domestic environment in the two countries remained stable. The Iranian revolution in 1979, and its indirect consequence, the war between Iraq and Iran, quickly destroyed the elegant and profitable edifice that had been built by the two diplomatic, political, and industrial establishments. At first the Iran-Iraq War proved very profitable for some French firms, in particular Matra, but a muted debate rapidly arose within the French administration. Could France remain so one-sided, so ostensibly on the side of Iraq? Should Paris abstain from selling weapons to the two belligerents, or should France distribute favors more equally by discreetly contributing to both sides?

France's combination of visibility, engagement, and vulnerability led to a direct, unplanned, and unwanted consequence: terrorism. The waves of terrorist bombings that struck at the very heart of French cities, Paris in particular, have been shown to have been direct "punishment" for French involvement on Iraq's side by Iranian-led or inspired commandos. Still, such terrorist attacks did not seriously alter France's fundamental orientations and choices in the region if for no other reason than that France's perception of its interests remained constant.

France's Arab policy, one of the key components of General de Gaulle's foreign policy legacy, was partially reviewed by President François Mitterrand upon his arrival to power in 1981.[10] The new president was critical of his predecessor's approach to the Arab-Israeli conflict. For Mitterrand, Valéry Giscard d'Estaing had been too negative toward the peace process that had led, under the auspices of the United States, to a separate peace between Israel and Egypt in 1979. Giscard had rallied successfully the members of the European Community behind French skepticism toward the peace process but to what purpose? France was right in saying that the fate of the Palestinian people was central to the future of the region, but Europe, like the Greek chorus in the antique drama, was commenting on events more than acting upon them. According to Mitterrand, this policy had to be adapted to new realities. France had antagonized the United States without seriously influencing the peace process. The time had come for a different policy, one that was at once more pro-Israeli and more pro-Palestinian and one that would reflect the dual sensitivities of the new Socialist elites that had come to power. The old guard wanted to reestablish at least part of the special relationship that had existed between Israel and France during

the Fourth Republic, while the "young Turks" of the May 1968 generation felt much closer to the sensitivities of the Palestinians. The Foreign
Ministry, however, was keen to return to a traditional policy more in
tune with the eternal interests of France, which meant a pro-Arab policy
in a classical sense. For them, only one policy was possible and made
sense. In fact, the more France gave the impression of a shift in its approach toward the Arab-Israeli conflict (François Mitterrand's trip to
Jerusalem being one example),[11] the more the Foreign Ministry argued
for continued support to Iraq. How else could France appear credible in
Riyadh or in the United Arab Emirates, who feared above all the revolutionary and regional ambitions of a non-Arab and Shi'ite country
such as Iran? The more ambivalent the policy of the United States appeared (because of the decision to provide arms to Iran in 1985 and the
resulting Iran-Contra affair), the more important it became to demonstrate to the Arab world that only France was a friend and reliable partner who contributed to Iran's containment through its military
equipment and diplomatic support to Iraq.

With the end of the Iran-Iraq War in 1988, France was at last in a
position to slowly restore a more normal and open relationship with
Baghdad. This was all the more necessary since the irresponsible miscal-
culations of Saddam Hussein had created a desperate economic situation for his country, which had clear and painful consequences for France.
The enormity of the Iraqi debt to France, made possible through the
mechanisms of the Compagnie Française d'Assurance pour le Commerce Extérieur (COFACE), the French agency set up to guarantee
French firms against export risks, was estimated by the early 1990s to be
as high as four billion dollars.[12]

Two years later, the continued adventures of the master of Baghdad
once more unsettled the rational certainties of Paris. This time France
had no choice but to oppose Iraq. The Iraqi invasion of Kuwait on
August 2, 1990, had to be condemned by France, but Paris contributed
to the Washington-led coalition without real enthusiasm. The political
cost of not participating in the military intervention led by Washington
under the umbrella of the United Nations would simply have been too
high. It would have led to the self-exclusion of Paris, not only from the
Middle East peace process but more globally from the possibility of
playing a significant diplomatic role within the Atlantic alliance or anywhere with the United States. Furthermore, after the end of the cold

war, at least, the perception prevailed in Europe that the countries of Europe should work together, and France's *not* acting with its allies (given Saddam Hussein's clear violation of international norms) could have injured the French drive for more *European* unity.

François Mitterrand had a clear vision of where the fundamental interests of France lay. It was not the case with all the members of his government. The defense minister at the time, Jean-Pierre Chevènement, had another vision of French interests. After describing in apocalyptic terms the potential casualties France's military contingents would suffer from their participation in the war, he chose to resign.[13] This incident constitutes a perfect illustration of the importance of the "American factor" in the definition of France's policy toward Iraq. For Chevènement, France should not become an instrument of a dangerously misguided American strategy. One of the key members of the "Franco-Iraq friendship" group, Chevènement (however misguided), was faithful to his vision of the world and to his principles.

Europe and Iraq

The Iraqi invasion of Kuwait was unsettling not just for French policy in the Middle East but also for the rest of Europe. Before the end of the cold war, Europe, if it could be considered as a whole, generally acted as a counterweight in the region to the United States and Soviet Union. Both France and Great Britain had historical ties as colonial powers in this area that continued to shape their policies. Great Britain, in contrast to France, leaned decidedly toward the U.S. view of the Middle East, especially on the question of the Arab-Israeli peace process. The Federal Republic of Germany played a much more muted role. It had a special relationship with Israel, given its Nazi past, but rarely took the lead in other policy initiatives. Europe as an entity pursued a dual policy in the region that could be described as "declaratory policy through political cooperation; economic orientation through the Euro-Arab dialogue."[14]

The end of the cold war and the Iraqi invasion of Kuwait magnified the weaknesses in the European Community. Whereas broad agreement existed on condemnation of the Iraqi aggression, differences existed on the national level, as exemplified by the French reaction described above, by British political and military support of the United States, and by

Germany's policy of "checkbook" diplomacy. Furthermore, while the end of the cold war paved the way for fairly broad international cooperation (under UN auspices but with U.S. leadership), it did not automatically create European political unity. Despite the European desire to pursue common policy, the mechanisms for such coordination did not yet fully exist. The upheavals caused by the revolutions of 1989–90 also preoccupied most European governments, leading to some degree of unpreparedness for the events in the Gulf.[15] The U.S. emergence as the sole superpower—militarily (and politically) capable of meeting challenges like that in the Persian Gulf—reinforced the perception of European weakness[16] and exacerbated French feelings of insecurity in relation to the United States.[17]

France's Obsession with the United States

The United States continues to occupy a central place in French thinking about its place and role in the world. It also constitutes a dilemma. On one hand, and as demonstrated by France's role in Operations Desert Shield and Desert Storm, the need to avoid alienating the world's most powerful and influential country is understood. On the other hand, the question of how to resist the United States, given its power and its influence, arises. But resistance per se does not constitute a viable or sustainable policy path. With the disappearance of the unifying threat of the Soviet Union, Franco-American tensions can only be offset by common interests and by the requirements of European unity. The French know too well, even if it is not always apparent in their diplomatic choices, that their secret dream—to build a Europe distinct from if not against the United States—is a nightmare for all their European partners. France's open expression of its differences vis-à-vis Washington in the Middle East or the Persian Gulf will in most cases isolate Paris from London or Bonn, not to mention the rest of the European pack. But this is not always the case. If France has at times been isolated over differences on Iraq, on Iran the split today is much clearer between Europe and the United States than between Paris and Washington. What motivates France in instances such as these is not simply French interests or judgments about which policy might prove best but rather something larger.

The French authorities tend to project their own rules of the game on the American political system. Even the best-informed French citizens have difficulty fully appreciating the balance of power in American democracy. For a country where the Parliament plays only a minimal role in foreign affairs, the very idea that another country could take seriously Montesquieu's principles is difficult to believe. Deep inside, French elites believe that the American executive uses Congress in a most Machiavellian manner, that is, to provide an excuse for doing things that the president favors but for which he wants to avoid responsibility. The mixture of legalism, moralism, paralysis, and sometimes brutality that characterizes American diplomacy in the eyes of the French is nowhere more visible than in Middle East politics. If the French are stooping for oil, the Americans are prisoners of a pro-Israel lobby. American nuclear nonproliferation policy is seen by Paris as especially selective and erratic and demonstrates unjustifiable double standards. Why emphasize Iraq, when Israel has been allowed the "bomb in the basement" for more than thirty years, and when nuclear proliferation by India and Pakistan is much more worrisome for the global balance and safety of the world?

French frustrations are greatly increased by the mixture of benign neglect, sheer indifference, or controlled irritation with which Washington considers initiatives from Paris. France's nuisance value no longer has the flamboyant qualities that were the direct result of General de Gaulle's inimitable style and made possible by the cold war and the mutual French and American need for one another on matters of substance. Today the relationship has become unbalanced. There is by far too much passion on the French side and too little interest on the U.S. side. It is this imbalance—one that stems from uneven power and influence—that generates the misunderstanding and tension that permeate all aspects of Franco-American relations as allies, partners, competitors, or rivals.

In security terms, Paris and Washington are at the same time allies and competitors. France's ambition to create an autonomous European identity in foreign and security policy, though formally welcomed by Washington, clashes in fact with American reflexes based on unquestioned U.S. leadership and not on equal partnership, declaratory policy notwithstanding.

On regional issues, the French have benefited (in the 1997–98 Gulf crisis, for example) from U.S. limitations, which stemmed from a lack of clear military options. But the cosmetic or real success of French diplomacy materialized only because Saddam Hussein, unlike in 1991, took seriously the American military threat. What happened did not, as was the case in the mid-1970s, constitute a division of labor between France and the United States. In early 1998 this implicit and neat division of labor did not exist and can only be seen as a rationalization of otherwise antithetical policies, the French excluding the military option and the Americans giving little weight to the diplomatic alternative.

From the vantage point of Paris, Washington's policy of sanctions and isolation toward Baghdad has failed.[18] Saddam Hussein is still in power and well in control of the situation. The human cost of the U.S. policy to the average Iraqi citizen and for Iraqi children in particular is enormous, especially if one considers its political consequences. An exit strategy must be devised, which would allow the reintegration of Iraq into the international community. The sensitivities of Arab public opinion must be taken into consideration at a time when the Americans demonstrate double standards in their diplomacy, that is, one characterized by a lenient understanding toward Israel and absolute rigor toward Iraq.

How Serious Is the Iraqi Threat?

Beyond the issue of sanctions, the main source of disagreement between Paris and Washington lies in differing interpretations of the seriousness of the military threat presented by Iraq's programs of unconventional weapons or weapons of mass destruction. If the French scientific experts in the various UN agencies have been among the first to single out and denounce the dangers of Iraqi accumulation of weapons of mass destruction, be they of a chemical or biological nature, the political authorities in Paris have been, to say the least, much more "relaxed" in their interpretations of the figures released by their experts.

Since August 5, 1998, when the United Nations Special Commission's (UNSCOM) regime of challenge inspections was in effect ended by Saddam, the situation has deteriorated, exposing the obvious duplicity of Saddam Hussein and the limits of American strategy. The August 1998 resignation from UNSCOM of an American inspector,

Scott Ritter, which reinforced Paris in its suspicion that U.S. policy lacked long-term vision, suggested there might be some merit to the reluctance of countries such as France or Russia to accept at face value the proofs of misconduct submitted by UNSCOM or the Clinton administration.[19] Still, the French denounced without ambiguity the Iraqi decision to suspend their cooperation with UNSCOM and the IAEA. Together with the other members of the UN Security Council and individually through its bilateral channel, France reemphasized to Iraq's government that Iraqi collaboration with these institutions was an absolute must if a partial removal of sanctions were to be considered. But if, in the French view, the continuation of permanent and efficient control of Iraqi destructive capacities is to be maintained by UNSCOM and the IAEA, then it is in the interest of the international community and of the countries of the region to offer to Iraq some kind of "light at the end of the tunnel." The absence of such hope could only encourage, in the French administration's view, the worst suicidal tendencies of the Saddam Hussein regime. For France, it is therefore essential to recognize the disarmament progress made by Baghdad in the nuclear and missile areas. The compromise advocated by the French would provide Iraq with partial sanctions relief and move from active to long-term monitoring of its nuclear and missile efforts as long as Iraq resumed cooperation with the "special commission" on chemical and biological matters.[20]

These differences of emphasis between France and both the Americans and the British (who support fully the Americans in the position that there should not be any sanctions relief for Iraq unless it fully complies with all its obligations regarding weapons of mass destruction and maybe not even then) on the reality and significance of the Iraqi military threat can only be interpreted as reflecting different political priorities. The Americans say that as strategic backbenchers, the French are abandoning strategic responsibility to the Americans. The French, by contrast, emphasize their more subtle and global political, social, and human understanding of the issues at stake. For France the Iraqi humanitarian situation constitutes unacceptable and politically useless suffering. According to the United Nations Children's Fund (UNICEF), as many as one-third of the children below the age of five suffer from some form of malnutrition.[21] The situation in Iraq also constitutes a social and cultural time bomb, which in the short run also helps the present Iraqi regime to consolidate its power. For Paris it is essential to allow Iraq to rebuild its infrastructure and to accelerate the distribution of humanitarian goods to the Iraqi population. Support for the "oil-for-food" resolution does not constitute for France an alternative to the removal of the embargo but a partial and temporary derogation, justified by humanitarian reasons.[22]

The existing misunderstandings between Paris and Washington are far from dissipated and may rebound at the first opportunity, that is, when the unresolved dimensions of the crisis explode again. Style, of course, matters. French Foreign Minister Hubert Védrine, a close collaborator of François Mitterrand for years, is a clever diplomat, and more often than not, would replace an aggressive yes toward the United States with a mellow and attentive no. But no amount of style could eliminate the differences in policy or the resulting friction in politics.

In the Middle East, the election of Benjamin Netanyahu and its direct consequence of blocking the peace process gave a new legitimacy to Europe's and, in particular, France's role in the region. Frustrated to be seen only as the bankers of a peace process conducted by others, Europe pretends, with added legitimacy, that it has a role to play, which is political as well as economic. Having learned from past mistakes, Europeans do not intend to play a substitutive but instead a complementary role to America in the region. Europe does not have to balance an overly pro-Israeli position of the United States by being overly pro-Arab. Europe simply has to demonstrate that it is openly and seriously pro-peace without any of the domestic constraints the United States encounters: not a peacemaker but a peace facilitator whose role is made more necessary and more difficult at the same time by the U.S. electoral calendar.

Exploiting its position as a permanent member of the United Nations Security Council to the maximum, France presents itself as the embodiment of a different Western voice and a self-proclaimed "go-between" between Washington and the rest of the world, in particular the radical countries of the southern hemisphere. Such a strategy presupposes close contacts with the UN secretary general and a tacit, if not declared, objective alliance between France and the United Nations, something exemplified by the February 1998 crisis. The November 1998 crisis played out differently, given the ultimate failure of diplomacy. But unlike the previous crisis, France kept its objections to

American use of military force to a minimum and did not play a key role in the resolution of the crisis. Indeed, the silence of the French was one of many signs that Saddam Hussein had isolated himself from any international support by his decision in late October to end all cooperation with UN inspectors. It is likely that the perception of this isolation (and an imminent, massive U.S. military attack) led to the series of letters from Iraqi Deputy Prime Minsiter Tariq Aziz to the United Nations, expressing Iraqi willingness to allow UNSCOM inspectors to return to work.[23]

France cannot go too far in Iraq's direction without endangering its balancing act on the Middle East peace process. To manage the two policies at once in a region so full of passion and where images, stereotypes, and prejudices are an essential part of reality is a very delicate and difficult challenge. The Gulf region is not the African continent, where the United States may need France's experience and presence, and France has to admit that it needs Washington's clout. Rivals in economics and trade, Paris and Washington are necessary partners in geopolitical terms on the African continent but not in the Gulf.

France's interests and ambitions in the Gulf are not even close to those of the United States. Meanwhile, many Americans believe they have a global security responsibility, which no one else can or wants to fulfill. Whereas the French would use the word "stability," Americans emphasize the concept of "security." For Paris, an obsession with security could easily lead to greater instability. This is a way of saying that popular emotions coming from the Arab world have to be taken into account. France and the United States may share common objectives when it comes to oil and arms sales—they want guaranteed access of the first and maximization of sales on the second—but this desire does not translate into common policy.

France's main dilemma in relations with the United States occurs because in diplomatic and security terms Europe does not exist, a reality that is unlikely to be transformed in the near future. Certainly since the Gulf War, progress has been made. The Maastricht Treaty committed the European Union to develop a common foreign and security policy (CFSP) and the 1997 Amsterdam Treaty anointed the idea of a high representative for the CFSP. But as noted, Maastricht did not automatically create the mechanisms and political will necessary to act in unison against problem states like Iraq. By contrast in trade and economic terms,

Europe is a real actor whose clout and influence have only been strengthened by the euro initiated on January 1, 1999. The only hope for the Europeans to balance the Americans is in the monetary field, where bipolarity does not seem out of reach.

There is an irony in the French situation. France's only card for challenging the U.S. power monopoly is Europe. Yet to play such a card, Paris has to abandon a significant part of its sovereignty to Europe if one distant day, Europe wants to enjoy the dream of playing the role of a modern Byzantium toward the new Rome that is today the United States. To indulge in such fantasy would not make sense. In the Gulf, Europe may exist vis-à-vis Iran but certainly not vis-à-vis Iraq, and France is not about to convince its partners to join it in a common policy along French lines. This suggests that Franco-American differences toward Iraq (even if there appeared to be a truce in the November 1998 standoff) are here to stay, a state of affairs that works to the detriment of common interests in Iraq, the overall U.S.-French relationship, and the ability of the two countries to work together elsewhere. Yet the need for France and the United States to work with each other despite their differences must override the desire to disagree.

The latest escalation of violence in December 1998—an air campaign known as Operation Desert Fox— showed that neither Washington nor Paris knew what to do about Iraq and Saddam Hussein. A policy of air strikes leads nowhere in either political or strategic terms. To simply abstain from military retaliation may damage the credibility of Western deterrence. The alternative control regime suggested by the French did not represent a credible solution in itself but highlighted the failures and contradictions of Washington's policy. Only one thing is clear. Saddam Hussein will very likely, unless some "miracle" happens, continue to represent a serious obstacle to better relations between Washington and Paris.

Notes

1. Jean-François Poncet, quoted in Dominique Moïsi, "France and the Middle East," in Colin Legum, Haim Shaked, and Daniel Dishon, eds., *Middle East Contemporary Survey*, vol. 4, *1979-80* (Holmes and Meier Publishers, 1981), p. 77.

2. See "Hubert Vedrine, France's Clever Cockerel," *Economist*, February 28, 1998, p. 57.

3. Dominique Moïsi, "Europe and the Middle East," in Steven L. Spiegel, ed., *The Middle East and the Western Alliance* (London: George, Allen and Unwin, 1982), pp. 18–32, especially p. 19.

4. Morton Kondracke, "She Stoops for Oil," *New Republic*, October 6, 1979, pp. 12, 14–15.

5. Moïsi, "Europe and the Middle East," p. 20. See also Paul Balta and Claudine Rulleau, *La Politique arabe de la France de De Gaulle à Pompidou* (Paris: Sindbad, 1973).

6. Prime Minister Chirac visited Iraq November 30–December 2, 1974. The result of the visit was the signature of an economic accord, primarily concerning oil. See *L'Année Politique Économique Sociale et Diplomatique en France 1974* (Paris: Presses Universitaires de France, 1975), pp. 263, 273–74.

7. The sale of weapons to Iraq was controversial—at once arming an already volatile region and limiting Soviet influence through the French arms sales. "For these sales constitute an integral part of France's close relations to Iraq, a relationship that is appreciated by the USA, which sees it as a guarantee that Iraq will not move too close to the Soviet camp." Moïsi, "Europe and the Middle East," p. 29.

8. See, for example, Balta and Rulleau, *La Politique arabe*.

9. Osiraq, the nuclear reactor in Iraq, was destroyed by Israel in 1981.

10. "M. Mitterrand et la monde arabe," *Le Monde*, May 28, 1981, p. 4d.

11. Mitterrand visited Jerusalem on March 3-5, 1982.

12. Peter Truell, "The Mideast Conflict: Some Nations Might Face Big Bill for Loan Guarantees," *Wall Street Journal*, August 8, 1990, p. A7.

13. "J.-P. Chevènement démissionne en raison de ses différends avec F. Mitterrand sur guerre du Golfe; P. Joxe est nommé ministre de défense," *Le Monde*, January 30, 1991, p. 16.

14. Moïsi, "Europe and the Middle East," p. 24.

15. See Nicole Gnesotto and John Roper, "Introduction," in Nicole Gnesotto and John Roper, eds., *Western Europe and the Gulf: A Study of Western European Reactions to the Gulf War Carried Out under the Auspices of the Institute for Security Studies of the Western European Union* (Paris: Institute for Security Studies of Western European Union, 1992), pp. 1–6.

16. It also created the impetus for more European cooperation, which ultimately culminated in the Treaty of European Union (the Maastricht Treaty).

17. See François Heisbourg, "France and the Gulf Crisis," in Gnesotto and Roper, *Western Europe and the Gulf*, pp. 17–38.

18. See Dominique Moïsi, "The Trouble with France," *Foreign Affairs*, vol. 77 (May-June 1998), pp. 94–104.

19. William Scott Ritter, Jr., the senior inspector for UNSCOM, resigned in August 1998, citing U.S. and UN inconstancy in their battle against Iraq. Judith Miller, "American Inspector on Iraq Quits, Accusing U.N. and U.S. of Cave-In," *New York Times*, August 27, 1998, p. A1.

20. See, for example, interviews given by Prime Minister Lionel Jospin and

President Jacques Chirac. "Iraq Entretien du Premier Ministre, M. Lionel Jospin, avec 'France 3' – Extraits," February 26, 1998, as found on the Internet at http://www.france.diplomatie.fr; "Interview de Monsieur Jacques Chirac, Président de la République au Journal Le Monde," February 27, 1998, as found on the Internet at http://www.elysee.fr/discours/discour_.htm.

21. United Nations Children's Fund, "Statistics: Iraq" (January 4, 1998), as found on the Internet at http://www.unicef.org/statis/.

22. See "Irak Intervention du Representant Permanent de la France aux Nations Unies," April 14, 1995, as found on the Internet at http://www.france.diplomatie.fr.

23. See "Excerpts from Iraqi Letter: 'Not Out of Fear' but 'Responsibility,'" *New York Times*, November 15, 1998, p. 16.

GIDEON ROSE

8 | *The United States and Libya*

Libyan leader Muammar Qaddafi has aggravated the United States for more than two decades, ever since he began using his country's oil revenues to harass enemies, sponsor terrorism, and export his "revolution." In the 1970s American officials expressed their diplomatic disapproval. In the 1980s they used unilateral economic and military sanctions to punish and, they hoped, oust him. In the 1990s they resigned themselves to isolating and containing him, using the limited Lockerbie-related UN sanctions to gain the support of a reluctant Europe.

By the mid-1990s a de facto transatlantic compromise on Libya had emerged, in which a complex array of sanctions kept Libya on the sidelines of regional and world politics but allowed its oil to flow onto international markets. Then domestic political developments led the United States to embark on a new anti-Qaddafi crusade, threatening the imposition of secondary sanctions against Libya's European economic partners in order to prevent new investment. Libya, however, actually played only a minor role in the ensuing transatlantic dispute. The real battles between the United States and its European allies were

140

fought on the Iranian and Cuban fronts instead and pushed to a back burner by a deal cut in May 1998.

Three months later, U.S. and British officials announced their willingness to hold the trial of the Lockerbie suspects in the Netherlands, although still using Scottish law and Scottish judges. Qaddafi had indicated earlier that he would accept such a proposal, but his initial response to the announcement was inconclusive. Nevertheless, to the surprise of many, he signed on to the plan in early 1999, apparently motivated by a combination of economic pressure and the blandishments offered by a series of diplomatic intermediaries including South African President Nelson Mandela, Saudi Arabian Crown Prince Abdullah, Egyptian President Hosni Mubarak, Russian Prime Minister Yevgeny Primakov, and U.N. Secretary General Kofi Annan. The United States, for its part, "assured Libya that the trial would not be used to undermine [Qaddafi's] rule."[1] When the two suspects were handed over in April, the UN sanctions against Libya were suspended, although the unilateral American sanctions dating from the pre-Lockerbie era remained in place. In an instant, therefore, the transatlantic debate over how to handle Libya snapped back to its late-1980s impasse, as Europe rushed toward accommodation while the United States held itself aloof. The extent of the rancor this time around seemed likely to depend on the length, revelations, and verdict of the Lockerbie trial, along with the future behavior of the ever-unpredictable Libyan leader.

Libyan Policy during the 1970s and 1980s

The United States' troubles with Libya began with Qaddafi's rise to power in 1969 and his decision to pursue a foreign policy based on radical activism. Challenging the West in both word and deed, Qaddafi supported numerous terrorist groups and revisionist causes (particularly those opposing Israel and its American patron) and was linked to atrocities such as the killing of Israeli athletes at the Munich Olympics in 1972 and the assassination of the U.S. ambassador to Sudan in 1973. In the mid-1970s, accordingly, the United States declared a unilateral embargo against arms sales to Libya, and in 1980 closed its Tripoli embassy.

In this area as in others, President Ronald Reagan and his administration took office determined to be more assertive than its predecessor and, in May 1981, citing Libyan support for terrorism and regional subversion, ordered the Libyan mission in Washington closed. Three months later, U.S. Navy jets downed two Libyan warplanes after being fired on during an exercise over the Gulf of Sidra. That fall officials debated what else could be done; they considered but rejected a unilateral U.S. oil embargo because it would do little to pressure Libya unless the Europeans joined, and confidential soundings revealed they would refuse to do so. In December reports circulated about Libyan "hit-squads" sent to assassinate U.S. officials, and in response the administration banned U.S. citizens from using American passports and money for travel to Libya and asked U.S. citizens there to leave.[2] Secretary of State Alexander Haig presented the U.S. case against Libya to NATO, but the Europeans refused to take similar measures. On March 10, 1982, nevertheless, the administration imposed a unilateral U.S. boycott of Libyan crude oil and established export controls for goods and technology; the rationale given for these actions was that they would curtail the revenues used by Qaddafi to finance terrorist groups.[3]

Several U.S. companies including Exxon and Mobil ceased operations in Libya once the boycott was announced, but others remained and continued production (although not exploration) over the next few years. Libya's revenues from oil exports dropped by more than half in the early 1980s, but the chief reason was not the U.S. boycott but rather a worldwide oil glut. In 1984 Great Britain cut off diplomatic relations with Libya after a policewoman was killed by fire from within the Libyan embassy in London, but the Europeans still generally refused to join the Americans in a tougher anti-Libya line.

During the first half of the 1980s, Libya's actions, primarily within the Middle East and North Africa, contributed to a general rise in international terrorism (although Iran and Syria played an even greater role). The Reagan administration's frustration continued to mount and during 1985 the president authorized a covert operation designed to undermine the Libyan regime. Like other efforts to destabilize Qaddafi, it did not succeed. Following the discovery of some Libyan oil sales within the United States, moreover, the administration extended the ban on the importation of Libyan crude oil to cover refined products.

At the end of 1985 dramatic terrorist attacks took place at the Rome and Vienna airports. When evidence emerged pointing to Libyan involvement, the Reagan administration stepped up its campaign to get its allies involved in strict anti-Libya measures, but the Europeans again refused. The administration decided to move forward unilaterally, and in January 1986 it announced the imposition of a new set of sanctions designed "to stop all American economic activity with Libya and bring all Americans home." The actions, officials said, were "necessary to make the [Libyan] regime . . . pay a price for its support of international terrorism and render it a 'pariah' among nations."[4] The administration soon announced, however, that foreign subsidiaries of American firms would not be affected and that the embargo was being modified to permit certain firms to retain their assets in Libya temporarily and to continue certain operations. Foreign subsidiaries of U.S. firms were excluded from the embargo because Secretary of State George Shultz wanted to avoid another dispute with Europe like the one over the Soviet gas pipeline a few years earlier. In addition to the embargo, Reagan ordered Libyan government assets in the United States frozen.

Reagan opted to increase sanctions and to freeze assets at this point rather than respond militarily, aides said, because he felt the latter course would raise unacceptable risks and because it was difficult to link specific targets for retaliation to the relevant terrorists. Also, according to administration officials, at least as important as the expected economic impact of these new measures was the extent to which they would exhaust all U.S. options short of future military action and perhaps provoke Qaddafi into a response that could serve as a pretext for such action.

With its various exemptions and modifications, the U.S. embargo represented an economic nuisance for both countries rather than a heavy blow to either. U.S. trade with Libya had declined beforehand, and U.S. investment there represented a trivial part of total U.S. overseas investment. U.S. companies were still the main operators of Libyan oil fields, accounting for roughly three-quarters of the country's total production of 1.1 million barrels a day. U.S. firms also marketed at least one-third of Libya's production to customers in Europe and elsewhere, but practically all U.S. business in Libya operated through subsidiaries based in London or Rome.

After the embargo was announced, Qaddafi maintained his challenging posture, and at the end of March, the U.S. Sixth Fleet deliberately crossed Libya's self-proclaimed "line of death" (32° 30' north latitude) in the Gulf of Sidra. The Libyans responded by firing some missiles at U.S. planes, and American forces retaliated by silencing the air-defense battery involved and sinking some Libyan patrol boats. In early April a bomb exploded at a West Berlin disco favored by American servicemen, and evidence pointed to Libyan involvement. In response, the United States launched a bombing raid on various Libyan targets including Qaddafi's residence, trying simultaneously to punish him for supporting terrorism, incite a coup, and ideally remove him from the scene completely. The raid killed a number of Libyans and damaged Qaddafi's quarters, but the Libyan leader survived and his rule was not seriously challenged. (The effect of this bombing on Libyan support for terrorism is disputed. Some observers feel that it led to Libyan restraint; others that it led directly to later attacks, including the downing of Pan Am Flight 103.)

In the wake of the bombing, which European countries other than Great Britain had refused to facilitate or endorse, European Commission members imposed a modest set of diplomatic sanctions on Libya and banned arms sales. Buoyed by this partial change in attitude as well as the agreement of a Group of Seven (G-7) summit to condemn Libyan terrorism, the Reagan administration launched a broad effort to get the Europeans to join in a variety of further sanctions, but none was adopted. The administration and Congress then decided to impose a deadline for the cessation of all direct involvement in Libya by U.S. firms. Eventually, the affected companies managed to negotiate three-year "standstill agreements" with Qaddafi that suspended their operations without prejudice to their interests or concessions while allowing the Libyan government to sell the companies' share of Libyan oil.

After a year, the full American embargo had neither made a significant impact on Libya's economy nor prevented some trade from taking place there by U.S. firms, mostly legally through their foreign subsidiaries. In May 1987 the General Accounting Office reported that "the practical impact of the U.S. trade sanctions on Libyan oil production is minimal because of the extensive foreign availability of oilfield equipment, services and supplies. . . . The short-term effect of the sanctions on the U.S. oil companies has been a loss of revenue while Libya continues to reap the full benefit of their oilfield operations."[5]

By the beginning of 1988, the Reagan administration had resigned itself to the fact of Qaddafi's existence and moved away from attempts to overthrow or intimidate him. As a White House official put it, "If one characterizes our earlier policy as one of active destabilization, one could say we're now trying to further isolate him." Another official was more blunt, "We finally decided we cannot remove the man from the outside by military means."[6] Hallmarks of the new policy included lowered rhetorical attacks, an end to U.S. Navy maneuvers in the Gulf of Sidra, and a decline in funding for Libyan exile groups. Among the reasons for the shift were Qaddafi's persistence in power despite U.S. actions, his diminished momentum and external activities, and a post–Iran-Contra change in Reagan administration personnel.

As one of its final acts, in January 1989 the Reagan administration granted permission for the major U.S. oil companies to resume operations in Libya through their European subsidiaries. The standstill agreements they had negotiated with Libya in mid-1986 were set to expire. These companies had lobbied the administration passionately to avoid any situation that would force them to sell off their Libyan assets, collectively estimated to be worth at least $2 billion and possibly twice that.[7] The administration kept a number of restrictions in place, however, which failed to satisfy Qaddafi. The companies were not permitted to return. Over the next few years this situation continued to fester, with the future of the U.S. oil companies' Libyan holdings in lasting limbo. The result has been that they have lost ground in Libya to their European competitors.[8]

During 1989 Qaddafi set out on a new foreign policy tack designed to reduce his isolation, playing down his links with terrorism, making peace with some regional governments he had earlier tried to subvert, and seeking wider diplomatic contacts. These moves brought better relations with Europe but were soon offset by Qaddafi's support for Saddam Hussein following the Iraqi invasion of Kuwait and his continued radical rhetoric and opposition to the Middle East peace process. As far as Libya-watchers could determine, for Qaddafi the continuing U.S. sanctions were, on balance, "a headache. It is very difficult to build anything [in Libya] in the [energy] sector without U.S. technology and equipment. In addition, some major European firms have shied away from Libya, not only for fear of treading on American assets but also because the sanctions prohibit companies prospecting in the U.S. to offset exploration costs against Libyan equity production."[9] At this point, however, fresh developments in an old investigation produced a new crisis.

Lockerbie and the 1992 UN Sanctions

On December 21, 1988, Pan Am Flight 103 exploded in the air over Lockerbie, Scotland, killing all 259 passengers and crew on board and 11 people on the ground. Among the dead were 189 American citizens. On September 19, 1989, moreover, the French airliner UTA Flight 772 exploded over Niger, killing all 171 passengers and crew. Evidence eventually emerged that seemed to establish that the Lockerbie explosion had been the work of two Libyan intelligence agents operating out of Malta. French authorities investigating the UTA bombing, meanwhile, uncovered evidence that it, too, was the handiwork of Libyan agents. In October 1991 a Parisian judge issued a warrant for the arrest of four Libyan intelligence officers charged with complicity in the UTA bombing, including Abdallah Senoussi, Qaddafi's brother-in-law. Two weeks later the United States and Great Britain jointly announced the indictment of two Libyan security officials, Abdelbaset Ali Mohamed Al Mehgrahi and Al-Amin Khalifa Fhimah, for the Lockerbie attack.[10]

In November 1991, the three Western nations issued a joint declaration on the two cases. Regarding Lockerbie, the Americans and British declared that the Libyan government had to "surrender for trial all those charged with the crime; accept responsibility for the actions of Libyan officials; disclose all it knows of this crime, including the names of all those responsible, and allow full access to all witnesses, documents and other material evidence, including all the remaining timers [of the type used in the attack]; [and] pay appropriate compensation." The three countries together declared that Libya had to comply with their demands regarding the two cases and prove by concrete actions that it renounced support for terrorism.[11]

The next month the European Commission called on Libya to comply with the American-British-French demands and raised the possibility of imposing economic sanctions if it did not. With Resolution 731 of January 1992, the UN Security Council endorsed the American-British-French statement of the previous November. Attempting to stave off the imposition of sanctions, Qaddafi offered to hand over the Lockerbie suspects to an international tribunal and allow the UTA suspects to appear before a French court, but this response was deemed insufficient. At the end of March, the Security Council passed Resolution 748, calling for sanctions on Libya unless it complied with Resolution 731 and handed over the Lockerbie suspects within two weeks. The measures specified were a ban on all air links with Libya, a ban on arms sales, and a reduction in personnel at Libyan embassies abroad.

Officials hoped that these sanctions would result in Libya's turning over the two Lockerbie suspects, who would then be prosecuted, fulfilling the demands of the Western governments and publics for judgment and punishment in the bombing cases. The suspects would presumably be convicted and perhaps implicate Qaddafi directly, thus providing grounds for further anti-Libya measures. More speculatively, U.S. and other Western officials hoped that the sanctions would undermine Qaddafi's regime by resulting in either a humiliating loss of face (if he complied) or the ratcheting up of domestic discontent one more notch (if he did not). These outcomes were not considered especially likely, but the sanctions were expected nevertheless to serve a useful purpose in further isolating Qaddafi and restraining his ability and will to make trouble for others.

Over the next several years the sanctions were renewed continually at three-month intervals, with occasional battles among countries trying to tighten them (led by the United States) and countries trying to limit or ease them (led by Italy, Germany, and Spain, which depend on Libyan oil supplies, and Russia and China, which generally oppose U.S. attempts to sanction "rogue" states). In August 1993, the United States, Great Britain, and France threatened new sanctions if Libya continued its noncompliance. This threat was followed up with action and resulted in the adoption of UN Security Council Resolution 883 in November. The resolution provided for a further tightening of restrictions on the Libyan aviation industry; a ban on exports to Libya of selected equipment for "downstream" oil and gas sectors (that is, refineries and distribution); a further reduction in staff levels at Libyan missions abroad; and a freezing of existing Libyan funds and financial resources overseas. The resolution stipulated that special accounts were to be set up from the sale of Libyan hydrocarbons and agricultural products, which would then be used to pay firms doing business with Libya.

This tightening of sanctions was designed primarily for psychological impact and to create further annoyances and uncertainty for the Libyans. The new measures were not designed to cripple the Libyan economy (for which a ban on oil sales would be required), nor were they expected to have real economic impact for a number of months—both because they were modest incremental measures and because the Libyans had been given ample time to prepare for them by stockpiling material and shifting liquid assets around. Qaddafi remained obstinate and soon renewed his violent rhetoric and announced that his war on exiled Libyan opponents would continue.

The Causes and Consequences of the UN Sanctions

The United States had sought cooperation on anti-Libyan measures from its European allies and the international community numerous times before Lockerbie, to little avail. The outcome after Lockerbie was different for five separate reasons.

First, the scale of the Lockerbie and UTA attacks was dramatically higher than that of previous cases of Libyan troublemaking. Together more than 400 people were killed, creating a deep sense of popular outrage in the West and a real constituency pressing for redress. Second, the victims included scores of British and French citizens in addition to Americans, ensuring that these countries would join the United States in demanding a response of some sort. Third, evidence of Libyan complicity in these attacks was much more damning than it had been in the past. Fourth, the demonstrated willingness of the United States to use force in the region during previous crises helped the Europeans recognize that agreeing to sanctions might actually be the best way to keep the crisis from escalating further—one of their perpetual goals. Fifth, the end of the cold war made it easier for major Western nations to use the UN Security Council for their own purposes. If the first four reasons had been present without the fifth, multilateral sanctions probably would still have been imposed but under different institutional auspices.

While less critical, two additional factors also played a role. Since the mid-1980s a change had taken place in the general Western attitude toward terrorism. The international community grew more disposed to regard it as a legal (as opposed to a political) issue and decided that it should be combated through collective international action. This shift made it easier for U.S. officials in the early 1990s to move logically from evidence of Libyan complicity in the airplane bombings to the imposition of multilateral sanctions under UN auspices. It also accounts for the sanctions' narrow focus—the fact that they were imposed not in response to a perceived Libyan strategic threat, but rather as (at least overtly) a lever designed to pry loose some defendants for trial.

Finally, during the late 1980s and early 1990s, the demise of the Soviet bloc, the 1990–91 Gulf War, and progress in the Middle East peace process had isolated the Arab rejectionist bloc from the mainstream of world and regional politics. This made collective action against Libya less controversial than it would have been even a few years earlier. (This last factor, to be sure, also made it more difficult to portray Libyan activities as part of a broader, larger threat.)

The particular UN sanctions adopted were selected because the governments involved wanted to do something to demonstrate their outrage, but the European countries that consumed Libyan oil were opposed to more stringent measures that would have had a much greater impact but also much higher costs. Foreign exchange receipts from hydrocarbon exports accounted for more than 95 percent of Libya's total hard currency earnings during the period in question; all parties involved knew that these were the truly important potential target for any sanctions. (The most reputable study of the subject suggests that a full-scale international oil embargo would force the Libyan economy to collapse within a year because the country has neither an independent industrial base nor sufficient agricultural production to feed its population.)[12] Yet roughly three-quarters of Libyan oil is purchased by European customers—chiefly Italian and German—and even in a globalized energy market, substitution would be expensive because of the close location and extremely high quality of Libyan crude oil. Any comprehensive oil embargo of Libya would thus impose serious costs on Europe, something European leaders are naturally loath to do. By exempting oil sales and purchases of basic oil drilling equipment from the measures, in other words, the sanctions chosen would at best merely harass and humiliate the Libyan regime rather than cripple it.

As for why the United States pursued a multilateral economic response in 1991–92 instead of the unilateral military response it had selected in 1986, the answer relates to the timing of the Lockerbie and UTA revelations. The crucial links between Libya and the bombings emerged years after the tragedies occurred, when public passions had cooled significantly and the issue had lost its urgency. If the Libyan connection had come to light in the immediate wake of the explosions, a military response might well have followed—as happened, for example, in 1998 after a link was quickly established between the free-lance terrorist network run by Osama bin Laden and the bombings of the U.S. embassies in Kenya and Tanzania. By the time the Lockerbie and UTA bombings were linked to Libya in late 1991, moreover, the Bush administration had its hands full in the Middle East maintaining support for the containment and isolation of Iraq as well as managing the emerging Arab-Israeli peace process. U.S. officials deemed these higher priorities than striking Libya, and decided not to risk overloading the circuits of the Arab world by launching another attack on Qaddafi.

The families of the Lockerbie victims have constituted an important Libya-related interest group during the 1990s, pressing the U.S. government to impose stiffer penalties. Many family members were upset that the official Lockerbie investigation came to concentrate solely on Libya, and many became frustrated at the lack of progress in the case. Although their pressure did not result in the imposition of new measures (at least until 1996), it did keep the issue alive and reminded officials that backsliding would carry public relations costs.[13]

As for their practical consequences, the UN sanctions further isolated Libya and produced some minor changes in its behavior, but for more than half a decade they did not result in the handing over of the Lockerbie or UTA suspects, nor did they significantly undermine the Libyan regime or economy. A reputable December 1994 study of the sanctions' effects found them to be real but limited and argued that the arms embargo in particular had actually had a beneficial impact on the Libyan economy, preventing Qaddafi from wasting resources in that area.[14] Uncertainty over future UN moves did not keep Western firms from carrying out existing contracts but did dramatically curtail their signing of new ones. Because gas contracts are long term and place a premium on stability, they were hit harder by the uncertainty than oil contracts. The ban on external flights doubled the time it took to get in and out of the country.

Libya's general economic performance continues to depend primarily on oil exports, which earned the country $7 billion in 1994, $8 billion in 1995, and $8.5 billion in 1996. Libya has remained by far the richest country in Africa on a per capita basis, with its current and future resources entirely at the regime's disposal. Like so many dictators, Qaddafi is economically his own worst enemy, wasting tens of billions of dollars on grandiose but worthless public works such as the "Great Man-Made River" project. Corrupt, statist, and grossly inefficient, Libya remains a backward country in which neither the central bank's governor nor its head of research can say what the inflation rate is.[15]

Another reason why the UN sanctions had only a limited effect is that previous sanctions had already driven out all businesses except those with deep roots or incentives to continue operating. By the time the new measures were imposed, "Business activity [was] dominated by firms that, in some cases, [could] boast up to 20 years of experience in avoiding the more obvious practical and financial pitfalls. Everyone [had] become well accustomed to shocks, having weathered the idiosyncrasies of Qaddafi's economic policy, the 1986 bombing of Tripoli and the . . . U.S. sanctions. . . . A company [was] therefore not going to relinquish its market share purely because the UN [was] threatening to make travel arrangements more problematic." Libyan arrears in payments, moreover, were a sunk cost difficult to leave behind: "Companies believe[d] that the only way to stand any chance of retrieving outstanding payments [was] to continue operating, even in the most trying circumstances."[16] The Libyan regime has also offered powerful incentives for individual businesses to remain or invest, largely off-setting pressures on those firms to stay out.

Some observers feel the UN sanctions have allowed Qaddafi to divert blame for economic hardship in Libya onto foreigners and away from the regime's own mismanagement—although other observers believe the opposite, and the difficulty of assessing Libyan domestic political currents from the outside makes it impossible to know for certain which view is correct. Fierce domestic repression, meanwhile, has ensured that anti-Qaddafi coup attempts have been unsuccessful, while the recent rise of an indigenous radical Islamic opposition has led some to ask whether Qaddafi himself might represent a lesser evil compared with the available alternatives. Many Europeans, for example, place a high priority on preserving domestic stability in Libya and are not eager to see Qaddafi leave because of fears that turmoil might follow.[17]

The Iran and Libya Sanctions Act of 1996

With Lockerbie more than a decade in the past, most of the international community thought the UN sanctions against Libya are too stringent and would probably have eased them if given the chance. The opposite feeling was prevalent in the United States, where domestic political incentives led politicians to ever-increasing paroxysms of outrage against rogue states. This climate produced another ratcheting up of the Libyan sanctions, this time directed less against Libya itself than against its European business partners.

In February 1993 Senator Edward M. Kennedy (D-Mass.), who has Lockerbie family members among his constituents, introduced a bill calling for the tightening of Libyan sanctions and gained twenty-eight cosponsors. That summer Kennedy and Senator Alfonse D'Amato (R-N.Y.), together with more than fifty colleagues, sent a letter to President Clinton calling for stronger action against Libya, and later in the year the Senate urged the administration to seek a full international oil embargo.

With the Republican takeover of Congress in 1994, the campaign to step up pressure on rogue states increased, as D'Amato became an influential figure and Iran his chief target. By the end of 1995, thanks indirectly to pressure from D'Amato and the American Israel Public Affairs Committee (AIPAC, the pro-Israel lobby in Washington), the Clinton administration had announced a unilateral commercial embargo on Iran and Congress was considering D'Amato-sponsored legislation that would impose a secondary boycott on Iran's European trading partners. To D'Amato's surprise and discomfiture, when his bill was on the Senate floor, Kennedy intervened to insert Libya as an additional target—as a gesture to the families of the Lockerbie victims on the seventh anniversary of the bombing. Kennedy refused to hold back even after being asked to do so by D'Amato, AIPAC, and the White House; once he acted, however, the others decided to go along rather than appear soft on terrorism.[18]

In an unrelated event during early 1996, a similar piece of legislation dealing with Cuba—the so-called Helms-Burton bill—passed Congress and was signed into law, thus setting a precedent for the enactment of extraterritorial sanctions by the United States against foreign business partners of regimes it disliked.[19] By the summer of 1996, therefore, the Clinton administration had little principled ground to stand on when opposing what had now become known as the Iran and Libya Sanctions Act of 1996 (ILSA), even had it wanted to, and so chose to focus instead on moderating its provisions. As Acting Assistant Secretary of State for

Near East Affairs C. David Welch testified before Congress, the administration supported the D'Amato legislation subject to various modifications, which it believed would "permit us to succeed in imposing
additional economic pressure on Iran and Libya, without causing a boo-
merang effect that unnecessarily hurts other American interests."[20]

ILSA was signed into law on August 5, 1996, with politicians rush-
ing to capitalize on the wave of antiterrorist sentiment that followed the
explosion of TWA Flight 800 off Long Island, New York. The act's
Libya-related sections forced the president to impose at least two out of
six possible sanctions on any foreign company that invested more than
$40 million in any year for the development of Libyan petroleum re-
sources or on any company that violated the UN sanctions.[21] President
Clinton invited family members of the Lockerbie victims to the signing
ceremony, and he declared that the measure "will help to deny [Iran and
Libya] the money they need to finance international terrorism. It will
limit the flow of resources necessary to obtain weapons of mass destruction. It will heighten pressure on Libya to extradite the suspects in the
bombing of Pan Am Flight 103."[22]

Even in its modified form, which gave the president some leeway to
blunt its impact, ILSA was strongly opposed by Europeans. Their primary concerns were pride (they resent being bullied) and economic interest (they see Iran and Libya as important commercial partners); they
are also motivated by principle (secondary sanctions are seen as a need-
less restriction on international trade) and political interest (some fear
that removing Qaddafi will lead to instability or worse). In November
1996 the European Union (EU) passed a blocking statute making it
illegal for European companies to comply with extraterritorial measures like ILSA and vowed to challenge their legality through the World
Trade Organization (WTO) if the United States did not back down.

Since Helms-Burton was passed first, it rather than ILSA became
the principal object of transatlantic legal skirmishing and negotiations.
Deadlines for resolving the dispute passed unheeded throughout 1997,
as Europeans held off pressing their suit in apparent return for the Clinton
administration's agreement to waive certain of Helms-Burton's more
objectionable provisions. In the fall of 1997, however, the announcement of a $2 billion investment deal in Iran by French, Russian, and
Malaysian companies seemed to flout ILSA directly and thus brought
the extraterritoriality dispute to a boil once again. The Clinton admin-

istration was caught in a difficult position, drawing fire from the U.S. Congress demanding that penalties be levied and European allies vowing a trade war if they were.

In May 1998 the administration announced that it had agreed to a deal with its European allies that would go a long way toward settling the disputes over both Helms-Burton and ILSA. The administration agreed to waive sanctions for the companies involved in the France-Russia-Malaysia-Iran deal, to continue its waiver of certain Helms-Burton sanctions, and to seek legislation allowing it to waive the remaining Helms-Burton measures. In return, the Europeans agreed to tighten their controls on exports of weapons technology to Iran and cooperate on efforts to block deals involving illegally expropriated property in Cuba.[23]

This compromise appeared likely to lessen transatlantic tensions rather than fully resolve them, both because Congress was not eager to pass the legislative changes the administration desired and because domestic political constraints made it difficult for the administration to reverse course entirely. It claims to continue to oppose foreign investment in the countries at issue, for example, and the scope and binding nature of the deal remains unclear. Italian Foreign Minister Lamberto Dini was reported to have claimed that Italian pressure forced the United States to agree to exempt future investments in Libya from sanctions as well as those in Iran.[24] Undersecretary of State Stuart Eizenstat, however, testified before Congress, "Let me state categorically [that] our policy on Libya has not changed. We strongly oppose any investment in Libya's petroleum sector, and we will continue our efforts to discourage and prevent it. We will continue to examine all such investments under ILSA and take appropriate action if any activity is found to be sanctionable. We have offered no expectation for firms from any country or group of countries, with respect to investments there or about the results of any review of our national interests with respect to Libya."[25]

Gauging ILSA's practical impact is difficult because much would have depended on how the United States responded to its bluff being called. The ILSA provision that punished those who violate the UN sanctions against Libya was uncontroversial but also trivial; the key Libya-related issues surrounded future development of Libyan oil and gas resources by European firms—whether there would be any and if so how the United States would react. The *Economist Intelligence Unit* noted that the law "will almost certainly hurt the medium- to long-term development of Libya's oil sector. In the short term, however, most international oil companies are waiting to see how the law is interpreted in practice."[26]

Libya, the United States, and Europe

During the 1980s the United States and its allies clashed repeatedly over how to handle Libya. At times U.S. officials viewed their European counterparts as skirting close to appeasement, while at times European officials viewed American actions as dangerous games played by trigger-happy cowboys. These attitudes could have important practical consequences, as when most European countries refused to have anything to do with the U.S. air raid on Libya in 1986—even to the point of denying permission for the planes involved to fly over their territory en route to the target, making the mission significantly more complicated and more dangerous.

By the late 1980s, however, the U.S. position on Libya had softened a bit, and after the emergence of evidence tying Libya to the Lockerbie and UTA bombings, the European position hardened somewhat. During the first half of the 1990s, therefore, the United States and Europe essentially agreed to disagree about Libya because both sides found the status quo tolerable: Libya was stable but kept in strategic isolation, politicians in the United States were able to claim that terrorism was being punished, and Libyan oil flowed to those in Europe who wanted it. The Western allies would politely try to convince one another about the merits of their preferred approaches but not press the matter too strongly because no significantly better or permanent solution to the problem was available. Europeans were skeptical of containment because they would bear the brunt of its economic costs and because they feared what might follow Qaddafi's demise, while Americans were skeptical of engagement because they saw Qaddafi as a sinister and untrustworthy character who would exploit any freedom of action he was given in pernicious ways.

This situation changed in 1996 with the passage of ILSA, because any substantial European investment in Libya now required a punitive response by the United States. By forcing the issue and binding the administration's hands, Congress deliberately tried to disrupt the status quo and turn transatlantic relations on this issue into a game of chicken, hoping that the threat of a trade war would lead the Europeans to change their policies. As noted above, the Clinton administration was forced to swerve first, at least on Iran and Cuba. Until the hand-over of the Lockerbie suspects, Libya remained in contention, which was ironic because for practically everybody in the United States the Libyan aspect of ILSA was a complete afterthought. One has to search diligently, for example, to find a few trivial references to Libya in the transcripts of two lengthy congressional hearings held on ILSA after its passage.[27]

In the end it is likely that, despite its protestations, the administration would have felt obliged to accede to European investments in Libya, as it did in Iran and for similar reasons. If there had been no break in the Lockerbie case, therefore, it is quite possible that the Libyan issue might well have reverted to its pre-ILSA status quo. And in spite of their public statements to the contrary, many U.S. officials would have found that outcome acceptable—because that status quo represented the most sensible way of dealing with the four major domestic constituencies concerned with Libyan policy. Ordinarily the only Americans who care very strongly about Libya are the Lockerbie families, who want to see a much tougher line imposed, and the energy companies, who want to see sanctions removed eventually. These competing pressures cancel each other out, making it difficult for officials to stray far from a middle course. In times of crisis two other groups come into play, but these merely recreate the stalemate at a higher level: Congress tends to favor a harsh anti-Libya line because it is a cheap way of sounding tough, while foreign policy professionals and those interested in interallied relations tend to favor a softer line in order to avoid transatlantic troubles.

In fact, the pre-ILSA status quo made not only political sense but policy sense as well; Libya is one of the rare cases where limited sanctions actually represent the least bad course of action available.[28] Because of his proven hostility to the West, penchant for violence, and erratic behavior, Qaddafi has always represented a real but low-level threat to American and Western interests. Appeasing him is not a good idea because it would involve a significant moral hazard and might exacerbate the problem rather than end it. Moving decisively to oust him is also out of the question because it would be extremely difficult, costly, and far more trouble than it is worth. Containment is therefore the only option left.

Critics are correct to point out that the U.S. and UN sanctions have not toppled Qaddafi, did not for many years produce the Lockerbie suspects for trial, and have cost some American and other firms real economic opportunities. Yet the sanctions have helped keep Qaddafi on the margins of world politics and prevented him from causing too much trouble beyond his borders, without requiring the United States and its allies to spend vast amounts of blood, treasure, or effort. The years of sanctions have hobbled Libya's conventional military capability, grounded its air force, and crimped its weapons of mass destruction programs. All this has substantially reduced the threat Qaddafi poses to his neighbors and the world at large, at least compared with what would have been the case had he been allowed to carry on business as usual. The tough stance taken by the United States on Libya over the years, furthermore, has contributed in important ways to the stigmatization of terrorism as an illegitimate activity and to the partial isolation of its state sponsors. The sanctions yielded modest benefits for a modest price.

In August 1998, three months after the Clinton administration cut its deal with the Europeans over secondary sanctions, officials announced another major development. The United States and Great Britain, they said, were prepared to accept a plan Qaddafi had suggested earlier—to hold a trial of the Lockerbie suspects in a third country—as long as the trial were held according to Scottish law and presided over by Scottish judges.

At the time, cynical observers saw this as a clever move in the ongoing battle for world opinion rather than a harbinger of an actual resolution to the Lockerbie dispute. The wisest course for the Western alliance, after all, seemed to be to return to the pre-ILSA status quo and extend it indefinitely. As long as Qaddafi remained in power, the cynics argued, a policy of benign neglect was the best that could be achieved and was better suited to the full range of Western interests involved than a policy designed to force a showdown or pursue some seemingly more "lasting" solution to the Libya conundrum. But for such policy to be sustained, something would have to be done to stop the gradual erosion in international compliance with the Libyan sanctions.

In June 1998, for example, the Organization of African Unity (OAU) had passed a resolution calling on its members to ignore the UN sanctions starting in September unless the United States and Great Britain agreed to hold the Lockerbie trial in a third country. The Non-Aligned

Movement (NAM) had made it clear that it intended to pass a similar resolution at the end of the summer. And eagerness to embrace Qaddafi could be found in the West as well: in August it was revealed that British Aerospace, Europe's largest defense contractor, was negotiating a multi-billion-deal to rebuild Libya's civilian and possibly even military capabilities and infrastructure as soon as legally possible.[29] By announcing that they were calling Qaddafi's bluff and making the very concession that the OAU, the NAM, and the Arab League had recommended, American and British officials seemed to have come up with a way to combat sanctions fatigue and put the diplomatic ball back into the Libyan court. U.S. officials proudly noted, for example, that the UN Security Council—which had not shown any interest in tightening the sanctions regime for a long time—adopted the new proposal unanimously while expressing its "intention to consider additional measures if the two accused have not arrived [in the Netherlands] or appeared for trial [in the United Kingdom or the United States] promptly."[30]

To the surprise of many, however, after much hemming and hawing Qaddafi actually accepted the deal, and in April 1999 Abdelbaset Ali Mohamed Al Mehgrahi and Al-Amin Khalifa Fhimah traveled from Libya to the Netherlands for trial. Why he changed his mind and allowed them to go, what the trial will show and what its consequences will be, and who will benefit most from this turn of events are all crucial questions to which only the most preliminary answers can be given at the time of writing.

Three factors—economic pressure, weariness, and peace of mind—seem to have driven Qaddafi to accept the deal. Low oil prices were inflicting serious damage on Libya (1999 oil revenues were predicted to be down 24 percent over the previous year), and one of the few ways he could quell domestic discontent and improve the country's economic position was to accelerate the development of its energy resources—something which could not happen until the UN sanctions were lifted.[31] According to some observers, moreover, the Libyan leader was growing increasingly weary of his personal and national isolation and wanted to preside over the reintegration of Libya into the international community himself rather than leave the issue to a successor. And significant concessions from the United States and Britain apparently reassured him that surrendering the suspects for trial would mean the end of one crisis, not the start of another. The change in venue, in other words, was important as a symbol of what might lie ahead. UN Secretary General Kofi Annan, for example, pledged that during the trial the "prosecutors would not attempt to embarrass or implicate the Libyan government," thus removing the threat that Qaddafi himself or his regime in general would be held accountable for the crime.[32] The *Washington Post*, meanwhile, reported that according to Arab diplomats "privy to the negotiations," before Qaddafi would agree to the deal he "wanted to be sure the buck stopped with the trial of the two men, irrespective of a finding of guilt, and not enmesh other Libyans who may be mentioned during the trial and create new obstacles to the freeing of Libya from international sanctions. 'Theoretically, it can go up to Gadhafi himself, and he wanted to prevent that,' one diplomat said."[33]

As for what the trial will bring and who will benefit, with one exception it is too soon to tell. Very few people familiar with the evidence doubt that Libya was responsible for the bombing, but that does not mean a conviction is certain. It bears pondering that the one familiar aspect of Scottish law is its countenance of a third possible verdict— "not proven." The presentation of the prosecution's case will probably inflame American opinion and make it unlikely that the unilateral American embargo on Libya will be lifted in the near future. As soon as the suspects were handed over, however, the UN sanctions were suspended and European firms practically trampled each other in their rush to formalize a wide array of Libyan deals. The likeliest outcome, therefore, is that the Libya policy debate will revert to the impasse of the late 1980s. The mutual congratulations that accompanied the arrival of the suspects for trial, in other words, will likely dissolve into transatlantic recriminations over the challenge still posed by Qaddafi's Libya.

Notes

1. Judith Miller, "How Suspects Were Moved, Very Discreetly, to Court," *New York Times*, April 7, 1999, p. A6.

2. Although widely believed at the time, these reports are now considered by U.S. intelligence officials to have been almost certainly greatly exaggerated and perhaps entirely inaccurate.

3. For a full discussion of U.S. sanctions against Libya see Gideon Rose, "Libya," in Richard N. Haass, ed., *Economic Sanctions and American Diplomacy* (New York: Council on Foreign Relations, 1998), pp. 129–56.

4. Don Oberdorfer and David B. Ottaway, "President Imposes Boycott on Business with Libya," *Washington Post*, January 8, 1986, p. A1.

5. *EIU Libya Country Report*, vol. 3 (1987), pp. 21–22.

6. Elaine Sciolino, "U.S. Sees Qaddafi as Being Weaker," *New York Times*, January 10, 1988, p. A9.

7. Under the sanctions and stand-still agreements the companies collectively were losing earnings of $100–$120 million annually. The sanctions also prevented the sale of oil drilling equipment and spare parts to other companies in Libya; that market was taken over by British and other European firms. *EIU Libya Country Report*, vol. 4 (1988), p. 11.

8. "European firms have benefited greatly from the absence of U.S. oil majors since 1987. . . . Italian and French firms have used their wide influence in the Libyan oil sector to position themselves for a greater role in Libyan development if restrictions are relaxed in the future." *EIU Libya Country Report*, vol. 4 (1995), p. 19.

9. Angus Hindley, "Qaddafi Aims for Respectability," *MEED Middle East Business Weekly*, June 28, 1991, p. 4.

10. Accurately parceling out responsibility for these attacks is extremely difficult, not only because of the scarcity of information about them but also because of the close contact and cooperation during the 1980s among the Iranian, Syrian, and Libyan intelligence agencies, together with various Palestinian groups. Many U.S. intelligence officials familiar with all the evidence, for example, believe that Lockerbie might have been the product of Iran's desire to strike back at the United States in retaliation for the downing of Iran Air 655. In this scenario the Iranians, with fairly limited ability to mount such an operation themselves, turned to the Libyans for help because of their extensive foreign operational network. Syrian operatives, furthermore, might have played some role in the attack without that country's leadership specifically authorizing it; some officials feel that there might also have been a Syrian role in the UTA 772 attack.

11. Office of the Federal Register, "Statement Announcing Joint Declarations on the Libyan Indictments," *Weekly Compilation of Presidential Documents*, vol. 27, December 2, 1991 (Government Printing Office), p. 1735.

12. See *EIU Libya Country Report*, vol. 2 (1995), p. 16.

13. Lockerbie family members met repeatedly with senior officials of both the Bush and the Clinton administrations. During the 1992 campaign, Clinton promised the families that he would not relent until the two suspects were turned over; he reiterated his determination not to back down at the groundbreaking of a memorial for the Lockerbie victims in December 1993, at the dedication of the monument in November 1995, and on anniversaries of the bombing.

14. See the *EIU Libya Country Report*, vol. 2 (1995), p. 16.

15. "Mystery of the Vanishing Oil Money," *Economist*, February 7, 1998, p. 48.

16. Angus Hindley, "Qaddafi's Battle for Survival," *MEED Middle East Business Weekly*, April 17, 1992, p. 4.

17. For an overview of recent domestic political trends in Libya, see Ray Takeyh, "Qadhafi and the Challenge of Militant Islam," *Washington Quarterly*, vol. 21 (Summer 1998), pp. 159–72.

18. "D'Amato and AIPAC preferred to focus on Iran but could not afford to be seen to be somehow supporting . . . Qaddafi." Vahe Petrossian, "A Winning Alliance," *MEED Middle East Economic Digest*, August 19, 1996, p. 23. See also R. Jeffrey Smith and Thomas W. Lippman, "White House Agrees to Bill Allowing Covert Operations against Iran," *Washington Post*, December 22, 1995, p. A27.

19. The event was the downing of two U.S.-licensed airplanes in Cuban air space on February 24, 1996. This led directly to the passage of the Cuban Liberty and Democratic Solidarity (LIBERTAD) Act of 1996 (also known as Helms-Burton).

20. C. David Welch, "Striking a Balance: Maximum Pressure on Iran and Libya, Minimum Cost to American Interests," testimony before the Subcommittee on Trade of the House Ways and Means Committee, 104 Cong. 2 sess., May 22, 1996 (Government Printing Office, 1996).

21. The six possible sanctions include a ban on U.S. Export-Import Bank assistance; a ban on U.S. export licenses to receive goods; a ban on eligibility for loans totaling more than $10 million a year from U.S. financial institutions; a denial of the right to be a primary dealer in U.S. government bonds; a denial of the right to bid on U.S. government contracts; and a denial of the right to export goods to the United States. For a clear discussion of ILSA and its legal context, see Bruno Cova, "Extra-Territorial Reach of the US Iran and Libya Sanctions Act of 1996," *Oil and Gas Law and Taxation Review*, vol. 14 (November 1996), pp. 449–58; and see also Patrick Clawson, "Iran," in Haass, ed., *Economic Sanctions*, pp. 85–106.

22. "Remarks by President Bill Clinton at Signing Ceremony for the Iran and Libya Oil Sanctions Act," *Federal News Service*, August 5, 1996.

23. For details see James Bennet, "To Clear Air with Europe, U.S. Waives Some Sanctions," *New York Times*, May 19, 1998, p. A6.

24. "Italy Pleased with EU-U.S. Sanction Compromise," Xinhua News Agency, May 22, 1998.

25. Stuart Eizenstat, "Hearings on Sanctions in U.S. Policy," testimony before House International Relations Committee, June 3, 1998, 105 Cong. 2 sess. (GPO, 1998), p. 15.

26. "Libya Industry," *EIU ViewsWire*, December 5, 1996.

27. See "Hearing on the Implementation of the Iran-Libya Sanctions Act," before the Senate Banking, Housing and Urban Affairs Committee, 105 Cong. 1 sess. October 30, 1997 (GPO, 1997); and "Iran-Libya Sanctions Act—One Year Later," Hearing before the House International Relations Committee, July 23, 1997, 105 Cong. 1 sess. (GPO, 1997).

28. The U.S. sanctions are limited because they are unilateral, while the UN sanctions are limited because they do not involve significant restrictions on the flow of Libyan oil or gas.

29. David Gow and Richard Norton-Taylor, "BAe admits to Libya Talks," *Guardian* (London), August 20, 1998, p. 3.

30. U.N.S.C. Resolution 1192, August 27, 1998.

31. Mark Huband, "Foreign Companies Set to Gain from End of Sanctions," *Financial Times*, April 6, 1999, p. 4.

32. Ray Takeyh, "An End to the Lockerbie Morass? The Libyan Angle," *Policywatch* 378 (Washington Institute for Near East Policy, April 5, 1999).

33. Nora Boustany, "The Delicate Art of Determined Diplomacy," *Washington Post*, April 7, 1999, p. A14.

STEFANO SILVESTRI

9 | *Libya and Transatlantic Relations: An Italian View*

Compared with Iran, the Libyan case has not been a major problem for transatlantic relations, even though Colonel Muammar Qaddafi has tried to increase his nuisance value in words and deeds. The approval by the U.S. Congress of the Iran and Libya Sanctions Act of 1996 (ILSA), however, gave new importance to Libya, adding it to the list of transatlantic problems that could lead to serious political and economic disagreements and crises.

There are no major differences in the European and American evaluation of Libya as a "rogue" state, a country that flouts the norms and rules of responsible international behavior. On both sides of the Atlantic worries arise about possible Libyan attempts to acquire capabilities to produce weapons of mass destruction. Each side has also suffered from terrorist attacks on its nationals perpetrated by Libyans, most notably in the downings of aircraft in Scotland and Niger. If anything, Europeans are more likely than Americans to suffer because of Libyan acts of hostility, simply because the distance between them and Libya is smaller and the dependence on Libyan oil and gas is greater.

Yet a major perceptual difference arises from American and European assessments of Qaddafi's and Libya's role in world security. The United States mainly stresses the negative aspects of Qaddafi's support for terrorism, his attempts to develop weapons of mass destruction, and his militant stance against Israel and the Arab-Israeli peace negotiations. European states generally assess the situation more optimistically based on Qaddafi's limited options, his anti-Islamic fundamentalist stance, and his cooperation, from time to time, with Western intelligence services. The question is whether the largely erratic behavior of the colonel, and his nuisance value, can be better controlled through military threats, sanctions, and undercover actions or through a mixture of pressure and political and economic incentives.

In recent years, some European governments demonstrated a greater willingness to join Washington in constraining Qaddafi's regime. In March 1992, France and Great Britain, with the United States, were instrumental in pushing the passage of UN Security Council Resolution 748 (1992), which placed mandatory sanctions on Libya as long as that country was in noncompliance with the requirements of the previous Security Council Resolution (731/1992). This resolution called for the extradition of two Libyan citizens deemed directly responsible for the bombing of Pan Am Flight 103 in December 1988 and required the payment of appropriate compensation. Resolution 748 ordered an aviation and arms embargo, various curtailments on Libya's diplomatic apparatus, and a boycott of the national airline, Libyan Arab Airlines. Libya's persistent refusal to comply led to further freezing of some assets and to the ban of some oil-related equipment.[1]

When President Bill Clinton, citing worries about chemical weapons production facilities, proposed a complete, worldwide trade and oil embargo against Libya, however, the European Union was unwilling to participate in such drastic actions. As a result of pressure from domestic constituents, the United States decided to take unilateral steps, which led to ILSA and the proposition, strongly rebuffed by American allies, of a secondary unilateral American boycott of those foreign companies dealing with Libya.

It is likely, however, that the Libyan question will not be decided only on its own merits but rather in relation to the question of policy toward Iran. The situation is tricky. Recent positive evolutions in Iranian-Western relations could produce the opposite result in Libya. Generally speaking, it would appear obvious that a possible softening of the sanctions against Iran would positively affect the Western stance toward Libya. Yet, it is also possible that, in order to reaffirm its tough stance against terrorism and rogue states, the United States would harden its position on Libya while allowing for a greater margin of maneuver for U.S. allies on Iran. In fact, the two cases differ radically at least on one key point: Iran has a new, popularly elected government, thus giving more credibility to the possibility of real political change. In Libya the maverick Qaddafi still rules. An opposite scenario is more straightforward. If the U.S. government applies ILSA sanctions against the South Pars deal with Iran, it seems unlikely that Libya would receive more liberal treatment.[2] Libya most likely would fade into the background and be treated as a secondary venue for confrontation between Europe and the United States.

Transatlantic consultations and cooperation on sanction policies against countries such as Libya and Iran do seem to have improved. The transatlantic summit in May 1998 between the U.S. government and the European Union led to a general understanding on the questions of Cuba, Libya, and Iran, whereby the American president would waive implementation of secondary sanctions identified in ILSA, while the European Union would cooperate more strictly with the United States to curb the risks of proliferation of weapons of mass destruction and of international terrorist and attempt a coordinated policy of pressure and dialogue with these "rogue" states.[3]

Italy and Libya

Italian policy toward Libya has been shaped by two factors: energy and proximity (both geographical and historical). The first one does not require much explanation. Libya is the principal supplier of oil to Italy (providing about one-third of total oil imports, the rest coming mainly from Iran and Saudi Arabia). Italy's increasing consumption of natural gas may further increase these ties thanks to the planned building of a new trans-Mediterranean pipeline from Libya to Italy.[4] If that happens, about one-fourth of Italian imports of natural gas will come from there. (The other main sources are Algeria, Russia, and the Netherlands.) This would require huge investments that may possibly run counter to ILSA.

Proximity has been a mixed blessing for both countries. Libya was the nearest Italian colony but also one of the most difficult to curb through several major and bloody military campaigns, starting in 1911 and ending well into the 1930s. After World War II, Libya became independent under British guidance. These were relatively quiet years that were swiftly ended by Qaddafi's arrival. The colonel emphasized historical Italian responsibilities toward Libya: a number of agreements, already signed and implemented, have failed to fully convince Qaddafi of the opportunity to close that chapter of Libyan bilateral relations with Italy. Meanwhile, former Italian settlers in Libya have been expelled (and their properties confiscated). Yet this conflictual posture has continuously and consistently proceeded with a parallel approach of cooperation, both in the economic and in the political field. The latter is the most surprising.

Qaddafi presents himself as the new revolutionary guide of the third world. His curious *Green Book* is the foundation of Qaddafi's *Third Universal Theory*, which bypasses capitalism and communism and even organized religious systems. (Islam is not even mentioned in the *Green Book*.) Such a third way has frequently put the colonel at odds with both communists and Islamists, giving support to the idea that, while he could be seen as a strategic enemy of the West, in practice he could constitute a tactical asset. In the long run, however, Qaddafi's ability to steer through a path of multiple confrontations has also deprived him of allies, increasing his overall marginality. The colonel's attempts to alter this situation by increasing his ties and support of international terrorism have worsened the situation, reducing Libya to the level of a "pariah" state.

The problem remains of what to do with Libya and thus with Qaddafi. Libya is a useful case study of the effectiveness of a policy of sanctions and imposed isolation, both because of the length of time for which sanctions of one kind or another have been applied and because of the differentiated enthusiasm felt for them by Western states.

The Political and Military Setting

To better understand the Libyan problem it is useful to assess the present international position of this country, including its potential role and threat to international security. Qaddafi came to power in 1969 and, barring unforeseen developments, is likely to remain in power indefinitely. The only credible alternative to his rule is a possible military coup by the army. Qaddafi is perfectly aware of this possibility and has maintained tight control over all military affairs, directly controlling the careers of all military officers and maintaining constant pressure over the institutions as a whole; for example, after the army's defeat in Chad, he threatened to disband the armed forces.[5]

Qaddafi's rule is also affected by difficult relations between the regime and the traditional tribal power system. Many tribes, particularly from the Cyrenaica region in northeast Libya, actively demonstrate their disaffection toward the colonel and his regime. The other significant opposition comes from the civilian society and has mainly taken the form of radical religious fundamentalism. Apparently, however, these radical militants have been unable to gather sufficient domestic support and are mostly linked to the large number of foreign (mainly Egyptian and Sudanese) workers in Libya. The exiled opposition leaders, based in Cairo and in Khartoum, live under the continuous threat of murderous attacks engineered by the Libyan services and are usually considered of limited influence and capability.[6]

The Libyan authorities stress the "Islamic threat" against their regime. The small flow of information coming out of Libya, however, fails to confirm this claim. Few radical Islamic groups are known to be active in the country. A so-called Armed Islamic Group (Groupe Islamique Armee, or GIA) has called for a jihad against Qaddafi. The small but well-organized Al-Gama'at al-Islamiyya (the Islamic Group), inspired by Afghan leaders, seems to be particularly active. The Fighting Islamic Group has organized terrorist attacks against high officials (especially during 1996). The Movement of the Islamist Martyrs has been active in Benghazi, organizing some uprisings. Yet these groups have limited popular appeal and derive most of their support from the many foreigners (mainly from Egypt and Sudan) working or living in Libya. That Libyan authorities consistently extradite the majority of the people arrested seems to confirm this hypothesis.

Libya is isolated both in the Arab and the African worlds, even if the visit to Libya by South African President Nelson Mandela in October 1997 constituted a propaganda success for the colonel.[7] Yet Mandela's visit was carefully designed as a personal mission of thanks for the past support given by Libya to the African National Congress (ANC) rather than a political move of significance for the future, and it has not been followed by other, more significant initiatives. Similarly, the generally positive attitude of the Tunisian government toward Qaddafi should be read as part of the global Tunisian strategy against the threat of radical Islam rather than specific support for the colonel's regime. Moreover, Syrian control over Lebanon and the process of peace negotiations with Israel have further isolated Libya in the Arab world. Although its relations with Egypt have somewhat recovered from the bitter period following the Libyan-sponsored assassination of President Anwar Sadat of Egypt, they remain poor and mostly conflictual. Furthermore, the European Union has never included Libya in its Mediterranean policy, which commenced in the early 1970s, nor in its more recent and far-reaching Euro-Mediterranean partnership.[8]

If the policy of economic and political sanctions applied by the United States and by the Europeans (with only minor differences in intensity) is added to this picture, it can be concluded that Libya is one of the most isolated and impotent countries in the world.[9] Even its military capabilities have been severely constrained by its inability to maintain its large arsenal in an acceptable working condition and the poor state of its armed forces. The Libyan military arsenal, particularly the air force, has been severely hit by the implementation of the UN sanctions, further diminishing its readiness and effectiveness. However, Qaddafi has demonstrated his ability to use his limited arsenal as propaganda: the firing of a couple of Scud missiles at (or in the direction of) a U.S. Coastal Guard Loran station on the Italian island of Lampedusa on April 15, 1986, and the threat of disseminating some mines in the Red Sea. These actions may have achieved some success in the media but essentially have achieved nothing, except to confirm the very limitation of Libyan military options.

No one believes that Libya could develop its own nuclear weapons, even if it attempts to buy some readymade warheads and to recruit some nuclear scientists. Presently Libya has only a small 10-MW light water research reactor bought from the Soviet Union. Libya was rumored to be trying to acquire a second and bigger 440-MW research reactor.[10] Yet Libya ratified the Non-Proliferation Treaty in 1975 and accepted the controls of the International Atomic Energy Agency (IAEA). The only real issue, in military terms, seems to be the attempt to produce chemical and possibly biological weapons. The available information is insufficient and somewhat contradictory as far as the ability of Libya to develop these weapons is concerned, but all indications seem to confirm a definite attempt to do that, even though Libya has signed the Biological Weapons Convention (but not the Chemical Weapons Convention).[11] Moreover, Libya, as well as many other countries, has officially reserved the right to use chemical weapons if attacked in kind.

It is worth noting that in 1986 the government of Chad claimed that Libyan forces used chemical weapons. Confirmation came in 1987 when gravity bombs charged with gas (probably hyprite) were dropped by the Libyan air force on the troops of Chadian President Hissene Habré. At least two major Libyan chemical complexes also arouse suspicions—large facilities at Rabta and a second southeast of Tripoli, at Wafa—and there are reports that a third one may be under development. According to some estimates, Rabta alone could have the capacity to produce up to 1.2 tons a day of chemical agents, as well as the necessary containers, bombs, and warheads.[12] No serious information is available on biological weapons.

These weapons, if and when available, could be provided to terrorists, dropped by plane, or placed in the warhead of a missile. Libya has some of the latter, mainly the Soviet-era Scud-B (possibly some Scud-C) missiles, and has tried without success to acquire more capable, long-range missiles from China and North Korea. Missiles with a range of 1,000 kilometers would threaten a large part of Italian territory. Modified, Iraq-like Scuds could reach a 900-kilometer range. Libya may also attempt to develop some new medium-range missiles utilizing German or Brazilian technologies. One thing should be underlined: among the various "proliferators" of the third world, Libya is probably the only one that explicitly links its desire to acquire long-range missiles and weapons of mass destruction with its aim of threatening the northern shore of the Mediterranean and the West. With the exception of Chad (where Libya was on the offensive) and its difficult relations with Sudan, at least officially Libya has no regional enemies. (In contrast, even Iran has a more "defensive" strategic posture.)

A large gap exists between Libya's words and deeds (and capabilities). The arms embargo has greatly damaged all Libya's conventional military capabilities and curtailed its ability to acquire new technologies, buy spare parts, and perform maintenance. It is estimated that about two-thirds of its aircraft cannot be considered operational, with the notable exception of Mirage and some of its Soviet-era Su-24 bombers.[12] Libya also has a limited capacity for in-air refueling, thanks to two modified Soviet-era tankers (one Il-76 and one Il-78). Defense expenditures have consistently declined (by approximately 30 percent from 1985 to 1998), parallel to the reduction in oil revenues.[14]

As a whole, Libya cannot be considered a major military threat but could nonetheless carry out an exceptional military attack, possibly employing chemical weapons, against its neighbors' territory, including Italy. Such an attack could not achieve any significant military objective, but it could have a serious political and psychological impact on the civilian population. Libya's capabilities can be defined more accurately in terms of their scare value than of their military value. Yet they are serious enough to cause unease among its neighbors (Italy included).

Although Libya may not be considered a military threat, its sponsorship of terrorism is. How to respond to that threat remains a matter of dispute between the United States and Europe. In the 1980s the United States generally followed a more aggressive approach to state-sponsored terrorism, while Europe was more restrained. The U.S. response to the bombing of a West Berlin night club frequented by Americans in April 1986 exemplified the differences in approaches.

After the Berlin bombing, U.S. intelligence identified Libyan involvement in that bombing, and the Reagan administration chose to take a stand and responded by bombing a number of targets in Libya, namely, in Benghazi and Tripoli. The (implicit) aim of the attack was to remove Qaddafi from power (either by killing him or inciting a coup). This goal was not achieved, and relations with Europe were negatively affected. European governments (except for Great Britain) generally were critical of the U.S. action. France particularly disapproved and refused to grant the United States the right of overflight from bases in England. Italy and others questioned the legality of such military action without concrete proof of Libyan state involvement. Furthermore, there was concern among all European governments about the threat of a new terrorist attack in the wake of the raid.[15] Despite these concerns, the European Commission imposed some sanctions on Libya, but they were limited in scope and, despite U.S. urging, Europeans refused to take a more assertive stance by applying the tougher sanctions desired (and applied) by the United States. The U.S. bombing neither ended Qaddafi's rule nor ended terrorist attacks, believed to be state sponsored. However, two terrorist attacks in particular seemed to bring the allies closer.

The first attack was the bombing of Pan Am Flight 103 over Lockerbie, Scotland, on December 21, 1988. The second attack, which occurred on September 19, 1989, was the explosion of French UTA Flight 772 over Niger. Criminal links were made to Libyan operatives, and in both cases Libyans with close ties to Qaddafi were indicted for the attacks. The three countries with nationals killed in the two explosions—France, Great Britain, and the United States—were in agreement in their condemnation of the attacks and in their determination to take more concrete actions. This culminated in the passage in January 1992 of UN Security Council Resolution 731, which urged Libya to hand over the suspects in the two cases. When Libya failed to do so, the Security Council approved Resolution 748 in March 1992. The resolution banned flights to and from Libya and the sale of aircraft and related parts and labor, reduced significantly diplomatic personnel in Libya, and prohibited the sales of arms and related materials. The continued failure of Libya to comply with the Security Council resolutions led to further restrictions on Libya with the passage of Resolution 883 (1993). On all three Security Council actions, Europe and the United States seemed to find a measure of agreement. That confluence remained even though U.S. and European approaches to "rogue" states varied tremendously elsewhere, and differences over the application of sanctions threatened to permanently injure the relationship.

A Critical Assessment

The UN-mandated sanctions and military attacks on Libya severely constrained its ability to improve its international status and may even have had some positive effects on the colonel's behavior toward the West by decreasing his willingness to risk confrontation. But these actions also failed in their main objective of convincing Qaddafi to comply with UN Security Council resolutions, not to mention curbing Libya's revisionism and bellicose rhetoric. In imposing sanctions on Libya, moreover, the international community developed some ambiguous practices that eroded some of the credibility and effectiveness of its action.

The list of these ambiguities must begin with the decision to exclude oil and gas exports from the sanctions regime imposed on Libya.

Although this move was a necessary compromise in order not to punish Europe more strongly than Libya and also to gain European support for sanctions, the decision also reduced most subsequent restrictions to forms of marginal annoyance and low-level political harassment. The greatest achievement of the sanctions policy was the reduction of the Libyan military threat, but it had a limited impact on the only weapon really feared by the West—terrorism—-and has probably increased Libya's desire to acquire some weapons of mass destruction.

A second ambiguity is the singling out of Libya as a rogue state. None of this was designed to suggest that Libya can escape responsibility for its actions. There was plenty of evidence that Libya did support a range of revolutionary groups, particularly Palestinian, during the 1970s and early 1980s. The momentous change brought about by the Oslo agreements and the recognition of the political legitimacy of the Palestine Liberation Organization (PLO) diminished somewhat the credibility of this argument. Furthermore, one could doubt the effectiveness of the policy followed by the West if it is true that, immediately after the 1986 Tripoli and Benghazi bombings by the United States, there were up to fourteen incidents in which Libyans were unambiguously involved, including six massive arms shipments to the Irish Republican Army (IRA) of which only one, on the trawler *Eksund*, was intercepted.[16]

This brings us to the third and most difficult issue of the Pan Am flight and French UTA airliner explosions. In both cases considerable evidence linked Libyans with these events, although the evidence, in the case of the Lockerbie incident at least, is still disputed by some.[17] Even if Libyans were connected with the incidents, it is by no means absolutely certain (even if it is likely) that the Libyan government or Qaddafi's personal clique can also be implicated. The most important point is that the international community (and especially Great Britain and the United States) chose a path that seemed to humiliate Libya. Neither the United States nor Great Britain agreed to Libya exercising its right to an independent arbitration or, failing the occurrence of that within six months after the request, a hearing by the International Court of Justice (ICJ), as required by the Convention for the Suppression of Unlawful Acts against the Safety of Civil Aviation, which, as signatories, they were obliged to do.[18] The decision on February 27, 1998, by the ICJ reaffirming its competence to discuss the case might have been of limited practical importance insofar as the decisions of the UN Security Council were concerned, but it stressed the juridical aspects of the Libyan case that undermined a legal argument for continuing sanctions.[19] Furthermore, a French decision to carry out the judgment of the UTA affair *in absentia* of the Libyan defendants eroded the Western common front on Libya.

The decision by Great Britain and the United States to agree to the creation of a special court in the Hague to try the Lockerbie suspects using Scottish law represented a significant change in attitude.[20] Whereas continued U.S. and British demands for extradition of the suspects for trial in Scotland created an impression of intransigence, the decision to compromise creates the possibility for gathering renewed support from Italy and other countries. The onus has been placed on Libya to react in kind. Failing to do so will create a new dilemma for the international community. It will need to decide whether or not to reward or punish Libya, that is, to create a plan for how to deal with Libya in the future.

The fourth difficulty concerns the effectiveness of sanctions in changing Libyan behavior. The Qaddafi regime is still in power, and the Lockerbie accused were only delivered for trial after years of pressure.[21] Even the considerable economic costs imposed on Libya (variously estimated as four to ten billion dollars),[22] quite apart from the human cost caused by lack of access to foreign medical and other facilities, made little difference in the situation. Nor are continued U.S. sanctions likely to do so in the future. European interests in Libyan oil made any strengthening of the sanctions regime virtually impossible. The decision of the Italian Foreign Minister Lamberto Dini, at the end of 1996, to meet officially with his Libyan counterpart, Omar M. Mountasser, displayed a growing willingness at least on Italy's part to halt or modify the sanctions regime. In November 1996, Dini also published an article calling for a new Middle Eastern dialogue without further isolating the so-called rogue states.[23] In the same vein, the 1996 decision of Colonel Qaddafi to allow French Judge Jean-Louis Bruguière to visit Libya (to investigate the terrorist attack against the UTA DC-10) smoothed the way toward better relations with Paris.[24] Turkish Prime Minister Necmettin Erbakan's visit in October 1996 was interpreted by the international press as a bold initiative by the Turkish Islamic leader.[25] On the contrary, Erbakan's well-publicized moves toward Libya and Iran were simply the continuation of a long and steady policy followed by his predecessors and remain very much in the mainstream of the present Turkish foreign policy.

The Future

The approval of ILSA has serious implications for Euro-American relations. The threatened block on access to U.S. investment and domestic contracts for foreign firms engaged in projects with more than $40 million (later reduced to $20 million) in either Libya or Iran has raised the specter of extraterritoriality and a trade war between Europe and the United States. It is also a strong attack on the internationally accepted concept of state sovereignty—not in order to create new supranational institutions or body of laws but to support the unilateral decisions of the United States.

In an ideal world, the principles of accountable state behavior (respect for human rights, defense of the global environment, and the like) could not and should not be resisted in the name of national sovereignty. Yet such a development would require clear accountability of all states, a larger degree of impartiality of judges, and greater transparency for the entire system. Nor will it be possible to convince many people of the opportunity to continue to enforce and possibly toughen a sanctions regime against a country like Libya until those who enforce them demonstrate their own more moral evenhandedness. While Qaddafi's handover of the Lockerbie suspects for trial in the Hague might be enough to convince most of the world to drop sanctions against Libya, it has not ended U.S. sanctions.

So what should be done with Libya? Its regime is highly unattractive and despotic. It undoubtedly brutalizes, represses, and sometimes assassinates its domestic opponents. But as much as its behavior ought to be changed, it has not happened through the use of sanctions. All that sanctions seem likely to achieve is a strengthening of the regime, as has occurred with Saddam Hussein in Iraq. Sanctions look increasingly like a relatively cheap option, one that enables governments to appear to support the desires (and sometimes the prejudices) of their domestic public opinion without taking responsibility for their actions or embarking on more expensive and difficult undertakings, such as direct military interventions on the territory of rogue states. They also enable governments to avoid policies that would risk creating outcomes that are arguably worse. Who would like a power vacuum in Iraq, the enlargement of the fundamentalist grip in North Africa, or a new oil crisis?

These scenarios suggest why the approach taken by Italy toward

Libya as well as toward the problem of other rogue states stresses dialogue more than sanctions, or at least points to the possibility of graduating a sanctions regime according to a number of intermediary and concrete objectives, so that a process of real negotiations occurs.

In this respect, Italy's priorities are related more clearly to the future than to the past. Although Italy supported the British, American, and French request for extradition of the terrorists, the Italian government does not believe that this single issue embraced the entire Libyan question. It did welcome the British and American decision to allow a trial of the Lockerbie suspects to take place in the Netherlands and the handover of the suspects in April 1999. There is certainly interest in developing Libya's ability to export energy, but there are also real concerns over the possible development of weapons of mass destruction. Thus, as in the Iranian case, the Italian government would like to see a progressive shift from the moralistic nature of present American policy (which renders sanctions particularly rigid and possibly ineffective) to a more flexible approach that could be more strictly related to specific and attainable objectives likely to increase overall security and the stability of the regions concerned. This is not meant to say that the Italian or the European approaches are as straightforward as they should be. On the contrary, the experience of the European "critical dialogue" with Iran has been a modest and ambiguous one. For all its shortcomings (that should and could be corrected), an approach that emphasizes small steps toward a more amicable relationship with Libya and other rogue states looks more rational and promising—and could have the significant bonus of avoiding a dangerous rift between Europe and the United States.

In spite of the suspension of UN sanctions, specific objectives for Libya should be identified, addressing various concerns, starting with the control and destruction of weapons of mass destruction and their construction facilities (if they are confirmed to be such by agreed international inspection), and then moving against Libyan support of international terrorism (which seems to be waning anyway) and to the acceptance or at least the nonrejection of the Arab-Israeli peace process, provided that it survives periods of stagnation. Specific and credible compensation should accompany Libya's eventual acceptance of these objectives.

Libya's return to the international community should be handled carefully. Allowing Libya to take part in regional and subregional dialogues, like the Euro-Mediterranean one or possibly, at first, as part of a Maghreb multilateral delegation (as a goodwill gesture), will give Libya an opportunity to positively raise its profile. Along this path, Libya may even come to play a positive role in the economic development of the Maghreb region as well as a political role regarding the Islamist threat in Algeria and Tunisia.

Notes

1. The United Nations Security Council took these measures with the adoption of Resolution 883 on November 11, 1993. See, for example, Paul Lewis, "U.N. Tightens Sanctions against Libya," *New York Times*, November 12, 1993, p. A10.

2. The South Pars oilfield will be developed by the French oil company Total together with the Russian Gazprom and the Malaysian Petronas.

3. See the "Understanding with Respect to Disciplines for the Strengthening of Investment Protection," signed by the United States and the European Union on May 18, 1998, as found on the Internet at http://www.eurunion.org. An illustration of the new coordination was the growing political contact between the Italian and Iranian governments (including a visit to Teheran by Prime Minister Romano Prodi on July 1, 1998) following careful bilateral preparation by the United States and Italy.

4. See "World Wire: Italy's ENI Has Deal with Libya," *Wall Street Journal*, November 5, 1996, p. A19; and John L. Wright, *Libya: A Modern History* (Johns Hopkins University Press, 1982), p. 245.

5. See, for example, Dirk Vandewalle, ed., *Qadhafi's Libya, 1969–1994* (St. Martin's Press, 1995).

6. For a general assessment of the state and society in Libya, see Moncef Djaziri, *Etat e société en Libye: islam, politique et modernité* (Paris: Harmattan, 1996).

7. "Despite U.N. Ban, Mandela Meets Qaddafi in Libya," *New York Times*, October 23, 1997, p. A3.

8. For general information on Libya's foreign policy, see Mary Jane Deeb, *Libya's Foreign Policy in North Africa* (Westview Press, 1991); and *The Middle East and North Africa, 1997* (London: Europa Publications, 1996). For information on European-Mediterranean policy, see the "Barcelona Declaration Adopted at the Euro-Mediterranean Conference," November 27–28, 1995, as found on the Internet at http://europa.eu.int. For more information, see F. Stephen Larrabee, and others, *NATO's Mediterranean Initiative: Policy Issues and Dilemmas* (Santa Monica, Calif.: Rand Corporation, 1998); and Roberto Aliboni, "The Euro-Mediterranean Charter for Peace and Stability: Perspectives and Priorities," paper presented at the Conferenza annuale Euromesco, London, 1998.

9. This situation may be set to change given the suspension of UN sanctions on April 5, 1999, after Libya handed over the two suspects in the Lockerbie case.

10. Libya does not appear, at least for now, to be pursuing construction of the reactor. See Rodney W. Jones and Mark G. McDonough with Toby F. Dalton and Gregory D. Koblentz, *Tracking Nuclear Proliferation: A Guide in Maps and Charts, 1998* (Washington: Carnegie Endowment for International Peace, 1998), p. 215.

11. As of March 1999 Libya has not signed the Chemical Weapons Convention. This, and conflicting estimates, makes determining the extent of Libya's chemical weapons ability extremely difficult. See Jones and McDonough, *Tracking Nuclear Proliferation,* pp. 215–16.

12. Maurizio Cremasco, *Libya* (Rome: Istituto Affari Internazionali, 1995).

13. See Alessandro Politi, *The Threat from North Africa* (Rome: Istituto Affari Internazionali, 1996).

14. Defense expenditures in millions of U.S. dollars were as follows: 1,844 in 1985; 1,401 in 1995, and 1,300 in 1998. Between 1985 and 1998, expenditures declined by 30 percent. See International Instititute for Strategic Studies, *The Military 1998/99* (London: Oxford University Press, 1998), p. 134.

15. Ronald Bruce St. John, *Qaddafi's World Design: Libyan Foreign Policy, 1969–1987* (London: Saqi Books, 1987), pp. 88–91.

16. Moncef Djaziri, "Europe, the U.S., and Libya," Working Paper (Gütersloh: Bertlesmann Foundation, December 1996), and comments to the paper by Josef Joffé.

17. Ibid.

18. The Convention was signed in Montreal on September 23, 1971. Article 14, paragraph 1 was used as the basis for Libya's filing of its complaint with the ICJ. Text of the convention as found on the Internet at http://www.tufts.edu/fletcher/multi/texts/BH586.txt.

19. International Court of Justice, "Summary of the Judgment of 27 February 1998," *Press Communiqué* 98/5bis, as found on the Internet at http://www.icj-cij.org/icjwww/Presscom/Press1998/ipr9805bis.html. The judgment recognizes the applicability of the Montreal Convention and Libya's right to a hearing at the ICJ. Furthermore, it declares that the United States failed to comply with its obligations under the Convention to allow a hearing to take place.

20. Philip Shenon, "It's Official: U.S. to Consider Dutch Trial in Lockerbie Case," *New York Times,* July 22, 1998, p. A3.

21. UN Secretary General Kofi Annan met with Qaddafi on December 5, 1998, in the hope that his visit would lead to the handover of the suspects. This meeting and much backroom political dealing led to the transfer of the suspects to the Netherlands on April 5, 1999. UN sanctions were immediately suspended, while it was expected that U.S. sanctions would not be withdrawn any time soon. See Judith Miller, "How Suspects Were Moved, Very Discreetly, to Court," *New York Times,* April 7, 1999, p. A6.

22. Author's estimates.

23. ". . . July 9, 1998, following a number of meetings of a bilateral Italian-Libyan Committee, the two Foreign Ministers have signed a joint document to *'close once and for all the negative legacy of the past'* " [from official communiqué of the Italian Ministry of Foreign Affairs]. The document states the commitment of both countries to fight all kinds of terrorism, to contribute to the nonproliferation of weapons of mass destruction, to reduce the factors of regional instability, to abide by the human rights [agreements], to search for disarmament agreements and others. On the purely bilateral side, this document reaches a number of agreements closing the thorny issue of "colonial damages" claimed by Colonel Qaddafi (and already settled by Italy under the terms of a bilateral agreement signed in 1956 with King Idris), establishing technical cooperation on the humanitarian issue of the minefields laid during Word War II and paving the way for the payment of a number of credits and claims by Italian firms and individuals, frozen by the Libyan government pending a solution of the other litigations (variously estimated at $1–3 billion). More significantly, this agreement is the necessary preliminary to the implementation of new investment and cooperation projects, particularly in the natural gas field. The most interesting feature of this document, significantly different from past commercial and diplomatic agreements, is the insistence on the general political issues of terrorism, nonproliferation, regional stability, and disarmament. See Lamberto Dini, in *Energia* (November 1996), Bologna, Italy.

24. "Libya Admits Magistrate," *Financial Times*, July 6, 1997, p. 1.

25. The trip caused some consternation with Turkey's Western allies, given their views of Libya as a primary sponsor of terrorism. Erbakan hoped to improve ties in the Islamic world by making this trip to Libya as well as Nigeria and Egypt. However, the visit to Libya backfired. Qaddafi stunned Erbakan by calling for a Kurdish homeland; and the Turkish parliament reacted by criticizing Erbakan's visit and calling for his resignation. His government only narrowly escaped a vote of no confidence over the issue. See Kelly Couturier, "Erbakan Trip Prompts Policy Fears: PM's Itinerary Has the Secular Establishment in an Uproar," *Financial Times*, October 3, 1996, p. 3; "U.S. Criticizes Turkish Leader for Libya Trip and Trade Deal," *New York Times*, October 8, 1996, p. A5; Kelly Couturier, "Turk's Libya Trip Causes Political Crisis at Home," *Washington Post*, October 8, 1996, p. A16; and Kelly Couturier, "Erbakan Survives Criticism on Libya," *Financial Times*, October 17, 1996, p. A3.

PAULINE H. BAKER
JOHN J. STREMLAU

10 | Nigeria: U.S.–European Stakes in Africa's Largest State

Thirty years ago the deadliest conflict in African history raged in Nigeria. World media coverage of starving children trapped in the secessionist enclave of Biafra briefly pushed the Nigerian crisis ahead of Vietnam as the international problem of greatest concern to public opinion in Europe and America. This generated an unprecedented international humanitarian intervention, which prevented the starvation of several millions of Biafrans while helping to sustain a military rebellion that lasted two and a half years.[1]

Today, many crisis managers in Europe and the United States recall that remarkable intervention as a precursor to the numerous, more costly, complex humanitarian emergencies that bedevil Western governments in the 1990s.[2] Ironically, despite Nigeria's regional role in taming the civil conflicts in Liberia and Sierra Leone, it was deteriorating conditions within Nigeria itself that once again brought that troubled state to a crisis point. By 1998 the world's tenth most populous country, which once described itself as "a showcase of democracy," had become the most brutal military dictatorship in sub-Saharan Africa. With the death of Gen. Sani Abacha in June 1998 and the installation of the army chief of staff Abdulsalam Abubakar as head of state,[3] the country stood on a precipice, facing three possible futures: a descent into violence, precipi-

179

tating another horrendous humanitarian crisis; deeper levels of repression, making the country an unstable and dangerous outlaw state; or a return to civilian rule and the path to democracy. The election of Gen. Olusegun Obasanjo as president on February 27, 1999, appears to have put Nigeria on the third path—a return to civilian rule. However, widespread electoral malpractices plunged that contest into political controversy. Many alleged that Obasanjo, who was backed by retired generals, did not represent a genuine return to civilian rule. Thus depending upon how Obasanjo rules, either of the first two scenarios could still come to pass. If that happens, Nigeria could present an even larger challenge than the crisis of a generation ago, straining relations between Americans and Europeans in ways more reminiscent of Bosnia than Biafra.

Yet, the worst case scenarios in Nigeria may be averted, especially in the post-Abacha era. Nigeria illustrates how members of the Atlantic alliance might act in concert to minimize potential violence stemming from complex humanitarian emergencies. What is not certain is whether these countries have the political will to act boldly with preventive diplomacy in a country of enormous importance.

During the 1967–70 Nigerian Civil War, Western governments were more at odds with their own citizens than they were with one another over whether, when, or how to intervene. While they generously provided money, food, and equipment to religious and other private humanitarian agencies that ran Biafra's relief airlift, U.S. and European governments consistently upheld Nigeria's right to suppress the rebellion. However, although in theory they upheld the principle of noninterference in the internal affairs of sovereign states, in practice they took sides. Great Britain remained Nigeria's principal arms supplier, with strong political backing from the United States. Paris covertly aided Biafra for commercial gain and for greater influence in Anglophone West Africa; French companies purchased the biggest share of Nigeria's wartime agricultural production. France thus kept its influence with both sides, simultaneously financing the federal war effort and arming and assisting the rebel forces. Soviet overtures to Nigeria, strong diplomatic support from most of Africa, and a shared judgment that the Federal Military Government (FMG) commanded the resources, legitimacy, and firepower to win combined to help reinforce the West's resolve. No one threatened UN sanctions, either to restrain the FMG or to force a peaceful resolution of the conflict. In contrast to recent human-itarian emergencies, Western governments did not press UN agencies or other multilateral organizations to shoulder the burden of humani-tarian intervention. In a unique commercial arrangement, Nigerian oil continued to be produced, with the proceeds due to the government deposited into an escrow account that accrued to the winner of the war. Remarkably, both sides in the Nigerian Civil War accepted that for-mula, and the oil industry avoided becoming embroiled in the conflict.

This scenario would not play out that way now.[4] Conditions within Nigeria and internationally have changed fundamentally since 1970. The need to understand these conditions, to find ways to prevent a recurrence of mass violence in Nigeria, and to remove any risk that it would cause political conflict within and between members of the At-lantic Community motivates this case study.

Nigeria's Simmering Crisis

Nigeria's current crisis has been slowly escalating since the arbitrary annulment by Gen. Ibrahim Babangida of the June 12, 1993, national elections, which were widely believed to have been won by Chief Moshood Abiola, a Muslim Yoruba businessman from the Southwest who reportedly received 59 percent of the vote. Some 14 million people, or 36 percent of the registered electorate, cast ballots. Abiola's support included four states in the politically dominant North, including the home state of his opponent. Despite administrative problems, most in-ternational observers regarded the conduct of this election to have been better than past elections and an accurate reflection of voter support, which cut across ethnic and religious lines. The annulment by an un-popular military junta resulted in an outcry that eventually led to the forced retirement of Babangida and the appointment of an interim na-tional government headed by Chief Ernest Shonekan, another Yoruba businessman from the Southwest. But within three months, this care-taker government was dissolved and the then defense minister and close associate of Babangida, Gen. Sani Abacha, assumed power.

Abacha's five-year reign of power was the most repressive period Nigeria had experienced since it gained independence in 1960. Shortly after Abacha seized power, he dissolved all remaining elected bodies at the national, state, and local government levels, banned political parties, appointed military commanders to head all state governments, and initiated a form of absolute military rule. Although Abacha recruited some civilians into his government to soften his image, there was unprecedented concentration of power in Abacha's hands and the regime never gained legitimacy. When Abacha conducted elections for delegates to a constitutional conference in May 1994, for example, fewer than 400,000 voters participated. At the same time, General Abacha took extreme measures to eliminate all opposition, including executing, assassinating, and jailing political dissidents, pro-democracy and human rights activists, journalists and intellectuals, and politically outspoken Nigerians.[5] Abacha purged the military, banned legal challenges to military rule, shut down independent newspapers, and ignored the judiciary.

The range of local and religious conflicts that spread throughout the country was indicative of the extent to which Abacha had infected Nigeria with the symptoms of a failing rogue state. Although no one can predict with certainty the staying power of repressive regimes, a U.S. government survey of global humanitarian emergencies in 1996, based on the estimates of the Central Intelligence Agency's National Intelligence Council, placed Nigeria at the top of a "watch list" of potential crises, noting that if widespread ethnic- or religious-based violence were to erupt, the conflict would be a huge catastrophe for Nigeria and all of West Africa.[6] Even African diplomats began to refer to Nigeria as "the sick man of Africa."[7]

Applying an analytical model that assesses the characteristics of failing states, Nigeria clearly was at risk of violence or collapse by mid-1998, despite the death of Abacha and the lessening of tensions under his successor, General Abubakar. Nigeria fulfilled ten of twelve indicators of potential state collapse: demographic pressures (particularly among groups competing for land, resources, and jobs); sustained human flight (an estimated 10 million, mostly skilled, Nigerians are in exile, 1 million in the United States)[8]; sharp and severe economic distress; uneven economic development along group lines; a legacy of vengeance-seeking group grievance (especially among the Ogoni, Ijaw and other Niger Delta groups, and the Yoruba people); criminalization or delegitimization of the state; a progressive deterioration or elimination of public services; and the factionalization of elites. Two other indicators—a suspension of the rule of law and widespread human rights violations; and a security apparatus operating as a "state within a state"[9]—were present but somewhat relieved with Abubakar's release of prominent prisoners, a new election plan, and the removal from office of Abacha's security chiefs. The consequences of some of these danger signs had been held in check for years by repression.

Especially worrisome was the reopening of ethnic and religious antagonisms that abated after the 1967–70 civil war and the international drift of Nigeria toward association with anti-Western powers that exacerbated domestic conflict. The economy has also spiraled downward. Some $280 billion in oil revenues over the past twenty years have been largely squandered as Nigeria has slumped from a middle-income status to a low-income country over the last decade. Its population suffers from intermittent shortages of fuel, owing to the poor maintenance of the refineries, and from income levels too low to purchase adequate food and medicine. The income of average Nigerians in 1960, at the time of independence, was on a par with Malaysians; in 1998 it was no higher than that of Malians. Per capita income has plummeted from $1,000 in 1980 to less than $250 in 1998. Aggregate growth rates over this period have averaged 1.6 percent, significantly lower than the rise in population of about 3.1 percent. State revenues of Nigeria's vast oil production have been dissipated and appropriated by a privileged and corrupt elite, with little of it filtering down to the people. More than a third of Nigeria's population live in poverty, and some 40 percent of children under five are seriously malnourished—this in a country that was once one of the most agriculturally productive and best educated in Africa.[10]

Sharply deteriorating political conditions in Nigeria led to a failing economy. Foreign investment outside the oil and gas sector has virtually collapsed. Foreign assistance and a World Bank program to restructure Nigeria's debt and rekindle economic growth have also been stymied. Without a viable and legitimate form of government, the prospects for reversing the economic decline are grim. At the same time, national impoverishment makes the task of political reform all the more difficult. A lack of funds for education, health care, basic infrastructure maintenance and development, and public administration deprive the government of the means to build minimal popular support. The continued flow of oil revenues, however, is probably sufficient for Nigeria's leaders, if they choose, to exert control through intimidation, bribery, and corruption, just as Abacha did, undermining the legitimacy of the state.[11] However, the export earnings in 1999 of almost $8 billion are less than half of Nigeria's 1996 earnings, which reached more than $16 billion. Much of this was funneled into private bank accounts of the ruling junta. Nigeria has been rated by Transparency International, an independent organization that bases its ratings on the assessments of international business respondents, as among the most corrupt countries in the world.

Abacha and other military hard-liners apparently had concluded that the international community lacked sufficient will, and certainly sufficient interest, in taking strong actions. At several points, when the international community could have reacted to deteriorating conditions, it did not. For example, when Shehu Yar'Adua died under suspicious circumstances in prison, this produced no meaningful reaction from Western governments. When Abacha slipped behind in his own schedule of elections, there was no sustained protest. When Abacha announced in December 1997 that he had foiled a coup attempt allegedly led by his second in command, Lt. Gen. Oladipo Diya, a Yoruba, the world simply waited.[12] And when Nigeria announced that Abacha would be the sole political candidate in the presidential race, there was simply exasperation expressed.[13]

Nevertheless, accumulating frustrations could boil over into generalized violence and renewed civil conflict even after a return to civilian rule if the military tries to "civilianize" its authority or seizes power after the transition. The shift to civilian rule, in other words, is not sufficient to avoid potential unrest stemming from deep-seated ethnic and economic grievances. Given the political, economic, and social deterioration that has occurred under military rule, internal violence, should it break out, could quickly ignite into a major conflict that could affect neighboring countries throughout West Africa. In fact, the widespread disaffection throughout the country, the weak economy, and the decay of national political institutions put Nigeria at a higher risk of "implosion" and state collapse during the Abacha regime than during its civil war three decades ago.[14]

After coming to power in June 1998, General Abubakar announced a ten-month transition plan to return the country to civilian rule by May 29, 1999. He also disbanded the five political parties fostered by Abacha, released some political prisoners, reassigned or forced the resignation of military officers close to Abacha, and appointed an electoral commission headed by a former supreme court justice to oversee elections. He was applauded internationally for these steps.

However, severe internal tensions persisted as Abubakar tentatively loosened the tight controls imposed by Abacha. One indication was the crackdown on demonstrators commemorating the fifth anniversary of the military annulment of the June 12, 1993, election and the continuing opposition of pro-democracy forces to Abubakar's announced transition plan.[15] Another was the initial hesitancy Abubakar showed in releasing political prisoners and his delay in releasing several remaining prisoners, including the alleged anti-Abacha coup plotters. Ogoni activists protesting against the oil industry in the Niger Delta also continued to agitate. Twenty Ogoni defendants had been released after having been detained for four years despite a court ruling that had granted them bail. Nonetheless, production shutdowns by Shell and Agip in the Niger Delta continued as a result of ongoing sabotage of oil installations and violent protests by villagers. In essence, a full scale, if uncoordinated, revolt exists in an area that covers six of Nigeria's thirty-six states, where the bulk of the country's oil resources are derived.

Given this background, it is critical for the Western powers and pro-democracy forces in Africa to ensure that the Nigerian military, and the successive civilian government, uphold the objective stated by Abubakar to democratize fully.

U.S. Policy Adrift

Nigeria is the most important bilateral relationship the United States has in sub-Saharan Africa, after South Africa. This has been so since the 1960s, when Britain withdrew as a colonial power. Nigeria quickly emerged as a leading moderate, with views that contrasted with the socialist rhetoric of Ghana's Kwame Nkrumah and other so-called pan-African leaders.[16] As the United States became overextended in its global campaign against the spread of communism, particularly in the quagmire of Vietnam, it increasingly sought to encourage the emergence of friendly "regional influentials." Nigeria was happy to oblige for its own interests.[17] In the 1990s, the United States no longer needed "regional influentials" to help contain communism. However, it discovered a new need for regional partners capable of containing the chaos of ethnic and other forms of intergroup violence. This became a particularly useful relationship when Liberia collapsed into civil war. The United States was relieved when Nigeria came forward with the troops and money to support a regional initiative to dampen West African civil unrest. This was accomplished first in Liberia, and then in Sierra Leone, where Nigeria intervened, paradoxically, to restore an elected government that had been toppled in a military coup.

The Abacha regime had several good reasons for investing heavily in regional and international affairs. First and foremost, it was a way to deflect international criticism and the threat of sanctions from the West over escalating human rights abuses at home. Second, it provided a way to garner African support for noninterference in Nigerian affairs. A third reason for Nigeria's military involvement in West Africa was that it deflected dissent in the military, where internal purges and rivalries were rife. Finally, there was the geopolitical dimension. Nigeria's regional domination undermines the influence of France, its traditional regional competitor, which is reducing its military role, while extending its cultural and economic influence, in sub-Saharan Africa. Showing much more flexibility in foreign policy than in domestic affairs, Nigeria's military leaders sought to ingratiate themselves with Paris while replacing France as the regional hegemon. When excluded from Commonwealth proceedings, Abacha proposed that Nigeria join the Francophone economic community, proclaimed French as an official language, and stated that it would become the main foreign language in Nigeria's schools. In return, France became one of Nigeria's greatest defenders against international criticism and a staunch opponent of sanctions, stirring divisions within the Atlantic Community. Presumably, for the military regime, these combined political interests outweighed the mounting financial costs, casualties, and domestic criticism of external intervention.[18]

A double irony has thus developed in U.S.-Nigerian relations in the 1990s: Washington relied on Nigeria to relieve the burden of West African peacekeeping, even though it was increasingly concerned about rising repression and instability within Nigeria itself. And Nigeria was applauded for defending democracy in Africa, even though it had hijacked democracy at home. This contradiction between the peacekeeping role that Nigeria played externally and the self-destructive behavior it exhibited internally complicated decisionmaking in the West. Indecision was compounded by an inability to establish priorities among foreign policy objectives and to reconcile opposing domestic interests.

Policy indecision appeared to be more pronounced in the United States than in Europe. For example, in advance of President Clinton's March 1998, five-nation, twelve-day tour of Africa, the most extensive African trip ever taken by a sitting U.S. president, the administration was unable to reach consensus on its policy toward Nigeria. There was no dissent regarding the decision to bypass Nigeria, and attention was focused instead on Ghana, Uganda, South Africa, Botswana, and Senegal. On policy toward the internal Nigerian situation, however, considerable disagreement took place. Clearance was given for Assistant Secretary of State for African Affairs Susan Rice to state at a Senate hearing on March 12, 1998, that the United States would find it "unacceptable" for Abacha, or any other military ruler, to win the election he had scheduled, although the operational implications of that warning were not spelled out. Two weeks later, while in South Africa, President Clinton contradicted his State Department aide when he said the United States would not object if Abacha succeeded himself, noting that several other African military leaders had undergone similar transformations. The remark was immediately "qualified" by White House aides who stressed that Abacha would have to comply with several democratic conditions before the United States would find his continuance in power acceptable. The mix-up exposed the confusion and paralysis that existed within the administration.

The one departure from this position was the decision in May 1998 to send a high-level U.S. delegation to Nigeria in June, an effort described as a "long shot" to appeal to Abacha to institute democratic reforms. Undersecretary of State Thomas Pickering, a former ambassador in Nigeria, was to lead the U.S. team, which was to include a four-star U.S. Air Force general to boost the credibility of the mission in the eyes of the Nigerian military. According to press reports, the Pickering mission was to tell Abacha that he would face further ostracism if he went through with his transition plan. The Nigerian government told the United States that the trip could only go forward if the administration lifted its visa restrictions on travel by Nigerian government officials. Because of these conditions, the trip was canceled—just days before Abacha's death—then revived as a mission to the new government.[19] It was not clear, however, if there had been plans to mount stiffer penalties on the Nigerian military if it had refused to take the opportunity, with Abacha out of the way, to turn toward democracy. Human rights groups and several prominent members of the African-American community had called repeatedly on the administration to apply stronger pressures, including the freezing of foreign assets of military leaders and the imposition of an oil embargo, in addition to the measures already in place: a ban on military aid and most other forms of bilateral foreign assistance plus visa and other restrictions on travel and cooperation with senior Nigerian officials.[20]

During Abacha's rule, Great Britain and Canada took somewhat stronger rhetorical stands, publicly declaring that they would not accept Abacha succeeding himself. However, the policy differences between the United States and its allies were more of tone than substance. Barring additional bloodshed, no one seemed prepared to apply stronger measures. The United States seemed more conflicted than others, buffeted by a cluster of commercial, cultural, human rights, and environmental lobbies, pulling Washington in different directions.

Whatever the extent of these complexities, the most important interest at stake, not only for the United States but also for Europe, was and remains the prevention of a potential disaster in Nigeria. This would have an impact on the region far more profound than that of Liberia and Sierra Leone combined, and it would affect economic, political, and social interests in the West.[21] The collapse of the continent's most populous state would reverberate throughout West Africa—creating a humanitarian crisis and political uncertainties for years to come—just as the collapse of the Democratic Republic of the Congo (formerly Zaire) has done in Central Africa. Alternatively, a stable and democratic Nigeria would have the kind of anchoring effect on the upper tier of sub-Saharan African states that a stable and democratic South Africa has had on the southern tier. Nigeria, in short, is a pivot upon which the stability of the entire region depends.

Besides concerns about regional stability, the United States and European countries have important bilateral interests. Nigeria is the world's sixth largest oil producer. The United States, which purchases half of Nigeria's output, receives 8 percent to 10 percent of its oil imports from Nigeria, much of it produced by American firms. Private foreign investment in Nigeria's resource sector is increasing, especially from Europe. A huge $3.8 billion investment to develop production of liquefied natural gas, for example, was announced by a major European consortium shortly after Ken Saro-Wiwa's execution in 1995. And in January 1998, Nigerian Liquefied Natural Gas (NLNG) signed a $10 billion contract with Enel, Italy's state electricity generator, to supply gas via France in a swap deal that is supposed to begin in 1999.[22]

Slated to last for twenty-two-and-one-half years, this contract launches the biggest industrial enterprise in sub-Saharan Africa. The Nigerian government, which owns 49 percent of NLNG, partnered with Shell Gas (25.6 percent), Elf Aquitaine (15 percent), and Agip (10.4 percent). With more natural gas reserves than crude oil, Nigeria has also signed long-term supply contracts with Spain, France, and Turkey. Not surprisingly, commercial interests had lobbied hard against any form of economic sanctions against Nigeria during the Abacha regime. This had undermined diplomatic efforts, as the Nigerian government was acutely aware of the primacy of commercial over political or security interests in the West. As a government official said, "Whatever the political situation, we sold all the gas and people are still interested in buying more."[23]

Both the United States and Europe also have an interest in stemming the activities of an extensive network of Nigerian drug traffickers, money launderers, counterfeiters, and swindlers who target the West. Nigerians are leading carriers of Asian heroin and South American cocaine destined for the U.S. and European markets. Rampant corruption at all levels of government fuels this traffic. Few concrete results have come out of Nigeria's campaign to counter the narcotics flow and international criminal activities. However, while the trafficking in drugs, stolen goods, and foreign currency fit the attributes of a rogue state, Nigeria has not exhibited other aspects of rogue behavior, such as active support of international terrorists or the development of weapons of mass destruction.[24]

The United States also has one special interest in Nigeria that is not shared by Europe—the concerns of the African-American community. Unlike South Africa, where apartheid stimulated widespread public opposition from African-Americans, Nigeria sharply divided African-American opinion. This was due in no small part to Nigeria's extensive lobbying campaign, estimated by one report to cost $10 million.[25] The campaign elicited the support of some prominent African-Americans, such as Nation of Islam leader Louis Farrakhan, CORE's Roy Innis, and Senator Carol Moseley-Braun (D-Ill.). Other African-

American voices called for stronger measures against Nigeria, such as Representative Don Payne (D-N.J.), TransAfrica's Randall Robinson, and former U.S. Ambassador Walter Carrington, who advocated oil sanctions against the Abacha regime.

Despite their differences, U.S. and European governments shared broad interests in wanting a peaceful, democratic, and prosperous Nigeria, notwithstanding residual postcolonial rivalries between France and Britain for influence in West Africa or the competition of rival oil companies for access to Nigerian reserves. The plain fact is that if Nigeria were to disintegrate, no one would gain significant national advantages. The costs of trying to alleviate another complex humanitarian emergency in Africa's most populous state would be enormous.

Nigeria's most ardent and consistent critics under military rule, and the strongest proponents of stiffer economic sanctions, have been members of the human rights community, in both private and government agencies.[26] Although it is a divided community, African-Americans have also been in the forefront, along with many in the Nigerian exile community, in calling for U.S. pressure to promote democracy and punish the military government for severe human rights abuses. Yet the Senate's first female black member, Carol Moseley-Braun, opposed sanctioning Nigeria. Her stated reason was that to isolate Nigeria, while continuing to trade with China and other countries that abuse human rights, was holding Nigeria to a double standard, possibly a racist one.[27] Policy-making had also been stymied by divided opinion on Capitol Hill and elsewhere in the black community. In May 1998, the U.S. House of Representatives and the U.S. Senate introduced companion bills on Nigeria, which called for codification of existing unilateral sanctions, the provision of $37 million in assistance for democracy and development, and mandated additional sports and visa restrictions if a free and fair election did not take place by December 31, 1998.[28] But the prospects for passage of the legislation were low in a Republican Congress, with the Congressional Black Caucus split, and with a new regime in Nigeria that promised a return to civilian rule.

The Clinton administration has also made much of consulting with African leaders, all of whom maintain good relations with Nigeria. In the immediate aftermath of the execution of Ken Saro-Wiwa and the other Ogoni activists, South African President Nelson Mandela condemned the Nigerian actions and raised the crucial issue of oil sanctions. For a brief period it seemed that a U.S.-South African effort to pressure Nigeria for human rights and democracy might be possible and provide the leadership for more concerted international action. But Nigeria immediately mounted a countercampaign and rallied African opinion to such a degree that South Africa pulled back, leaving the United States with no African allies against Nigeria.

Politics aside, there is little question that the most effective weapon available to the United States and Europe to influence Nigerian policy was oil sanctions. With oil traded in dollars and the Nigerian government's nearly total dependence on oil revenue to maintain political control and continue its self-enrichment, a multilateral embargo would have had a direct and rapid effect on the ability of the regime to survive. But, here again, Nigerians knew it was a double-edged sword. Nigerian "sweet crude" is plentiful and low in sulfur, which means that it produces less environmental damage. The populous and politically important northeastern United States relies heavily on Nigerian oil. At a time when the United States already had oil embargoes on three other major producers (Iraq, Iran, and Libya), when the State Department was reviewing its sanctions policy worldwide, few outside of the human rights community were advocating oil sanctions against Nigeria. Virtually no one did after Abubakar acceded to power and promised new elections. Generally, except for the pro-democracy and human rights constituencies, even under Abacha little enthusiasm existed in the U.S. foreign affairs community for additional sanctions against any country, other than those that supported international terrorism or engaged in weapons proliferation. The U.S. business community, especially the oil sector, strongly opposed sanctions. It organized an antisanctions lobbying office, U.S.A.*Engage, which quickly grew to over 500 members and lobbied Congress through the U.S.-Africa Corporate Council. Support for sanctions against Nigeria was even weaker in most European countries.

Nevertheless, in the opposite direction, grass-roots sentiment had been building. State and local government sanctions, and shareholder resolutions calling on U.S. firms to limit business ties with Nigeria, continued. An independent assessment concluded that "unconfirmed estimates value the direct economic impact of the [local government and shareholder] sanctions at some $200 million in lost revenues to companies with business ties in Nigeria—notably Chevron, Coca-Cola, Mobil, Motorola, and Shell Oil."[29] Several U.S. localities adopted legislation on either restricting purchases from companies doing business with Nigeria (Amherst, Mass.; Alameda County, Berkeley, and Oakland, Calif.) or condemning the government (Cambridge, Mass., New Orleans, New York, St. Louis), as had the U.S. Conference of Mayors and two Canadian cities, Toronto and Vancouver.

Abacha's death took much of the force out of these grass-roots efforts to press for economic sanctions and blunted the arguments of those within the Clinton administration who sought stronger measures against Nigeria. Since the execution of Ken Saro-Wiwa and the other Ogoni activists in 1995, U.S. officials had maintained, at least rhetorically, that all economic sanctions, including an oil embargo, were options in an emerging strategy to protect human rights and promote democracy in Nigeria. Yet for reasons already noted, the United States did not impose more severe sanctions either through executive or legislative action. The administration was not even able to reach an internal consensus on the role that sanctions should play in its overall policy toward Nigeria.

The issues posed by Nigeria had to be weighed against a broader debate about the utility of sanctions in U.S. foreign policy. In the view of most of the foreign policy establishment, Nigeria did not threaten vital national security interests in ways that justified embargoing oil imports as was done with respect to Libya, Iran, and Iraq. The Abacha regime never indicated any interest in acquiring weapons of mass destruction or in sponsoring international terrorism. Moreover, Nigeria is not located in a region of strategic importance comparable to the Persian Gulf and Middle East. Finally, the administration realized that under prevailing circumstances, other industrial countries would not join a U.S. oil embargo aimed at forcing a change in Abacha's policies. There was even less likelihood of consensus for such action among the five permanent members of the United Nations Security Council.

There was also an ironic twist in the Nigerian situation confounding U.S. policymakers during the final months of Abacha's repression: the question of who would be his successor. Abacha had centralized power in his own hands and jailed, killed, or otherwise neutralized potential competitors, including Abiola and Yar'Adua, his two most prominent rivals, both of whom died while in detention. No obvious civilian successor or political organization with a national following appeared ready and able to take the reins of power, even if Abacha had been persuaded to abandon his plan to run as the unopposed candidate for president. Thus, the deaths of Yar'Adua, Abacha, and Abiola and the ascension of General Abubakar, who denied having personal political ambitions, created huge uncertainties about who, ultimately, would fill the political vacuum.[30] With billions in oil revenues, the military repressed or coopted opponents, domestically and abroad. Regionally, Nigeria also had bought support through foreign aid or by underwriting much of the costs of oil imports to countries in western and southern Africa. Hence, as the state became perilously weaker in the 1990s, and with Western nations unwilling to intervene, the pro-democracy and human rights forces within Nigeria become more demoralized, frustrated, and fragmented. Even under Abubakar, they were filled with doubt that the military would honor their promises and go back to barracks.

Indications of a political revival, however, began to appear during the final months of Abacha's reign, when all five of the only political parties recognized by the government nominated him as the sole candidate for president. This produced a strong reaction from a prominent group of thirty-four citizens from across the country, who warned Abacha in an open letter published in most Nigerian newspapers that he should not succeed himself or the consequences would be "outlawry and anarchy."[31] The group included former civilian elected officials, former ministers in Abacha's government, and representatives from all major ethnic groups and regions. Nigerian opposition groups, many of whom had fought with one another, also began to work together, forming the Joint Action Committee of Nigeria, a group of forty-five smaller opposition organizations, including supporters of Abiola. Even former military rulers, Gen. Ibrahim Babangida (who was responsible for annulling the 1993 elections, which precipitated the ongoing political crisis in the first place) and Gen. Muhammadu Buhari, opposed Abacha publicly. Such actions suggest that Abacha may have finally overplayed his hand, fueling unsubstantiated rumors that he may have even been poisoned by disaffected members of his inner circle.

Abacha left Nigeria in a very precarious situation. To pull Nigeria back from the brink of collapse, Abubakar and the military had to take decisive, dramatic, and irrevocable steps to restore civilian rule. For someone who rose to the top of the Nigerian military by currying favor with the likes of Abacha, this was a tall order. The United States and other members of the Atlantic Community supported a rapid transition to civilian rule and continuing postelectoral support of democracy.

Up to that time, there had been only one precedent for enlightened military leadership, backed by strong Western support, able to facilitate the restoration of democracy in Nigeria. This occurred in the late 1970s when a Yoruba from the South of the country, Gen. Olusegun Obasanjo, led the country through a lengthy process of constitutional development that culminated with national elections in 1979. Although civilian politicians fell into the traps of corruption and sectarian rivalries, the process and constitutional framework of that transition served as a precedent. Unlike what happened in the 1970s, though, the Abubakar government chose to withhold promulgation of a constitution until after the election process was completed.

Other political transitions in Africa were successfully concluded with the vigorous orchestrated support of the Western powers. During the 1970s, the United States, Great Britain, France, and other European powers had worked closely to facilitate a peaceful end to white minority rule in the southern African territories of what became Zimbabwe and Namibia. In the 1990s, the West substantially assisted democratization in South Africa well after elections for majority rule were completed. Strategies based on these precedents could be applied to support the transition to democracy in Nigeria as well. They deserve to be recalled so that every opportunity is provided to discourage a backlash in the military and strengthen civil society. Nigeria may be poised at perhaps the most critical decision point in its history. The Western powers must carefully consider alternative contingencies and mount a collective effort in preventive diplomacy, taking advantage of the transition in civilian rule in what may be the last, best hope of keeping Nigeria from slipping onto the brink of chaos, where Abacha left it.

Conclusion

The strangely coincidental deaths within a month of each other of the head of state, Gen. Sani Abacha, and his leading civilian opponent, Chief Moshood Abiola, in mid-1998 dramatically altered the political landscape. It led to a transition process which many Nigerians deemed not fully democratic, but rather a step toward civilian control. But whether these events have created sufficient political space to resolve the country's long-term political tensions peacefully is unclear. Civilian rule will commence under a cloud of controversy. According to official results, Gen. Obasanjo won 63 percent of the vote (compared with Abiola's capturing 58 percent of the 1993 vote). Some 30 million people, or 55 percent of the registered electorate, were reported to have cast ballots (as compared to 14 million voters or a 36 percent turnout in 1993). However, even election officials suspected there were about 13 million falsely registered voters, and international observers reported far lower turnout in most states. Citing these and other irregularities, former President Jimmy Carter stated, "Regrettably, therefore, it is not possible for us to make an accurate judgment about the outcome of the presidential election." [32]

There nonetheless will be general international acceptance of the election. Many Nigerians will also prefer to accept the results rather than prolong the controversy and give the military a pretext to stay in power. However, a vast section of the populace—particularly the Yoruba and the peoples of the Niger Delta—feel marginalized, angry, and alienated. The election did not succeed in bringing political legitimacy to the state or in resolving the festering structural problems that the military left in its wake.

How the new civilian government deals with these problems will be critical for the peace and prosperity of Nigeria and West Africa, and for other countries with economic, political, and humanitarian stakes in this unstable region. Transition decisions, particularly how to restrain the military from getting involved in politics, should be a primary focus of a concerted and continuing effort by the members of the Atlantic Community aimed at preventing deadly conflict and facilitating a lasting, peaceful political settlement. But the staying power of the Western powers should go beyond the transition, if it succeeds, to ensure that the Nigerian military stays out of politics for good.

Although the Nigerian situation is complex and fraught with uncertainties, actions by the military before and following the May 1999 transition to civilian rule are likely to follow one of three possible scenarios:

—The first scenario is one in which the Abubakar military government continues with a political transition that turns out to be dissimilar in form, but not in substance, from the one under way at the time of Abacha's death. The aim of that exercise was to create the appearance of change, while allowing Abacha and his cohorts to continue to control Nigeria in a "civilianized" government. Abubakar has taken steps to differentiate himself from Abacha by dismantling the illegitimate party structures and electoral processes that would have left the country with no alternative to Abacha. But there are forces within the military who are seeking a formula for protecting and advancing the military's control over what remains of the Nigerian state. The danger of course is that this "military without a military" scenario might slow, but not stop, Nigeria's slide into conflict and chaos.

—The second scenario would be a blatant reassertion of military rule, either during the transition to civilian rule or after civilians are sworn into office, which would trigger a new and more deadly round of repression. While Abubakar appears to recognize the breadth and depth of the country's longing for an end to military rule, at least in its current form, there may well be others in his ruling council or in the lower ranks who see no better alternative. This, after all, has been the pattern over three decades of successive military rulers in Nigeria. Given the military's lack of political legitimacy, a military comeback, even under a benevolent strongman with a plausible claim to the standard of Ghana's Jerry Rawlings, would be hard-pressed to consolidate power in Nigeria. The one issue on which all Nigerians across ethnic, religious, and regional lines are agreed upon is that the military must go. The opposition would surely go underground and become violent, attacking oil installations and other vulnerable state assets. Nigeria would, under this "resurgence of repression leading to chaos" scenario, almost inevitably become a political and humanitarian catastrophe.

—The last scenario is one that offers some hope of averting the worse cases outlined above. Realistically, the only chance for putting Nigeria back on track is for the Abubakar-led transition to restore full constitutional democracy by May 29, 1999, and for the new civilian regime to act. It must be politically inclusive, curb corruption, decentralize power, and revive the economy. It will not be easy. After thirty years of increasingly oppressive, secretive, and corrupt military rule, pent-up popular grievances and suspicions demand a rapid and complete political transformation, with broad-based participation of all segments of Nigeria's diverse society. This will require an open process and complex negotiations to build consensus and political confidence.

The United States and those European governments with significant economic, political, and humanitarian interests at stake in Nigeria should focus their policies on influencing the military's actions affecting the prospects for each of these three contingencies. Clearly, genuine fulfillment of the third scenario is the most desirable for Nigerians, West Africans, and for the rest of the international community, all of whom should rally in support of a democratically elected government. Members of the Atlantic Community should consider resurrecting a consultative and policy coordinating process similar to that which helped facilitate democratic transitions in southern Africa. This need not take place at the level of foreign minister or higher, a habit that naturally developed for regional conflicts during the cold war and may still be appropriate for troubled states where weapons of mass destruction or other strategic interests are at stake. In the case of Nigeria, the hard work of preventive diplomacy may be better left to officials at the sub-cabinet level. But the effort must be energetic, sustained, well coordinated, and supported at the highest levels. To give this coordination structure and process, those countries most concerned—notably the United States, Great Britain, and France—should consider forming a "Contact" or "Friends of Nigeria" group. This could include other European states as well as those countries from the region, such as Ghana or South Africa, which also have vital stakes in Nigeria achieving a successful democratic transition. Such a group of like-minded states must also be sufficiently well organized and staffed to maintain regular contact with other interested parties, including the United Nations Secretariat, relevant UN specialized agencies, key African states and regional and subregional organizations, the most influential local and transnational nongovernmental organizations involved in Nigeria's transition, and the leaders of the international oil companies who, despite their intense competitiveness, share a common interest in reinstating the rule of law and due process in Nigeria.

The prevention agenda will be long and complicated. Ensuring the credibility of the military's promise to return to the barracks and stay there is critical. Military officials serving in high government positions must not be allowed to stand for political office for a specified number of years, including after they retire.[33] To build public confidence this ban may have to be imposed retroactively, at least to cover the period since the last national election that the military designed and then overthrew. The ambitions of current and retired military leaders are already evident and a source of popular unease. For example, Abacha's immediate predecessor, Gen. Ibrahim Babangida, is widely believed to have backed Obasanjo financially and is said to be still interested in returning to power some day. Although chances that he would ever win a free and fair national election are extremely slim, he may have sufficient resources and influence to corrupt the process and contrive another thinly veiled military takeover. At the same time, there is hope that Gen. Olusegun Obasanjo, who led the country back to civilian rule in 1979, will restrain the military and foster national reconciliation.

Members of the Atlantic Community have a window of opportunity to encourage a peaceful democratic transformation of Nigeria, but it must be carried out quickly, with governments taking the lead. The target of influence should be focused initially on guaranteeing that the Nigerian military ensures a peaceful transition to civilian rule. Emphasis should focus thereafter on the successor government, rebuilding professionalism and integrity of state institutions, and civil society, to ensure that the transition lasts.

Western powers should also press for a new constitutional formula to restore confidence among diverse and mutually suspicious groups. The Abacha constitution, which was not published during his reign, lacked legitimacy and was highly controversial. It proposed a complex system of regional or ethnic rotation of office, which may have the effect of entrenching rather than relieving ethnic rivalry. Constitution making is a process that must be driven by Nigerians, but Western allies can offer assistance that helps ensure that there is a shift from the rule of soldiers to the rule of law.

Western powers must also recognize the risk that the transition might be overthrown by reactionary military elements. Western powers must adhere to a common set of policies and principles and be prepared to offer a mixture of sufficiently attractive incentives and disincentives to influence local decisions. Incentives could include debt relief, aid in creating decentralized and accountable institutions and formulas for distribution of oil revenues, support for privatization and private foreign investment, infrastructure investment, and improved cooperation on a range of international activities and issues of mutual concern, including crime, drug trafficking, and corruption. In addition, military assistance could be considered under a democratic regime, especially in training for regional peacekeeping, public health, disaster relief, and civic action programs.[34]

If things go wrong, however, stiff measures may need to be taken. The allies should be prepared to act collectively to impose selected and targeted sanctions, if there is serious backsliding. These may include a ban on new investment, tighter travel restrictions, freezing the assets of the military elites, a sports ban, and—if all else fails—an oil embargo. As undesirable as that might be, it would be far preferable to Nigeria collapsing into chaos or acquiring more of the violent and criminal attributes of a failed state.

The United States should take the lead in building an allied effort, especially in light of the potential for positive change in the midst of a still shaky transition. In the other countries included in this study, the time has clearly passed for preventive diplomacy; the Western allies are at odds over how to approach Iraq, Iran, Libya, and Cuba. Nigeria has not yet reached that stage, and, indeed, may be able to avoid it. However, if it were to become a rogue state or a failed one, even under civilian rule, domestic and international factors would put the United States on the defensive for not having acted sooner, particularly during a time of unprecedented opportunity. Criticism in the United States would come primarily from human rights activists and the African-American community, dividing the United States even further from its Western allies.

Nigeria and the Western allies are at a critical decision point. Traditional friends of Nigeria have the opportunity to work with internal leaders to contain the forces for disintegration, foster regional and economic security, and promote long-term access of the West to oil supplies in a stable political environment.

Without a proactive allied effort, short-term parochial forces could drive policies not only in Nigeria but also within and among the members of the Atlantic Community. Rivalry by U.S. and European corporations to gain commercial advantage through a "wait and see" or competitive approach could undermine a comprehensive strategy toward Nigeria. If transatlantic competition for short-term commercial gain is allowed to prevail over effective diplomacy, then the West will simply play into the hands of the military hard-liners who are far more likely to lead Nigeria toward the darker scenarios of chaos, conflict, and state collapse. In the end, the West would probably be drawn in anyway, but at the worst possible time.

Notes

1. For information about the Nigerian Civil War and its international dimensions see AHM Kirk-Greene, *Crisis and Conflict in Nigeria: A Documentary Sourcebook 1966–1970,* 2 vols. (London: Oxford University Press, 1971); John de St. Jorre, *The Nigerian Civil War* (London: Hodder and Stoughton, 1972); and John J. Stremlau, *The International Politics of the Nigerian Civil War, 1967–1970* (Princeton University Press, 1977).

2. The term "complex emergency" emerged in the corridors of the UN General Assembly during negotiations in the early 1990s to establish the Department of Humanitarian Affairs. The term is ambiguous because it is often used to describe both the complex origins and nature of the conflict itself, as well as the complexity of the international response and engagement in attempting to ameliorate human suffering and contain local conflict. What is different about the 1967–70 Nigerian Civil War and most post–cold war humanitarian emergencies is not the complexity of local forces that spawn mass violence but the scope and nature of the international response. Before 1990, the intervention to aid Biafra was nearly unique; now complex interventions may occur at the rate of twenty to twenty-five a year, usually under the broad umbrella of a mandate by the UN or other international organizations. Also, the principle of noninterference in the internal affairs of sovereign states was widely accepted in international affairs; in the 1990s, there is less tolerance for sustaining that principle in the face of "ethnic cleansing," genocide, and mass starvation.

3. Gen. Sani Abacha died suddenly on June 8, 1998, without an autopsy or an official explanation of the cause of his death. Within twenty-four hours, Maj. Gen. Abdulsalam Abubakar, 55, was sworn in as Nigeria's tenth head of state. A member of a northern minority group from Minna in the Middle Belt, Abubakar was a member of the Provisional Ruling Council, a committee of top army officers, and a close ally of the former head of state, Maj. Gen. Ibrahim Babangida. Abubakar had never held a political post. He was the chief of defense staff but not Nigeria's most senior officer. In order to become president, he had to be promoted to full general.

4. The 1967–70 war over Biafran secession ended with a decisive federal military victory. Despite the deaths of well over an estimated 1 million people, there were no recriminations, and reconciliation was swift. Rapid development of Nigeria's vast oil reserves generated huge sums for reconstruction and development that over the next twenty years exceeded $250 billion for a country with a population that had grown to approximately 110 million, with an educated elite second only to South Africa, and an agriculturally rich territory four times larger than the United Kingdom. Nigeria of the early 1970s was poised to become Africa's leader and a country of great international influence. Instead, there was a succession of increasingly repressive and corrupt military dictatorships, interrupted only by four years of inept but democratically elected leadership. As a result, Nigeria in the 1990s was driven to the verge of ruin.

5. For a vivid and compelling account of the history of Nigeria's political failures, see Wole Soyinka, *An Open Sore of a Continent: A Personal Narrative of the Nigerian Crisis* (Oxford University Press, 1997).

6. U.S. Government, *Global Humanitarian Emergencies, 1996,* released by the U.S. Mission to the United Nations, February 1996, "Possible New Humanitarian Emergencies in 1996," pp. 17–18.

7. Howard W. French, "The Enemy Within: Dictator's Arrest of His Aides Shows Nigeria's Unsteadiness," *New York Times,* December 24, 1997, p. 6.

8. John N. Paden gave the estimate of Nigeria's brain drain in testimony before the Subcommittees on Africa and International Operations and Human Rights of the House Committee on International Relations, December 12, 1995, 104 Cong. 1 sess. (Government Printing Office, 1996).

9. For a detailed account of Nigeria's human rights violations at the time, see "Nigeria: Transition or Travesty?" *Human Rights Watch,* vol. 9 (October 1997). For a discussion of the analytical model, see Pauline H. Baker and John A. Ausink, "State Collapse and Ethnic Violence: Toward a Predictive Model," *Parameters,* vol. 26 (Spring 1996), pp. 19–31. For an updated version, see Pauline H. Baker and Angeli Weller, *An Analytical Model of Internal Conflict and State Collapse: Manual for Practitioners* (Washington: The Fund for Peace, 1998).

10. Peter M. Lewis, a professor at American University, Washington, D.C., compiled this information for the Center of Preventive Action of the Council on Foreign Relations. General Abubakar told his newly appointed cabinet at its swearing-in ceremony on August 22, 1998, that "every human-welfare and development index measuring the well-being of our people is on the decline." "First Things First," *Economist,* August 29, 1998, p. 45.

11. Gen. Abdulsalam Abubakar effectively scrapped the petroleum ministry, which over the years had won a reputation for being the most corrupt part of government, and transferred all its responsibilities to the office of the presidency. The move gave more power to both Abubakar and the state-run Nigerian National Petroleum Corporation (NNPC), run by a northerner, Dalhatu Bayero.

12. Abacha sentenced Diya to death, but Abubakar later commuted the sentence for him and other officers involved in the alleged plot to twenty-five years in prison. After the elections were completed in February 1999, Abubakar released Diya and ninety-five other prisoners.

13. However, U.S. officials concluded that Abacha's rigging of the election combined with the sagging economy and imprisonment of political opponents led to significantly rising tensions and that the purported transition could no longer be depicted as democratic. Thomas W. Lippman, "U.S. to Appeal to Nigeria to Launch Democratic Reforms," *Washington Post,* May 29, 1998, p. A4.

14. Although that risk had subsided with the conduct of violence-free elections in 1999, many unresolved issues remained.

15. For example, Dr. Beko Ransome-Kuti, chairman of the Campaign for Democracy, said he was unimpressed by the democratization moves of Abubakar

because he "was part and parcel of the Babangida and Abacha regimes." He insisted that the only way to resolve Nigeria's problems was to convene a sovereign national conference and form a government of national unity. See *Nigeria Today*, August 28, 1998, p. 3.

16. For a summary of Nigeria's foreign policy during this period, see Stremlau, *The International Politics of the Nigerian Civil War*, chap. 1.

17. For an account of Nigeria's expanding role in West Africa, see Pauline H. Baker, "A Giant Staggers: Nigeria as an Emerging Regional Power," in Bruce E. Arlinghaus, ed., *African Security Issues: Sovereignty, Stability and Solidarity* (Westview Press, 1984), pp. 76–88. For a summary of the expansive role of Nigeria in West Africa by the 1990s, see Howard W. French, "West Africa Trembles with Nigeria," *New York Times*, June 14, 1998, p. 6.

18. Nigerian radio broadcast August 3, 1997, as reported in FBIS-AFR-97-215, August 5, 1997. Interestingly, there has been little significant internal debate over Nigeria's peacekeeping activities. However, these factors are likely to lead a civilian government to reduce Nigeria's peacekeeping activities.

19. Lippman, "U.S. to Appeal to Nigerian Ruler to Launch Democratic Reforms." Ironically, the trip did not accomplish its intended goal. Instead of pressing the Abubakar regime to release Abiola and move toward democracy, U.S. officials became embroiled in the controversy surrounding Abiola's death. He was stricken with a heart attack while conferring with the Americans. The military had been pressuring Abiola to renounce his claim to the presidency as a condition of his release, but he refused. When U.S. officials announced that Abiola collapsed while they were talking to him and that they were sure that he had died of natural causes, they were accused of playing into the hands of the military, who, many Yorubas believed, wanted Abiola out of the way. Despite confirmation by an international team who performed the autopsy that Abiola had indeed died from a heart attack, his supporters clung to the belief that the military was responsible. Some maintained that the military induced the heart attack through poison; others faulted the military for failing to provide Abiola with medical attention during his detention.

20. See, for example, the April 24, 1998, letter to President Clinton rejecting the administration's "constructive engagement" accommodation with the Nigerian military, which called for unilateral oil sanctions. It was signed by twelve prominent African-Americans, including Julian Bond, Ambassador Walter Carrington, Kweisi Mfume, Donald Payne, Randall Robinson, Maxine Waters, Tilden LeMelle, Bill Lucy, Gay McDougall, and Wyatt Tee Walker, and supported by TransAfrica and the Africa Fund. However, other African-Americans opposed stiffer measures, including Jesse Jackson, who was President Clinton's special envoy on democracy in Africa, and Senator Carol Moseley-Braun, the only African-American member of the U.S. Senate.

21. See David Smock, "Can Nigeria Make a Peaceful Transition to Demo-

cratic Governance?" Special Report, Washington, U.S. Institute of Peace, December 1997, p. 5.

22. "NLNG Plans Big Gas Expansion in Nigeria," *Nigeria Today*, Internet news service, May 29, 1998, p. 4.

23. Ibid.

24. For a discussion of what U.S. policymakers consider to be the characteristics of a rogue state, see former National Security Advisor Anthony Lake's essay "Confronting Backlash States" in *Foreign Affairs*, vol. 73 (March–April 1994), p. 45. For a brief discussion of the inapplicability of the term for Nigeria, see John N. Paden's statement before the Subcommittees on Africa and International Operations and Human Rights, December 12, 1995, p. 111, which highlights Nigeria's positive international role. He notes, "Even ardent Nigerian critics say Nigeria is 'good abroad, bad at home.'"

25. John Cook, "Welcome to the New! and Improved! Nigeria," *Mother Jones*, vol. 23 (January–February 1998), p. 51.

26. Africa Watch, PEN, Amnesty International, the Sierra Club, and other groups belong to national and multilateral organizations and have found allies. For good independent assessments of Nigeria's bleak human rights situation, see Amnesty International's *Nigeria: No Significant Change—Human Rights Violations Continue*, AFR 44/20/97 (London: Amnesty International, September 22, 1997), and "Nigeria: Transition or Travesty?"

27. See Adonis Hoffman, "Politics to Statesmanship: Moseley-Braun Does the Right Thing with Vote on Nigeria," *Chicago Tribune*, May 20, 1996, p. 15.

28. The Nigeria Democracy and Civil Society Empowerment Act of 1998 (S. 2102/HR 3890) was sponsored by only four cosponsors in the Senate and two cosponsors in the House when it was introduced.

29. See "Human Rights Concerns Dog Nigeria," *IRRC Corporate Social Issues Reporter*, October 1997, p.12.

30. Abubakar was selected to head the government after Abacha's death, in part because he had a reputation of being a soldier without political ambitions. On a visit to South Africa, he stated that the thought of running for the presidency "had never crossed [his] mind." See "Nigeria Announces Election Dates and Rules," *Nigeria Today*, Internet news service, August 26, 1998.

31. "34 Prominent Nigerians Warn Abacha over Presidency," *Nigerian News Du Jour*, Internet news service, May 12, 1998, p. 2. In August 1998, this group formed a new political party, the People's Democratic Party, although a Yoruba grouping, the People's Consultative Forum, pulled out. See *Nigeria Today*, August 28, 1998, p. 3.

32. James Rupert, "Nigeria Confirms Vote Result," *Washington Post*, March 2, 1999, p. A14.

33. Nearly a dozen retired generals won seats in the 109-member Senate in the February 1999 parliamentary elections.

34. Because of Nigeria's poor record on human rights and democratization, it had been excluded from participation in the African Crisis Response Initiative (ACRI), the Clinton administration's program for strengthening the peacekeeping capabilities of African states. Under a democratic regime and with a reformed military that becomes more professional, Nigeria could be included in this initiative. Indeed, a democratic Nigeria could reclaim its historical role as a leader in resolving conflicts in the continent.

ANTONY GOLDMAN

11

Nigeria: Many Problems, Few Solutions

Nigeria matters. With a population estimated by the United Nations at over 100 million, Nigeria is by some margin Africa's most populous nation. It is also the continent's leading oil producer; indeed, current output of more than 2 million barrels a day places it comfortably inside the ten biggest oil exporters in the world. Economically and militarily, it dominates a region endemically unstable and impoverished. Historically, it has with confidence claimed a leadership role in Africa, in particular over the struggle for majority rule in the South. In recent years, Nigerian syndicates have also occupied an increasingly high profile in international organized crime, particularly the trade in illegal drugs and fraud. Since independence from Great Britain in 1960, Nigeria has witnessed one civil war, three constitutions—with a fourth on the way—six successful military coups, and innumerable unsuccessful plots. Stable civilian government has proved elusive in a society with a myriad of religious, ethnic, regional, linguistic, and class fault lines. Although Nigeria's civil war took place thirty years ago, the extent of the chaos and dislocation then continues to serve as a reminder that the consequences of a fundamental erosion of the state might prove so catastrophic as to draw in many outside interests. In the post–cold war environment, it is that endangered species, a developing country that has retained its geostrategic importance.

This chapter explores the historical perspective from which European states have approached policy toward Nigeria and the extent to which this created tension between Europe and the United States. It considers the difficult relations with the government of the late head of state, Gen. Sani Abacha (1993–98) as a case study in Western impotence. It also considers the factors likely to influence policy, the options now open to European decisionmakers, and whether a significant cleavage with the United States is likely to occur.

Europe and Nigeria: Common Policy versus National Interest

European states have been involved in West African affairs for five hundred years. As the former colonial power, Britain has a historical association with the territory now known as Nigeria that stretches back 120 years. Its interests in Nigeria far surpass those of other European Union (EU) member states, although in recent years that preeminence has to a degree been undermined. Britain is Nigeria's biggest bilateral creditor, with debts outstanding of around $6 billion, and is its main source of imports.[1] Britain maintains the largest foreign embassy in Nigeria and processes more visa applications than all other EU countries. Until the early 1990s, military ties between the two countries were especially close, with many senior officers receiving training in Britain. There are also close links with the political and business elite, while several hundred thousand people of Nigerian birth reside in Britain.

Several other EU members also have significant and sometimes contradictory interests in Nigeria. With the collapse of communism in the 1980s, the old-style, informal arrangement of postcolonial influence, by which Britain and the United States occupied a senior position in Nigeria, began to unravel. In Nigeria as elsewhere, there is now new competition in the diplomatic and commercial arena from a variety of sources inside Europe and farther afield. Germany is Nigeria's second biggest creditor, while France and Italy also have official loans outstanding of more than a billion dollars. Nigeria is also one of Germany's biggest markets in Africa. In the energy sector, private French companies have upstream and downstream interests as significant as anywhere in the world, as have their Italian counterparts. From 1999 onward, Italy will purchase $500 million of gas a year from Nigeria, and Nigeria will be Spain's second most important source of crude oil. Commercial considerations, therefore, have become an increasingly important influence on diplomatic relations for several EU states. In addition, France pursued, with some success, a long-standing regional agenda to raise its profile in Nigeria, an Anglophone country in an otherwise predominantly French-speaking region.[2]

Anatomy of a Problem

Since independence, Nigerian governments have on a number of occasions found themselves at odds with members of the international community over aspects of domestic policy. In the 1960s, speculation surrounding France's alleged support for Biafra's unsuccessful bid to secede during the civil war badly soured relations, as did the bungled effort by Nigeria to kidnap a former government minister from Britain in 1984. Broadly, however, there was a consensus in the West to support a strong, unitary Nigeria, even under military rule, as the most likely guarantor of a range of interests, which included the following:

—Strategic/defense. During and after the cold war, policymakers have judged a militarily powerful, West-leaning Nigeria as a useful ally in promoting regional stability and a potentially useful counterweight to South Africa and the emerging countries of northern Africa, as well as a secular bulwark against creeping Islamic radicalism in parts of western and eastern Africa.

—Energy/commerce. Nigeria is, and will remain, a globally significant producer of oil and natural gas. This provides lucrative opportunities to Western companies and also affects the world energy market. Oil revenue also makes Nigeria potentially one of the richest economies in sub-Saharan Africa, with enticing opportunities for the private sector in a range of industries, including telecommunications, manufacturing, pharmaceuticals, and defense.

—Human rights/democracy. In Nigeria, democracy has been a goal toward which successive administrations—civilian and military—have aspired more than achieved. In the post–cold war era, democracy and human rights have come increasingly to dominate the public policy agenda in the West toward Africa, however, which leaves the army's de facto tenureship at the center of government for all but four of the last thirty-two years increasingly problematic for officials under pressure from liberal, domestic constituencies.

—Drugs/international crime. During the past decade, Western governments have shared a growing concern about the rise of organized criminal networks of Nigerian origin that have increasingly come to dominate drug trafficking and fraud.

Nigeria under Abacha:
A Case Study in Western Impotence

Under the five-year military regime of Gen. Sani Abacha—who seized power in controversial circumstances in 1993 after the army annulled presidential elections—an already precarious situation in Nigeria deteriorated further. An unprecedented strain was placed on relations with the West, which nevertheless proved unable to produce an effective and united policy in support of muddled and sometimes conflicting national and commercial interests. It is, therefore, worth considering what Europeans, individually and collectively, found "difficult" about the former administration in Nigeria. Abacha's departure and its legacy affecting policy should also be studied.[3]

In Europe as elsewhere, critics of General Abacha generally focused on his record on democracy, human rights, corruption, and organized crime. They argued that Western policy must call to account a regime that failed to meet criteria for good governance and accountability on which EU members formally base their Africa policy. In particular, there was pressure on the Labor government in Britain elected in 1997 to honor its commitment to an ethical foreign policy. Critics complained that failure to act firmly would hasten the collapse of a state already in an advanced state of decay, with dire consequences not only for Nigeria but also for much of western Africa.

There is much evidence to support such a critique. General Abacha played a key role in his predecessor's decision to annul presidential elections in 1993 and ruled in a manner arbitrary even by the standards of a military government. He relied on cooption, coercion, and repression to maintain security, further undermining already shaky institutional integrity by establishing his own decisionmaking networks independent of government and military structures. Allegations of a manipulated political process were matched by complaints of human rights abuses. Most prominent among these was the execution in November 1995 of the minority rights activist Ken Saro-Wiwa and eight colleagues. General Abacha also used formal and informal instruments to undermine Nigeria's traditionally vibrant free press, dismantling organized labor and eroding the independence of the judiciary, dealing with his most vigorous opponents through special tribunals, detaining others without charge, and in some instances, sanctioning extrajudicial executions.

Abacha's political program lacked constitutional legitimacy, resembling by the end little more than an empty vehicle to enable his transformation from military ruler to elected president. Popular response to the transition was marked by apathy, with low turnout for local, state, and federal elections held in March and December 1997 amid familiar accusations of rigging, fraud, and influence peddling.[4] Although the constituent assembly charged with drafting a new (Fourth Republic) constitution completed its work in June 1995, its findings were never released, making it impossible to judge the rules under which Nigeria would be governed. The legal basis on which the five registered political parties agreed in April 1998 to select General Abacha as their consensus candidate was, for example, unclear, and the parties themselves acquired little legitimacy.

The United States and others have complained about the increasing evidence linking Nigerian networks to the global trade in illegal drugs, principally heroin but also cocaine. Privately, U.S. Drug Enforcement Agency officers in Nigeria say the problem has grown more acute in the past five years, with the country now a major transit point and clearing destination for dirty money. According to one official, more than 70 percent of the global heroin trade is organized by Nigerians.[5] This appears not to generate the same concern in Europe as on the other side of the Atlantic. In a separate indication of the growth of organized crime, the intelligence services in Britain have undertaken a new initiative to combat fraud and welfare abuses linked to Nigerians and said to cost the country a billion dollars a year.[6]

Such arguments, however, have had only a limited effect on policy. As will be discussed below, while sanctions adopted by the EU against

General Abacha's administration were far tougher than measures implemented by the United States, they were nevertheless limited in scope,
routinely ignored, and questionable in value, when it came to influencing developments in a manner regarded as positive by policymakers.
The Abacha years exposed the wide differences that exist within and
between European countries over the strategic objectives of Nigeria policy
and the tactical measures to be adopted in pursuit of such objectives.

Unlike other rogue states accused of posing a threat to regional and
international stability, such as Sudan or Iraq, Nigeria's military rulers
have been in the vanguard of successful peacekeeping efforts in a host of
African countries and maintain warm relations with several neighboring elected governments. Critics of General Abacha usually regarded
the tension between apparent repression at home and enlightenment
abroad as a paradox. It could, however, be argued that the image of
constitutional democracy that Nigeria supported in neighboring states
masked a collection of potentially unstable, thinly disguised dictator-
ships characterized by their loyalty to and dependence on Nigeria. For
while Nigeria led efforts to restore the elected government of Sierra
Leone in 1998, it actively courted the leaders of coups in Gambia in
1994 and Niger in 1996, indicating the general's preference for a regional security framework based more strongly on almost feudal-style
fealty than institutional democracy.

Nigeria also shares the concerns of some of its most vigorous critics
over the growth of radical Islam and has constituted a bulwark in efforts
to prevent its spread from north Africa and the Middle East to the predominantly Islamic populations of most west African countries. Efforts
to proselytize in Nigeria by radical Islamic groups have been met with
uncompromising firmness and violence by Nigeria's conservative, Muslim ruling elite, to whom potentially they present a very real threat.
However, while opposition to Islamic fundamentalism may garner as
much favor in Europe as in the United States, the government's exclusively security-oriented strategies have failed to deal with the underlying socioeconomic causes behind the rise in radical Islam in northern
Nigeria. It merely suppresses tensions that may yet explode.

Some officials even in states most hostile toward General Abacha,
such as Britain, argued that narrowly focusing on the shortcomings of
his government was overly simplistic: General Abacha's success—and
excesses—had not occurred in a vacuum but had rather reflected a wider

malaise in which the civilian political class and the established military hierarchy had failed to resolve fundamental tensions inhibiting the establishment of a stable constitutional system. Unlike Chile under General Augusto Pinochet or the present regime in Burma, a brittle civil society has succumbed not only to repression but also to cooption and factionalism, creating a crisis of leadership that has deepened popular skepticism. Although Abacha's government was in the formal sense a dictatorship, the coalition of constituencies on which General Abacha depended extended well beyond a northern, Islamic, conservative, military elite.

Indeed, some of the policies for which he was most reviled were in fact no more than extensions of what his predecessors had practiced. The assault on what is arguably Africa's most lively press may have intensified under General Abacha, but the assassination of the publisher of the independent weekly *Newswatch*, Dele Giwa, that is widely blamed on state security agents, took place in 1986, seven years before Abacha came to power. Although Abacha's proposed transition was widely criticized, his predecessor also sought to control the political environment, sanctioning only two parties that received funding from and had their manifestos written by the state. The security legislation Abacha used freely to deal with opponents was actually drafted by Gen. Olusegun Obasanjo, a former head of state widely respected abroad for relinquishing power to civilians in 1979.

Soundbite Diplomacy:
A Policy without Vision or Conviction

General Abacha's government did, however, increasingly begin to challenge some of the orthodoxies on which Western policy toward Nigeria had long been based. His proposals for self-succession challenged the convenient illusion that the military's occupation of power was not in conflict with the theoretical desirability of a conventional, civilian dispensation. In addition, his efforts at coopting the political class further undermined its already low popular credibility and limited self-confidence, highlighting its uncertain capacity to foster a system of government sufficiently robust and effective to prevent renewed military intervention. At the same time, the marginalization of several constituencies—the Yoruba elite, communities in the oil-producing Niger Delta, and an increasingly impoverished Islamic North—combined with accelerated economic decay created sometimes violent tensions with potential to undermine the fabric of Nigeria as a unitary state. Western oil companies also grew increasingly frustrated over the arbitrary and increasingly inefficient way in which the sector had been managed.[7] In turn this policy helped further depress the economy, limiting other Western commercial interests at a time when an awkward diplomatic environment constricted normally close and lucrative defense ties. This sense of unease within Europe and the United States over developments in Nigeria pointed to several scenarios, each of which remains problematic:

—A stable, democratic Nigeria, with a thriving, increasingly open economy. Support for such a scenario was publicly easy for Western powers. It proved more difficult to adopt measures to encourage such a move, however, in a country as divided over language, ethnicity, religion, class, and region as Nigeria, which has such a marked absence of democratic institutions. Indeed, previous efforts at civilian rule—the First Republic (1960–66) and the Second Republic (1979–83)—fell well short of most accepted criteria for democracy, and served to weaken further the concept of a stable, unitary Nigeria.

—An authoritarian, military-ruled Nigeria. Long accepted as the status quo and a precondition for stability in a country in which the civilian political class had proved so lacking, General Abacha judged that long-term stability could only be established by formally merging the military into the constitutional process. The path of self-succession was a pattern that had been repeated with some success and much Western support elsewhere in western Africa, for example, in Ghana, Burkina Faso, and Chad. Policymakers found it difficult to endorse such developments in Nigeria, however, given Abacha's track record on governance, human rights, and the economy, which also seemed likely to hasten the ultimate demise of the state.[8]

—The ethnic fragmentation of Nigeria. In a process similar to that which contributed to the collapse of the former Soviet Union and former Yugoslavia, the increasing atrophy of the state and disenfranchisement of citizens, and the difficulty in identifying any form of workable system to preserve a government increasingly built around the military's near monopoly on the exercise of force, has created concern over the viability of the Nigerian state. However, and although the three largest ethnic groups together constitute the majority in Nigeria, intragroup differences are sharp, and several minority communities equally have no wish to return to the regional domination characteristic of the First Republic.[9] This means that the collapse of the state would likely prove immensely difficult to manage, with potential for violence and dislocation on a massive scale, creating a crisis well beyond Nigeria's borders, which, although not directly affecting energy interests, would probably force a reluctant, costly, and difficult external intervention on humanitarian grounds.

This unpalatable array of options unfolding under General Abacha created a superficial veneer of unity within Europe that masked a multitude of divisions and empty commitments, with a pronounced lack of clarity over the ultimate goal of a common policy and how best it ought to be achieved. Broadly, the EU publicly declared itself in favor of an end to military rule and the establishment of a stable democracy built upon the rule of law, transparency, and respect for human rights. This, however, was also General Abacha's stated aim, and neither the EU or Abacha seemed clear as to how such noble ambitions could be translated into practical reality in the context of a society as divided as that in Nigeria, with a civilian political class so discredited and corrupted as twice before to have prompted coups widely welcomed by the public. Although radical opposition groups enjoyed some credibility abroad, they have very little profile in Nigeria itself. The movement was weakened by the detention of key leaders; more serious damage, however, was created by the willingness of some prodemocracy activists to be coopted by General Abacha, the domination of the movement by people from the Southwest, and the perpetual, personality-based infighting amongst the plethora of groups claiming to carry the challenge to military rule.

European powers, therefore, found themselves criticizing aspects of government in Nigeria without grasping the fundamental problem of how the country might escape its grim past of perpetual instability and institutionalized corruption. Rightly, they expressed skepticism over the prospect of General Abacha's transition delivering a stable democracy and acknowledged the gathering potential for a descent into chaos. They urged an easing of repression, the release of political prisoners, and the opening up of the political process. They offered little insight, however, as to how democracy could be achieved and sustained, with many in European policymaking circles conceding that neither inducements nor threats would influence the then government.

European policy was, as a result, half-hearted, driven to some degree by the legacy of international media pressure that surrounded two pivotal events: the annulment of the 1993 elections by a government in which General Abacha was a prominent member, and the execution of Ken Saro-Wiwa in 1995, an event regarded by General Abacha's opponents as symbolic of all that was worst about a regime apparently prepared to use violence and state repression freely to pursue its agenda. These two incidents prompted all the measures now in place against Nigeria by the EU.[10] Policy was defensive and reactive, created in response to wider media and lobby pressure generated by environmental groups over the fate of Ken Saro-Wiwa for the kind of soundbite diplomacy that demanded that "something" be done.

Indeed, while diplomats dismissed suggestions made by Tom Ikimi, then Nigeria's foreign minister, and others that foreign powers were involved in an alleged coup plot in late 1997, many believed that relations with Nigeria would only warm once General Abacha was out of office. They believed that with the present transition so flawed, and with the army the only political force to have retained any institutional integrity during the past thirty years, renewed political intervention by Nigeria's military would prove inevitable in the short to medium term. The hope was that a new, more accommodating personality would assume power. This apparent abdication of initiative on the part of some policymakers reflected not only a lack of clarity but also a recognition of the absence of easy levers and achievable goals to influence a particularly stubborn government.

Defining Policy: Weakness and Division

Policy by EU members toward Nigeria in recent years defies easy characterization. Briefly following the execution of Ken Saro-Wiwa in 1995, there was pressure to move toward the complete isolation of Nigeria, a pressure resisted by most European governments on the grounds that it might worsen rather than improve the situation. The cooling of media interest in Nigeria and waning environmentalist pressure subsequently allowed the remaining external influence on EU governments—the business lobby—to appeal to naturally cautious instincts of diplomats. Sanctions imposed in 1993–95, however, limited the opportunities for constructive engagement and dialogue. Relations might best be described as cool, although in critical situations, such as the response to the coup in Sierra Leone in May 1997, Britain, like the United States, worked closely with the Nigerian military over efforts to repatriate foreigners.

This ambiguity was keenly exploited by General Abacha's government. With some justification, ministers in Britain, for example, were accused of following the U.S. fashion for using foreign policy issues to play out parochial, domestic political concerns; issuing loud but empty rhetorical condemnations of Nigeria to curry favor with liberally inclined middle-class voters rather than adopting a genuine policy. In contrast to Britain, other EU member states with commercial and strategic aspirations in Nigeria—such as France, Italy, and Spain—were far more moderate in their public pronouncements and private deliberations.

Limited Levers, Limited Measures

In 1993 the EU introduced a ban on issuing visas to government officials and serving military officers in response to (and effectively as a punishment for) the annulment of presidential elections.[11] In mid-1995, unspecified measures were threatened if a controversial tribunal into an alleged coup plot ended with the execution of a well-connected former head of state, Gen. Olusegun Obasanjo. In any event, death sentences were commuted, with voices in Europe and the United States lauding the value of "quiet diplomacy." In November 1995, despite similar appeals from the West, Nigeria's military rulers proceeded with the execution of Ken Saro-Wiwa and other Ogoni activists, prompting a huge international outcry and the adoption of tougher measures, including the temporary withdrawal of heads of mission, a sporting ban, and a tightening of visa restrictions.

The handling of the Obasanjo and Saro-Wiwa cases is instructive: while at the time some diplomats felt their influence helped save the former head of state, it appears now that domestic factors determined the approach adopted by Nigeria's military authorities. Obasanjo, while politically awkward and internationally well-connected, enjoyed limited support in the army and even in his native Southwest and presented little real threat to General Abacha's position or to the security of his regime.[12] The execution of one former military ruler by a serving military ruler would also have set an uncomfortable precedent. Clemency might have helped appease critics abroad, while the commuting of death sentences to long prison terms would ensure that Obasanjo and his former deputy, the politically ambitious and equally well-connected Gen. Musa Yar'Adua, would nevertheless ensure that a potential challenge to the government could be dulled. Ken Saro-Wiwa, however, posed something close to a genuinely revolutionary threat to the survival of Nigeria in its present form. Although a figure of no national prominence, his campaign for the rights of the Ogoni people had begun to open debate on how little minority communities in Nigeria benefit from the state, something that might ultimately have led to demands for autonomy, self-determination, or even independence from a remote, centralized federal structure. For a clique of generals schooled in a civil war to preserve the integrity of Nigeria, the choice did not prove difficult to make, and there is little to suggest that international pressure made the government even hesitate, although the scale of the international response clearly came as a surprise.

EU Policy: A Qualified Failure?

European policy toward Nigeria under General Abacha, while tougher than that adopted by the United States, appears to have had at best only very limited success: the political process remained carefully managed; prominent political figures remained in detention; allegations of human rights abuses persisted; drug trafficking was an increasing problem; and prospects for a stable democracy in the medium and long term were not improved.

Part of the problem facing policymakers appeared to be a lack of confidence in the effectiveness of measures adopted to encourage policy objectives. Indeed, the sporting ban imposed in 1995, which might actually have carried some weight in Nigeria, was first bent and then effectively abandoned by EU member states. Reasons for the shift in thinking appear connected to political expediency rather than any particular change in Nigeria. Greece wanted no disruption of the world athletics championships in 1996 while bidding for the Olympics, and

France was especially keen for a controversy-free soccer world cup in 1998. Few European countries respected the terms of the visa ban first imposed in 1993, and still fewer, the spirit behind it. Loopholes allowed senior government ministers to visit France, Germany, and Italy without a fuss, while even in Britain, which complained about its partners' attitudes, a number of extremely prominent officials close to General Abacha met with government departments in London. No specific benchmarks were set to judge Nigeria's progress toward democracy according to which measures might be lifted. Member states agreed only to a periodic review of the situation, although in February 1998, the European Parliament passed a resolution listing such criteria, a move condemned by radicals in Nigeria as legitimizing Abacha's transition and conservatives who regarded such criteria as hypocritical interference.[13]

The apparently more hostile line pursued, at least rhetorically, by the Labor Party government in Britain produced unexpected consequences, indicating the dangers in adopting a policy long on image but short on substance. In May 1997, it introduced a ban on Nigerian aircraft flying to Britain after repeated complaints over safety standards were ignored. Although such concerns were genuine, Nigeria interpreted the move as political, an indication of the new government's avowedly tougher line, pursued by the transport minister, Glenda Jackson, who while in the opposition had been sharply critical of General Abacha's administration.[14] Nigeria slapped a reciprocal ban on British aircraft, which remained until July 1998 and a change of government, depriving British Airways of two of its most profitable routes. Although London insisted the dispute ought not be regarded as political, its decision to lift its ban in August 1997, without any apparent changes to the safety regime adopted by Nigerian carriers, served only to confirm the Nigerian military's initial interpretation of the act as politically motivated. As a result, Britain lost out commercially, saw its influence further eroded, and missed an opportunity to make an easy political—and an important safety—decision.

After Abacha: Widening the Options

The sudden death of General Abacha on June 8, 1998, apparently of a heart attack, has provided an opportunity for an opening up of the domestic political environment in Nigeria, and—as a consequence—a reevaluation of policy in the EU and the West.[15] The new head of state, Gen. Abdulsalam Abubakar, was formerly defense chief of staff under Gen. Abacha. Although a member of the Provisional Ruling Council, he had never before held political office. He moved quickly to present the image of a professional solider who was reluctantly pushed into center stage and had every intention of restoring the credibility of the military and leaving power as soon as possible. His first steps in government indicated a deft touch. Releasing prominent political prisoners, scrapping General Abacha's cabinet, and abandoning the discredited transition program represented, at least symbolically, a sharp change in direction that had few critics either in Nigeria or abroad. He was rewarded with early visits by the British foreign office minister, Tony Lloyd, who was also representing the EU, the secretary generals of the United Nations and the Commonwealth, and a top-level U.S. delegation led by Undersecretary of State Thomas Pickering. A sensitive response to the equally sudden death on July 7, 1998, of Nigeria's most prominent political prisoner, Moshood Abiola, helped check bloody riots in some parts of the Southwest, preserving stability without resorting to repression.

However, although the change of government has helped significantly ease bilateral tensions between Nigeria and the EU, and most especially between Britain and her former colony, awkward issues remain. General Abubakar, like most of his senior colleagues, was, at least formally, a prominent member of the former regime. It may be argued, with some justification, that real power under General Abacha had been appropriated by informal networks of trusted advisers rather than official military or government structures.[16] Nevertheless, this element of continuity is therefore something of an obstacle for those trying to blame all of Nigeria's ills on General Abacha.

In particular, the change of government, with its emphasis on the undesirability and inadequacy of General Abacha's transition program, has once again brought into focus the nature of the obstacles to establishing a stable, accountable system of government in Nigeria. This raises the question of whether the EU can adopt a common position on Nigeria and the extent to which this may strain transatlantic relations.

General Abacha, in a clumsy and incompetent manner, established a political program that finally formalized the army's position of authority, cloaking military rule in the clothes of constitutional government, much as several of his counterparts elsewhere in western Africa had done. Ideologically, this policy was an acknowledgment both of the inadequacy of Nigeria's civilian political class and of the political aspirations of junior- and middle-ranking officers. General Abubakar, however, has rejected this position, instead favoring a return to the conventional, theoretical distinction between the military and politics in Nigeria as the best route toward the establishment of stable democracy and the preservation of the army's institutional integrity. This approach places as much faith in the competence of the weak civilian political class as it does in the professionalism of a military now accustomed to the lucrative fruits of office.

Furthermore, while relaxing the spending constraints that allowed General Abacha to stabilize an unreformed, inefficient, state-dominated, oil-dependent economy—though at the cost of sharp recession—the new head of state appeared reluctant to adopt the radical reforms needed to facilitate more rapid growth, improve relations with creditors, and reduce the attractions of central government to those vulnerable to corruption.

Individually and collectively, EU member states have reacted with cautious optimism to the change in leadership and the new direction that General Abubakar has espoused. An elected government is likely to be a precondition for the lifting of existing sanctions. However, in the longer term, the weakness of the civilian political class, the decay of the economy, and the ambitions of junior officers make the fostering of a stable, constitutional dispensation only one, and by no means the most likely, of a number of scenarios. The EU and the United States will also have to consider more awkward options that might have a major impact on policy toward Nigeria.

In particular, if a civilian government racked by incompetence, tribalism, and corruption begins to implode, as was the case in 1966 and 1983, again ambitious young officers would find the temptation to intervene difficult to resist. Again Western policymakers would face an impossible choice between supporting a civilian government pulling the country to pieces, a military government with no base for establishing institutional stability, or the potentially chaotic balkanization of Africa's most populous nation.

The energy sector, which is of considerable importance to the international oil market, might continue to thrive irrespective of such changes, as has been the case in Angola despite thirty years of debilitating civil war. Strategically, some in Europe and the region might prefer a collection of much smaller, weaker states in the place of Nigeria. Overall, however, collective Western interests are likely to be better served by the preservation of a strong Nigeria, ideally under stable, civilian government. Potentially, such a government could act as a catalyst for rapid economic growth and a force for regional stability, as indeed it was even under General Abacha. Although such an outcome might be the most appealing for both the EU and the United States, policy levers to encourage such a development are limited, and their application may prove a source of mild tension across the Atlantic.

Policy Review: The Challenge before Dissenters

The absence of debate in Europe over Nigeria has proved an additional factor behind the reluctance of governments to engage what is an extremely complex and tricky issue. Despite the easing of diplomatic tensions following the death of General Abacha, the central question of how Nigeria may best be governed remains resolutely awkward. The opposition lobby that enjoyed some influence in 1993–95 in pushing for a more aggressive stance on Nigeria by the West was weakened as much by the engagement of so many of Nigeria's political class with General Abacha's transition program as by the detention of a few others, by a lack of resources, and by personality and ideological divisions.[17] In short, radical opposition groups have lost credibility despite such prominent figures within their ranks as the Nobel laureate Wole Soyinka and will struggle to influence the post-Abacha dispensation.

Debate is further narrowed by an absence of a media profile on Nigeria. As of this writing, there are just four Western journalists permanently based in Nigeria. This is only partially the fault of the local authorities, which in recent years have been famously slow to issue press visas. It also reflects the reluctance of the media to come to terms with an African story not easily represented in the moralistic, near biblical terms favored by the Western media in its coverage of the Ethiopian famine in 1984, the struggle against apartheid in South Africa, the violence in Rwanda, and the downfall of Mobutu Seso Seko. In Nigeria there are no Mandelas waiting to come out of prison, no handful of wicked men but for whom the whole country might run smoothly, no liberal democratic parties and a transparent government based on the rule of law and the dignity of its citizens. Nigeria defies one-dimensional analysis and is therefore increasingly either avoided or misrepresented by the mainstream media, most especially television.

Within Europe, pressure for a more relaxed approach has come principally from France, which in recent years has advocated an Africa policy built around support for governments in which strength is more prized than accountability. In Nigeria, this is complemented by aggressive lobbying from oil companies and a desire to raise a diplomatic profile in the biggest Anglophone country on the continent. Paris, with the backing of Italy and to a lesser extent Spain, succeeded in watering down measures adopted by the EU against General Abacha, and would prefer to maintain a low-key policy in which the local picture with regard to human rights and democracy is only a contributory factor to a policy equally informed by other national, strategic, commercial, and energy interests.

Prospects for Change

A return to the authoritarianism that developed under General Abacha could see pressure increase for the kind of punitive measures touted by lobbyists but rejected by policymakers in the mid-1990s. Exerting leverage over a more enlightened military regime or a civilian administration is, however, equally problematic.

Obstacles to a tough policy are many. A number of measures are sometimes offered as potential levers available to Western powers to push for greater democracy. These include a freezing of assets, an embargo on oil sales, and promoting Nigeria's isolation. Whether sanctions are practical or even desirable, however, is unclear. An oil embargo without the backing of a UN Security Council resolution would probably achieve little other than to shift the destination of Nigeria's main exports, despite the fact that the United States alone currently purchases around 40 percent of the country's total output. Barring some fantastic outrage, it is difficult to see the UN General Assembly, in which Nigeria has many friends, or the permanent members of the Security Council, principally France and China, ever accepting such a resolution. Even if it did, its implementation would probably require some form of naval monitoring of the Gulf of Guinea. And were that successful, the policy carries the risk of hardening the Nigerian government, heightening instability, and pushing the country into the very abyss that policymakers so fear. Other sanctions might prove an irritation but would not create the same kind of critical pressures, with Nigerian officials confident of circumventing measures like asset freezes.

If moves toward democracy falter, the most likely scenario is for European partners to paper over the wide differences among them. They could unite behind an empty common policy, while each member state pursues a distinct national agenda. This response would be facilitated by the absence of media pressure to act more positively and the lack of obvious solutions to Nigeria's myriad problems. Although some policymakers believe that such reactions amount to tacit approval for a process that will see Nigeria continue gradually to fall apart, elected governments will operate on the principle that if there is to be a catastrophe, it may not happen during their period in office. Meaningful alternatives to such a policy are difficult to determine and harder to defend. Creeping violence not only in Ogoniland but in a dozen other places and the growth of radical Islam in the North are indications of the new and potentially explosive forms in which the political vacuum created by the failure of civilian and military leadership over the past thirty years may be filled. However, unlike most other African countries, Nigeria is not vulnerable to the traditional levers available to donors, such as the withdrawal of credit, something tried since 1992 with no discernible effect other than the deepening of recession and the erosion of infrastructure. Indeed, the cooling of diplomatic ties between Nigeria and its transatlantic partners under General Abacha has been accompanied by a sharp rise in trade between Nigeria and countries such as India, China, North Korea and South Korea. Nor is there a form of government that has not been tried, tested, and failed in Nigeria. With influence so limited, the greatest danger, one into which Britain appears to have slipped, is for ministers to follow their American counterparts who promise more than they can deliver, to threaten tough action without actually adopting firm measures and clear goals. This weakness and unsureness undermine lingering diplomatic influence and compromise commercial advantage without making any material difference.

The United States and Europe

As they have among and within EU member states, so divisions between the broadly common approach adopted in 1993 and 1995 on both sides of the Atlantic unfolded and sharpened in the months leading up to General Abacha's death and indicate the potential for tension to emerge if events in Nigeria again begin to drift. In Europe, there was regret that the Clinton administration failed even to adopt the watery measures instituted by the EU—coupled with concern that a liberal-left constituency might succeed in pushing through a much tougher, potentially even more destructive policy. EU policymakers see the arguments over Nigeria in Washington principally as an exercise in local politics, with little genuine, informed debate as to how to influence the situation. In particular, Nigeria has worked hard to neutralize initiatives to mobilize the African-American lobby that could potentially push the United States into a tougher line than Europe, where no parallel lobby exists. Although Washington has eschewed the formal sanctions package adopted by the EU during the Abacha administration, it operated a similar restrictive visa policy. Like Britain, the United States was reluctant to cooperate with a military government on defense issues, while nevertheless acknowledging and supporting western African initiatives led by Nigeria to restore peace and stability to Liberia and Sierra Leone. The reality is that despite increased commercial competition and differences in emphasis—the United States is far more concerned over the drug question than Europe—the gap between the United States and Europe over Nigeria, even under General Abacha, was never as wide as with other so-called problem states and could not be described as in any sense a source of real tension.

This uneasy transatlantic fudge has been maintained since 1993. Defense and intelligence officials in Europe and the United States will continue to see the Nigerian military as the key political force, not only in Nigeria but also in the region, and will seek to prevent the adoption of policies that might undermine its integrity. At the same time, politicians, particularly in Washington, are likely to come under renewed pressure to "do something" about Nigeria should steps toward democracy falter. Action by the United Nations is unlikely, given the strength of support Nigeria enjoys not only in the General Assembly but also from China and France in the Security Council. Unilateral measures, along the lines of legislation enacted against Iran and Libya, would however further strain relations across the Atlantic, while additionally creating room for Nigeria to maneuver.

The U.S. interest in preserving the integrity of Nigeria as a state is probably greater than most EU member states, except for Britain. For Washington, a strong Nigeria can help provide a regional security framework and commercial opportunity, in contrast to the approach of some other European states that strategically and commercially might benefit from the erosion of Nigeria's regional domination. Although relations among France, the United States, and Great Britain were strained by policy differences over the civil war in Nigeria, when France had tacitly supported Biafran secession, moves toward a break-up of Nigeria again might also raise transatlantic tensions, particularly if an unmanaged break-up were accompanied by violence, atrocities, and a humanitarian crisis. Policymakers in Washington must therefore judge the extent to which they are prepared to support a compromise on democracy and good governance in Nigeria as a necessary condition for the preservation of the state and the avoidance of a messy implosion likely to strain relations with a Europe partly divided and partly disinterested in the country. Responsibility for holding Nigeria together, still less sustaining a democratic system, however, will remain the responsibility of Nigeria in a process in which both the United States and Europe—to the dismay of some lobbyists and the relief of many policymakers—will remain largely impotent.

Notes

1. *Budget of Economic Growth and Development,* Federal Ministry of Finance, Abuja, Nigeria, 1994. Nigeria is forty-fifth on the list of Britain's trading partners, an important factor that reflects the relatively marginal position Nigeria occupies on the foreign policy agenda compared with issues relating to, say, Europe, the Middle East, or North America.

2. After the biannual Franco-African summit in Ouagadougou, Burkina Faso, in December 1996, Nigeria's head of state, Gen. Sani Abacha, announced that the teaching of French would become compulsory.

3. Although a myriad of conspiracy theories mushroomed following Abacha's sudden demise, including poisoned apples and a Viagra overdose, persistent reports of ill health relating to a liver complaint circulated in the months before his death. On August 13, 1998, *Reuters* quoted local newspapers as saying that two

Indian prostitutes who had been with the head of state on that last, fateful night had been released after the authorities had concluded that foul play had not been involved in the head of state's death.

4. March 1997, December 1997, April 1998; many observers treat with profound skepticism claims by the Independent National Electoral Commission of a turnout of around 35 percent for each of the polls.

5. Personal communication, April 1997.

6. Jason Bennetto, "Nigerian Crime Wave Sweeps through Britain," *Independent*, February 2, 1998, p. 1.

7. Most of Nigeria's oil is produced by five Western operators—the Anglo-Dutch Shell Petroleum Development Company, Mobil Producing Nigeria (US), Elf Nigeria (France), Chevron (US), and Agip (Italy).

8. The British foreign office minister, Tony Lloyd, described General Abacha's self-succession as "unacceptable" in Michael Holman, "UK Minister Warns Nigeria over 'Flaws' in Election System," *Financial Times*, July 10, 1997, p. 30, a position echoed by the U.S. Assistant Secretary of State Susan Rice in March 1998 but contradicted by President Clinton during his trip to Africa later that month.

9. The Yoruba in the Southwest, the Igbo in the Southeast, and the Hausa-Fulani in the North.

10. *Official Journal of the European Communities,* December 12, 1995, 95/544/CFSP, reviewed by 97/820/CFSP, as published in *Official Journal of the European Communities,* December 9, 1997, bans entry to the EU of "members of Nigeria's Provisional Ruling Council and the Federal Executive Council, members of the Nigerian military and security forces and their families" although "exceptions . . . may also be allowed on urgent humanitarian grounds"; expulsion of Nigerian military attachés from the EU and withdrawal of EU military attachés from Nigeria; a ban on sporting links, with the exception of the 1998 football World Cup and the 1998 World Basketball Championships; cancellation of military training courses; suspension of development assistance, with the exception of poverty alleviation projects and support for human rights groups. No indication of benchmarks for what might constitute an early transition to democracy was given, nor what further measures might be considered.

11. Ibid.

12. Gen. Olusegun Obasanjo came to power in 1976 following the assassination of Murtala Mohammed in a failed coup; in 1979 he became Nigeria's only military ruler to hand over power to an elected civilian successor, subsequently becoming an international statesman of some repute.

13. European Parliament, "Resolution on the European Union's Attitude towards Nigeria. UN Human Rights Commission," R4-3018/98 (February 19, 1998).

14. Lords Hansard, Parliamentary debate, November 1995.

15. *Reuters*, June 8, 1998.

16. Within a month of General Abubakar coming to power, National Security Adviser Ismaila Gwarzo, Head of Presidential Security Hamza àl-Mustapha, and

Minister of the Federal Capital Territory Lt. Gen. Jeremiah Useni were, respectively, dismissed, redeployed, and retired.

17. In July 1998, Amnesty International estimated there were dozens of political prisoners in Nigeria, far fewer than Egypt or Algeria. *Amnesty Internationl News Release* AFR 44/38/98, July 8, 1998. Until his death on July 7, 1998, Chief Moshood Abiola was among those held in detention; he was widely held to have won the annulled 1993 presidential elections, although his then running mate, Babagana Kingibe, served as General Abacha's foreign and interior minister and remains in a cabinet that includes several other prominent civilian politicians.

RICHARD N. HAASS

12 | *Conclusion*

This volume makes clear that dealing with rogue regimes and difficult countries or situations beyond Europe can pose substantial problems for U.S.-European relations and for U.S. foreign policy more generally. As is often the case with foreign policy, no easy solutions are available. Still, there are steps that Americans and Europeans can and should take to bolster policies designed to promote constructive change in particular countries—steps that also limit any adverse consequences, or the potential for them, for transatlantic relations.

Even this relatively modest set of objectives will be difficult to realize. For the foreseeable future, differences over policy toward non-European events will likely constitute the greatest challenge to harmonious U.S.-European relations. This does not imply that Americans and Europeans cannot work together to their mutual benefit. Nor does it mean that difficulties will not arise within Europe, including both the former Yugoslavia and Cyprus. Rather, most of the challenges, including some of the most difficult and important for both Europe and the United States, will come from farther afield.

Some of the reasons were suggested in the introduction to this volume and reflect the end of the cold war and the resulting decline in transatlantic cohesion. The five case studies highlight additional factors. Americans are prone to act (or at least tempted to act) unilaterally and without formal authorization. Europeans see greater benefit in versions of multilateralism that emphasize standing institutions and international law. The United States tends to be quick to resort to confrontational instruments, such as economic sanctions or cruise missiles, whereas the European preference is for diplomacy and engagement. (This pattern is particularly pronounced when energy-related interests are at stake, something that may reflect Europe's greater dependence on the energy resources of problem states.) For reasons of history, culture, and domestic politics, American foreign policy tends to be more influenced by values than that of most European countries, whose foreign policy is defined more by interests—especially commercial ones. Indeed, in a world of reduced strategic risk, more scope for commercial competition exists among erstwhile allies, especially as governments on both sides of the Atlantic find themselves under great pressure to lower unemployment (or to keep it low). All of these differences create a backdrop for caricature: a European view of U.S. foreign policy as heavy handed and dominated by domestic politics, an American view of European foreign policy as amoral and dominated by a search for profit.

The Case Record

These caricatures need not become reality. All five of the cases surveyed in this volume by American and European experts contain clear potential for useful collaboration. In the case of Cuba, for example, implementation of the understanding of May 18, 1998—by which the European Union agreed to drop its challenge in the World Trade Organization (WTO) and curtail subsidies of European firms that are "trafficking" in confiscated properties in Cuba in exchange for the United States rescinding its threat to deny Europeans physical access to the United States and to take them to court in the United States over such investments—should remove (if Congress consents) the friction stemming from secondary sanctions.

Beyond this diplomatic cease-fire, however, a more concerted policy is necessary on how to promote what most people on both sides of the Atlantic agree is the right goal, namely, a peaceful transition to a more liberal and market-oriented Cuba. Some meeting in the middle may be required. The United States might choose to selectively lift its embargo, as suggested by Richard A. Nuccio, and Europe might engage Cuba in a more conditional fashion, as Joaquín Roy proposed. Adoption of a common set of investment guidelines to promote human rights and fair employment practices—akin to the Sullivan Principles adopted for American companies present in South Africa under apartheid—is one possibility that should be explored.[1] Another possibility would be for Europe and the United States to agree to a common road map for Cuba that lays out the details under which sanctions would be lifted (and incentives extended) as particular reforms occur. Europeans may object to this approach on the grounds that Cuba poses no strategic threat and that a policy of conditional engagement allows the Castro regime to block the very contacts with the outside that bring with them the potential to change Cuba for the better.[2] If Europe reacts this way, America's more restrictive policy would likely remain intact until either its domestic debate evolved or Cuba changed from within. The risk inherent in a continuing inability to agree to a common approach to Cuba is that it decreases the prospects for peaceful change within Cuba—and thereby increases the chance that a crisis may erupt that is dangerous not just for Cubans but for the United States and transatlantic relations as well.

Iran is a second case in which the May 18 understanding between the United States and the European Union removed some, if not all, of the animosity deriving from secondary sanctions. In this case, the package consisted of European agreement to implement tighter control over selective high-technology exports to Iran in exchange for a U.S. waiver of its objections to European investment in Iran's energy sector. Like the Cuban case, the complete disappearance of friction stemming from secondary sanctions will depend on amending existing legislation and, therefore, on whether and how Congress decides to implement the May 1998 understanding.

Iran, though, presents a fundamentally different sort of challenge than Cuba in that Iran poses an actual threat to U.S. and European interests. Iran's ambitions in the realm of weapons of mass destruction are particularly troubling, as is its record of sponsoring terrorism and subversion. It is thus difficult if not impossible to justify a stance of unconditional (or nearly unconditional) engagement. Instead, a conditional approach may be warranted, as suggested generally by Geoffrey Kemp's benchmark approach or, more narrowly, by Peter Rudolf's proposal for a U.S.-European Union (EU) initiative to limit Iran's nuclear ambitions. A related alternative would be for Europe to adopt a version of U.S. sanctions that would then be withdrawn only as Iran met negotiated criteria in such realms as terrorism, human rights, and nuclear weaponry.

An approach along these lines requires movement from both the United States and Europe. Washington for its part has begun. The effective jettisoning of "dual containment," a change implicit in Secretary of State Madeleine K. Albright's June 1998 address that recognized the significance of President Mohammed Khatami's electoral victory and called for a road map to guide U.S. and Iranian relations, was an important step—even if the speech failed to lay out specific milestones.[3] A series of consultations—involving the U.S. executive, Congress, and the EU—might be convened to flesh out such a road map, making clear the changes required in Iranian behavior and the parallel moves needed in the West. Reaching U.S.-European agreement on such a road map promises to be extraordinarily difficult—the two sides cannot even agree on whether Europe's engagement or American pressures resulted in the emergence of Khatami and a somewhat more moderate Iran—but it is a necessary first step if Iran is not to re-emerge as a major source of transatlantic discord.

Iraq is a case of growing transatlantic tensions—something that distinguishes it from the four other cases where it is possible to identify at least some narrowing of differences between Europe and the United States. Europe, or more accurately, France, appears anxious to reduce or eliminate economic sanctions against Iraq in order to bring about its rapid reintegration—whereas the United States is raising the requirements for a lifting of sanctions. Behind this divergence lies not only commercial calculations but a different assessment of both the humanitarian impact of sanctions and of the actual and potential threat posed by Saddam Hussein.

In this case, too, an argument exists for some compromise on both sides. The United States would be wise to reconsider its decision to link any lifting of sanctions to Iraqi compliance with *all* Security Council resolutions rather than to its behavior in regard to weapons of mass destruction as is stipulated (and as the United States voted for) in UN Security Council Resolution 687.[4] Moving the goalpost removes what incentive Iraq does have to comply with the most important of Western objectives and creates undesirable fissures between the United States and France, as accurately described by Dominique Moïsi. It is also unnecessary, in that there is no evidence that Iraq is prepared to comply in full with its obligations in this area, something underlined in June 1998 by revelations that Iraq had filled warheads with VX nerve gas and by subsequent Iraqi decisions to block the work of UN weapons inspectors.[5]

But France's haste to see sanctions relaxed is not only inconsistent with the facts of the case but strategically unwise. Iraq is a prime example of a country that poses a meaningful threat to U.S. and European interests—and a country that would be likely to carry out such threats if given half a chance. Any "engagement" would be exploited by Saddam Hussein to rebuild Iraq's capacities to repress its own population and to endanger its neighbors.

Nor is it possible to argue that sanctions themselves are responsible for the poor plight of the Iraqi people. From the outset, a humanitarian exception has allowed Iraq to import food and medicine. Iraq has also had the opportunity to export oil to raise additional revenues for just this purpose. For years it chose not to exercise this option, forfeiting some $20 billion in revenue on top of the approximately $100 billion it has forfeited by refusing to comply with UN Security Council Resolution 687. Now, under UN Security Council Resolution 1153 and subsequent decisions, Iraq has the option of selling more than $10 billion of oil a year to raise funds for a vastly expanded list of humanitarian imports.[6] Iraq's misery is a direct result of the regime's refusal to meet its international obligations and its unwillingness to avail itself of the humanitarian relief offered, preferring instead to increase hardship as a device to build international opposition to the sanctions.

A reasonable policy, then, is one that would follow Resolution 687, allowing Iraq to resume exports once it fulfilled all of its obligations regarding weapons of mass destruction. Limits on what it could import (especially in military and dual-use realms) would remain, as would a more modest weapons inspection regime. Proceeds from exports would continue to flow into an internationally supervised escrow account that would help ensure Iraqi compliance with open-ended restrictions and payment of compensation to past victims of Iraqi aggression. A European failure to sign on to such a policy would cause a major rift in relations with the United States. It would also leave Washington with few options (beyond those suggested by Kenneth I. Juster for strengthening domestic opposition to Saddam) other than to consider employing massive amounts of conventional military force whenever Iraq failed to meet its international obligations or began to reconstitute an unconventional weapons capability.

Libya has caused less transatlantic tension in recent years for several reasons, including the relative modesty of the interests at stake. (I say "in recent years," remembering the strains that accompanied the U.S. decision to attack Libya in April 1986 after intelligence pointed to Libyan complicity in the bombing of a West German nightclub frequented by American soldiers.) There also has been a consensus among the United States, Great Britain, and France that Libya must comply with UN Security Council resolutions stipulating its obligations in the realm of terrorism. But there have been problems all the same, stemming mostly from American secondary sanctions and from a view (widespread in Italy) that isolating Qaddafi risks bringing someone worse into power— akin to what we see in Sudan.

The May 18 understanding that eased tensions over Cuba and Iran also applied to Libya, although implementation remains at issue. Yet another factor that has eased potential problems is the absence of any American push to extend sanctions to cover oil. Also helping to defuse this issue was the Anglo-American decision in July 1998 to offer the Libyan government the option of submitting the two accused individuals to the jurisdiction of a special court in the Netherlands and the subsequent handover of the suspects in April 1999.[7]

However, some potential still exists for new transatlantic problems over Libya that transcend Lockerbie, if, for example, evidence should emerge of new Libyan support for terrorism or, even more seriously, of a credible program there to build weapons of mass destruction. (A similar and even more serious situation for transatlantic relations would arise if intelligence implicated Iran in such activities.) The United States may want to use covert action or military force to respond to any such developments, courses of action that are unlikely to find much support in Europe. Although the best that may be hoped for, as Gideon Rose and Stefano Silvestri implied, is a return to the status quo existing before the passage of the Iran and Libya Sanctions Act of 1996, consultations among the United States and, at a minimum, Italy, Great Britain, and France about how to deal with such contingencies are clearly in order.

Nigeria, as noted in the introduction, differs notably from the other cases. Thus far it has not been a serious source of transatlantic tensions. Moreover, it may not become one, owing to Gen. Sani Abacha's death and indications of internal change, including the decision to release some political prisoners and hold elections. Still, Nigeria's future is uncertain as Antony Goldman rightly suggested. Indeed, it has the potential to become a failed state that would pose a threat not simply to itself but to much of Africa. Nigeria thus represents a challenge for Americans and Europeans, namely, how best to promote desirable political and economic reform in a country of economic and political importance to both Africa and the West but one that has known considerable repression, corruption, and instability. This challenge presents—as Pauline H. Baker and John J. Stremlau indicated in their chapter—a prime opportunity to engage in preventive diplomacy.

Engaging successfully in preventive diplomacy in Nigeria of the sort suggested in this book most likely requires linking the availability of economic and political incentives (and limited but credible political and economic sanctions) to the behavior of Nigeria's new rulers. Far-reaching sanctions—measures that would significantly affect Nigeria's energy sector—are unlikely to be an option, both for commercial reasons and because of the view in Europe, one held by some Americans, that such penalties could exacerbate internal hardship and instability. As a result, some transatlantic understanding on a road map for Nigeria would seem possible and worth exploring. Such a road map would tie the provision of nonhumanitarian assistance, debt rescheduling and new investment, and contacts with Nigerian political and military figures to steps that would bring about a more open political and economic order, a further release of political prisoners, and economic reform that curtails corruption.

Assessing Relations

One thing this country-by-country review makes clear is that there is no mechanical or consultative fix to transatlantic tensions. Significant differences in thinking about threats and policy persist. Many Europeans reject the entire notion of characterizing selected states as "rogue" on the grounds that such characterization is bound to be self-fulfilling.

Still, consultations are critical. Surely the U.S. administration of the day needs to avoid "consulting" only after it has determined its own policy, be it by executive decision or congressional fiat. U.S. diplomatic efforts to build European support for a common approach to India and Pakistan in the aftermath of their May 1998 nuclear tests—and after the Clinton administration had put into effect comprehensive sanctions mandated by U.S. legislation—are an instructive example. Such consultation does little more than disguise unilateralism.

Similarly, European governments need to consult with Americans (in Congress as well as the executive branch) before acting or, just as important, before coming to a collective EU decision that can prove extraordinarily difficult to revise. The slowly growing relevance of Europe's common foreign and security policy (CFSP) makes such prior consultation even more important.

Many consultative mechanisms already exist for this purpose, including a multitude of bilateral channels in Washington and European capitals, various U.S.-EU forums ranging from an annual summit to more frequent foreign policy–oriented meetings among responsible officials, NATO, the Group of Eight (G-8), and the five permanent members of the UN Security Council, or P-5. None is perfect, however. Bilateral channels, however indispensable, by definition do not represent Europe. The U.S.-U.K. and, increasingly, the U.S.-France, networks require greater attention given the power and influence of these two countries. With CFSP more an objective than a reality, the EU rarely acts as a decisive foreign policy actor. One reform that would help here would be a decision by Europeans to replace current unwieldy and often ineffectual arrangements—the Troika (representing the most recent, current, and projected holders of the EU presidency), the presidency, and so on—with something akin to a European national security adviser who could speak for Europe in foreign policy and defense matters.[8] What would also contribute to better transatlantic understanding would be more frequent meetings involving members of Congress and European officials.

For now NATO remains the most important transatlantic venue for discussing traditional matters of security. But NATO's growing membership makes it more cumbersome. It is also oriented toward military solutions and limited in what it can do beyond Europe. The G-8 is uneven in that it simultaneously combines selected European governments (France, Germany, Great Britain, and Italy, as well as the president of the European Commission and leader of the country that holds the EU presidency during that six-month period). The P-5 excludes all Europeans except France and Great Britain. All such channels suffer from the reality that they often include actors whose participation is largely irrelevant or even counterproductive and exclude actors whose participation may be desirable, necessary, or both.

The inevitable result is a high degree of "forum shopping." For promoting support of economic sanctions, the broadest possible participation is desirable, something that argues for using UN, U.S.-EU, and NATO forums. For active diplomacy and the use of force, more selective approaches may be warranted. What will increasingly make the most sense are specific groups cobbled together to deal with specific challenges. Such factors as desire, capacity, and relevance will influence inclusion in ad hoc coalitions of the able and willing, combined joint task forces—CJTFs in NATO parlance—contact groups.[9]

One change that would contribute a great deal to calming transatlantic tensions would be an American decision to eliminate secondary sanctions. Much of the recent strain between Americans and Europeans stems from the U.S. resort to secondary sanctions against those European entities and persons who do not implement primary sanctions instituted by the United States against a specified target. Here little can be done other than for the United States to decide to eschew secondary sanctions as a tool of policy. Agreements announced in May 1998 appear to reflect a good deal of progress in regard to Iran, Libya, and Cuba.

But reducing or even eliminating secondary sanctions, while removing a significant source of friction from transatlantic ties, will in itself contribute little to better common policy toward problem states. This requires greater harmonizing of U.S. and European policy—and greater compromise by both sides.

For its part, the United States needs to further rein in its enthusiasm for primary sanctions. This should be done on its merits and not simply to facilitate better relations with Europe. Recent history suggests that sanctions (and unilateral sanctions in particular) all too often cannot accomplish the ambitious tasks set out for them and have unintended and often undesirable consequences extending beyond the forfeiture of economic gain, including strengthening authoritarian regimes and causing humanitarian hardship.

The path to improving relations across the Atlantic likely requires the brokering of a new understanding between the White House and Congress. Sanctions need to be targeted more carefully on those firms or entities involved in the offending activity. Humanitarian exceptions that allow for targets to import food and medicine should be the norm, as should the authority to waive particular sanctions if the president determines that it would serve the national interest. Such reform will only occur as a result of a concerted effort by the president and his senior aides with both Congress and the public at large, broad support from business interests, and congressional willingness to accept a more modest role for the institution.[10]

Although not discussed directly in this volume, the Middle East peace process also bears on transatlantic behavior toward problem countries. It is not simply that U.S. stewardship of the peace process affects Arab willingness to work with the United States against Iraq and Libya; it also affects European views of American leadership. European respect for American foreign policy falls off—and with it European willingness to follow America's lead—when the United States seems to follow a moral double standard by not asking that Israel do its fair share to contribute to peace with the Palestinians and its Arab neighbors.[11]

But increased Western effectiveness in the world and improved transatlantic relations also require changes in European thinking and behavior. Europe, and France in particular, should resist the temptation to oppose the United States for the sake of asserting European independence and identity at a time when the United States is the world's dominant power. Such posturing is not just simply unworthy, but it also entails real costs for transatlantic relations and for the ability to achieve common objectives vis-à-vis problem states.

Nor should Europeans insist on formal UN Security Council authorization as a prerequisite for common action toward a problem state. Such a requirement—one that emerged at various junctures during early transatlantic consultations over Kosovo—would provide Russia and China a veto over U.S. and European action. Legitimacy must stem in the first instance from the objectives of the policy and how it is implemented. Multilateralism is not "UN-ism" and should not be defined so narrowly.

A more serious problem in Europe comes from what appears to be little more than blind faith in the effectiveness of engagement. Antipathy toward sanctions is deep and wide. There is also a general reluctance (and a growing inability in the physical sense) to deploy military force outside Europe. Although unconditional engagement may be the right policy in those instances in which the target cannot endanger either European or American interests, it may not be the desired approach when normal economic interaction risks strengthening the hand of irresponsible leaders and providing them the means to seriously threaten U.S. and European interests. Moreover, even when unconditional engagement is called for, it needs to be buttressed by such initiatives as investment codes, support for nongovernmental organizations and civil society, and "free" radio broadcasting to maximize the pressure on the government to liberalize. Other options to consider include narrow sanctions and military interventions if a situation grows more serious. If Europeans correctly criticize certain American policies as all stick and no carrot, they risk the charge that their own approach boils down to all carrot and no stick. The notion of "good cop, bad cop," in which Europe acts as the former and the United States the latter, has the potential to contribute to a solution only if the good cop is willing to get tough if incentives fail to bring about the desired results. The "critical dialogue" with Iran is a case in point, as the lack of European willingness to introduce penalties into Europe's relations with Iran removed what interest Iran had in moderating its behavior. Easing sanctions against Iraq in the absence of full Iraqi compliance with its obligations to eliminate all of its weapons of mass destruction would constitute a major error. The same should apply to Libya in regard to terrorism and weapons of mass destruction.

As a rule of thumb, policies of conditional engagement—defined by road maps that commit the international community and the problem country to undertake a series of reciprocal actions—make the most sense in dealing with difficult or problem states that pose a threat to others. Sanctions and incentives should be manipulated depending on the behavior of the target state. A risk exists that such an approach allows disruptive elements within the target state to block normalization, but this is a price worth paying when the target still poses a threat and economic interaction only adds to it.

In some cases, and despite intense consultations, the United States and Europe may not be able to agree on the best way to deal with a problem state. Best efforts do not always succeed. The correct response for the United States in such situations is not to introduce secondary sanctions against European holdouts, something that would not resolve the matter and could introduce a new set of problems. Nor in most cases should the United States implement unilateral sanctions, which are likely to be feckless. Leadership requires a willingness to listen and, if need be, to modify ends and means in order to attract followers. The United States thus should do more to make its arguments public—to persuade public opinion in Europe as a means to influence governments. The United States also should make clear what the alternative policy to sanctions would be, including the use of military force.

Europeans should know, though, that repeated unwillingness on their part to join the United States in what appear to be fair and reasonable approaches toward problem states is shortsighted and dangerous in two ways. First, a lack of a common policy risks allowing certain dangerous actors to increase their capacity to threaten important European and American interests. Not working together to thwart the proliferation of weapons of mass destruction comes to mind.

Second, a pattern of European refusal to support important foreign policy initiatives supported by the U.S. executive branch and Congress will lead inexorably to a growing American alienation from Europe. Europeans cannot have it both ways. They cannot expect the United States to remain engaged in Europe if Europe is not an active partner with the United States beyond the continent. It is not simply that Europeans will lose influence in American decisionmaking councils. The result will also be greater American unilateralism around the world and more frequent American use of military force—combined with greater American detachment from Europe. The projects of enlarging NATO and the EU, whatever their merits, cannot substitute for the inability of Americans and Europeans to work out a common policy for dealing with the dominant challenges of the post–cold war world.

Notes

1. The text of the so-called Arcos Principles can be found in Rolando H. Castañeda and George Plinio Montalván, "The Arcos Principles," in George Plinio

Montalván, ed., *Cuba in Transition*, vol. 4 (Florida International University, 1994), pp. 360–67.

2. See "The Cuban Threat to U.S. National Security," a report prepared by the Defense Intelligence Agency and others pursuant to section 1228 of Public Law 105-85, 111 Stat. 1943-44, November 18, 1997. The unclassified report was passed to Congress by Secretary of Defense William Cohen on May 6, 1998 (Department of Defense, news release 213-98).

3. See remarks of Secretary of State Madeleine K. Albright before the Asia Society dinner, New York, June 17, 1998.

4. See remarks by Secretary of State Madeleine K. Albright at Georgetown University, March 26, 1997.

5. Jim Hoagland and Vernon Loeb, "Tests Show Nerve Gas in Iraqi Warheads; Finding Contradicts Claims by Baghdad," *Washington Post*, June 23, 1998, p. A1.

6. See also UN Security Council Resolution 986 (April 14, 1995), which initiated the "oil-for-food" program.

7. Philip Shenon, "It's Official: U.S. to Consider Dutch Trial in Lockerbie Case," *New York Times*, July 21, 1998, p. A3. Marlise Simora, "2 Libyan Suspects Handed to Court in Pan Am Bombing," *New York Times,* April 6, 1999, p. A1.

8. The Treaty of Amsterdam did make provisions for a high representative for CFSP. It remains to be seen who will fill this post and whether that person will be someone of international stature or rather an able technocrat.

9. Simon Serfaty has written recently of the desirability of resurrecting the decades-old notion of a "directoire" of selected, that is, leading, European states to work closely with the United States in meeting major challenges. See his "Bridging the Gulf across the Atlantic: Europe and the United States in the Persian Gulf," *Middle East Journal*, vol. 52 (Summer 1998), pp. 337–50. See also Richard N. Haass, *The Reluctant Sheriff: The United States after the Cold War* (New York: Council on Foreign Relations, 1997).

10. See Richard N. Haass, ed., *Economic Sanctions and American Diplomacy* (New York: Council on Foreign Relations, 1998).

11. See several of the pieces by European contributors in Robert D. Blackwill and Michael Stürmer, eds., *Allies Divided: Transatlantic Policies for the Greater Middle East* (MIT Press, 1997). Also see Philip H. Gordon, *The Transatlantic Allies and the Changing Middle East*, Adelphi Paper 322 (Oxford University Press and International Institute for Strategic Studies, September 1998).

Contributors

Pauline H. Baker
The Fund for Peace

Antony Goldman
The Economist Intelligence Unit

Richard N. Haass
The Brookings Institution

Kenneth I. Juster
Arnold and Porter

Geoffrey Kemp
*Nixon Center for Peace
and Freedom*

Dominique Moïsi
*Institut Français de Relations
Internationales*

Richard A. Nuccio
*Weatherhead Center for
International Affairs,
Harvard University*

Gideon Rose
Council on Foreign Relations

Joaquín Roy
*School of International Studies,
University of Miami*

Peter Rudolf
Stiftung Wissenschaft und Politik

Stefano Silvestri
Istituto Affari Internazionali

John J. Stremlau
*International Relations Department,
University of Witwatersrand*

Index